f**P**

VOWS

The Story of a Priest, a Nun, and Their Son

PETER MANSEAU

FREE PRESS

NEW YORK   LONDON   TORONTO   SYDNEY

FREE PRESS
A Division of Simon & Schuster, Inc.
1230 Avenue of the Americas
New York, NY 10020

FREE PRESS and colophon are trademarks of Simon & Schuster, Inc.
For information about special discounts for bulk purchases,
please contact Simon & Schuster Special Sales:
1-800-456-6798 or business@simonandschuster.com

Designed by Joseph Rutt

Manufactured in the United States of America

10 9 8 7 6 5 4 3 2 1

Library of Congress Cataloging-in-Publication Data

Manseau, Peter.
Vows : the story of a priest, a nun, and their son / Peter Manseau.
p.   cm.
1. Manseau, William J. (William Joseph) 2. Catholic Church—United States—Clergy—
Biography. 3. Manseau, Mary Doherty. 4. Ex-nuns—United States—Biography. 5.
Manseau, Peter. 6. Children of clergy—United States—Biography. I. Title.
BX4705.M3214M36 2005
282'.092'273—dc22
[B]
2005040151

ISBN-13: 978-0-7432-4907-2
ISBN-10:   0-7432-4907-0

For my parents:
Rev. Dr. William Joseph Manseau,
a good father in every sense of the word,
and Mary Doherty Manseau,
full of grace

CONTENTS

Part Three
REFORMATION

Part Four
PROCREATION

Part Five
REVELATION

VOWS

PROLOGUE

My parents don't remember their earliest conversation. What was said when, who spoke first and why: these are details almost forty years gone. All my father can tell me is that he met my mother in his storefront ministry center in Roxbury late in the spring of 1968. A year before, he had rented an abandoned funeral home on Shawmut Avenue, propped open the doors to thin the stench of flowers and embalming fluid, and hung a sign out front declaring that all were welcome. A few months later, someone threw a metal trash can through the plate-glass window beside the entrance. He covered the hole and cleaned up as best he could, but there was no end to the mess that had been made.

When my father describes the room in which he met my mother, he is always sure to mention the biblical murals that decorated the walls. I suppose he likes the image of the two of them surrounded by life-size portraits of prophets and saints, but my mind is drawn instead to all that stubborn glass, to tiny slivers working their way deep into the shag carpet, catching light whenever the overhead fluorescents were on.

Wednesday evenings, Dad tells me, he would walk down Fort Hill from the All Saints rectory and preach in his storefront to whomever would listen. Sometimes he drew a crowd that filled five rows of folding chairs: families from the Lenox Street housing projects, drunks from Blue Hill Avenue, a handful of sisters from the convent nearby.

One night the woman who would be my mother was among them. They all sat together with the soles of their shoes crunching the carpet below; singing, clapping, praying in a building that still wore scars from the previous summer, the season when the city burned.

That's how I imagine the scene of my parents' meeting, as a series of contrasts and contradictions. Standing between a cardboard-patched window and scripture-painted walls, half-buried shards twinkling like stars beneath them, they made their introductions in the middle of a storefront with nothing to sell. He was a Catholic priest wearing a white plastic collar like a lock around his neck. She was a nun in a virgin's black veil.

What did they say? Too much has happened since then; it's no surprise they can't remember the simple greeting that started it all. Whatever the words might have been, I know they were spoken in a place full of the kind of faith with which I was raised, the kind of faith that knows how close hope and pain are to moments of possibility; the kind that sees something holy in that broken glass at their feet, splinters of grace that cut as well as shine.

Part One

VOCATION

VIA CRUCIS

The sculpture in the corner is dark, the color of wet earth. Rising three feet or so above its pedestal, it could be the model of a tower or a knot-gnarled tree. In fact, it is a tangle of bodies, a doll-scale depiction of a scene usually associated with souls in eternal torment: bare arms, legs, and torsos wrapped around one another, grabbing and kicking as if being pulled from below; pained faces staring out in every direction. From a distance, the piece looks almost accidental, protuberances jutting out here and there, no logic to its shape. Only on closer inspection can you see the intersecting wooden beams, and the man nailed to them, buried under the odd bulk of the hardened clay. The bodies wind around a tilted crucifix like ribbons on a maypole fallen down. It's difficult to tell where one ends and the next begins. Jesus' dead hand rests on a muscular shoulder. A veiled woman writhes past his forearm, revealing her breasts. The bodies spiral upward from the cross of death at the base of the sculpture to another cross, much smaller, at the top, held by communal effort. Not by a particular body or by many, but as one. That's the message. The medium, however, is far more messy: up close the sculpture resembles nothing so much as a game of Twister played on the canvas of a late gothic crucifixion. Right hand, red. A fumbling group-grope of revelation.

If it's a sacrilege, it's a well-placed one. *Via Crucis*, the Way of the Cross, stands in a dim hallway of the Archbishop's Residence in

Brighton, Massachusetts, on the first floor of what was until recently one of the most prestigious addresses in the Roman Catholic Church, former home to the highest-ranking prelate in America. The sculpture doesn't at all match the decor of the manse, but still, it's a fitting spot. For all its physicality, its erotic detail, the tangle of bodies is meant to suggest the church itself; the cumulative experience of those whose lives have rested on a single sacrifice, building up through the centuries to a mountain of human endeavor that one day will reach its reward.

Yet whatever the artwork is supposed to represent, when I stood in the hallway in which it resides, it seemed unlikely many others had viewed the sculpture of late. A skin of dust covered the pedestal; a faded plaque was all that displayed the artist's name. Along with the usual effects of age and neglect, the piece was rather difficult to see. The whole house—quiet, empty, smelling of freshly vacuumed carpet—was cast in shadows, as if half the lightbulbs had burned out at once, or, more likely, as if they were keeping an eye on the electric bill, trying to save a nickel or two wherever they could. This was the spring of 2003. The Archdiocese of Boston had by then paid over $50 million in settlements to victims of sexual abuse by its clergy. They could barely afford what little light was left.

My father had an appointment that day to meet with the archdiocese's "Interim Apostolic Administrator," Bishop Richard G. Lennon, acting man-in-charge after Cardinal Bernard F. Law resigned in disgrace for his role in the abuse scandal. Law had insisted for months he knew nothing of the dangerous histories of the men involved. Then came the documents: his name, his blessing, on transfer after transfer, moving known pedophiles to unsuspecting parishes, sending wolves to tend his flock. It all resulted in a promotion for Lennon, but now he had the unenviable job of cleaning up the mess.

I had gone along with Dad that day to offer moral support. With nothing but bad news coming out of the Archbishop's Residence lately, he had been understandably anxious about the meeting. Yet it seemed possible at the time that Bishop Lennon agreed to speak with Dad more as a diversion than anything else. Compared with the scandal and the financial crisis it caused, my father should not have presented a pressing matter from the church's point of view. Dad's errand was merely to find out whether the Catholic hierarchy still considered him a priest. He had been ordained by the Archdiocese of Boston some forty years before. Eight years later he had married my mother, and had been excommunicated for refusing to resign his priestly status. Somewhere along the way, a change in canon law had reduced his penalty from excommunication to censure, and now, at sixty-seven, he was considering getting right with his church.

After thirty-four years as a devoted if disobedient Catholic married to the same, my father thought it might be time to have his union with my mother recognized by Rome. The church would do no such thing, however, if Dad remained unwilling to bend to its will on the question of his priesthood, his "clerical state." In other words, in order to have the primary relationship of his life affirmed by the church he loved, he would have to give up his primary identity within it. It's a kind of sacramental blackmail: not quite damned if you do, damned if you don't, but grace, authority, and even God are at stake if you take this kind of thing seriously. And Dad does. So he wanted to know where he stood, and what would be involved in being laicized, or, as the process is also called, "dispensed," "regularized," "reduced." The church has no shortage of terms for spiritual debasement.

We were sitting in the worn chairs of a dimly lit waiting area. Dad leaned forward, sat back, crossed and uncrossed his legs, trying to adjust, to settle into his chair and just wait patiently for the bishop to appear. At the far end of the hall, blue light shone from the windows of a small chapel: blue light on blue carpet, blue light on marble tabletops, blue light on an oak brown door.

"We used to come up here two at a time, once a week," Dad said. "Two seminarians would go into that chapel to help Cardinal Cushing with his radio broadcast. He'd intone the rosary into his microphone and it was our job to provide the responses. *Hail Mary, full of grace, the Lord is with thee,* he'd say, and we'd answer, *Holy Mary, Mother of God . . .* That was the whole show. People actually listened."

Dad straightened his glasses, glancing nervously around the hallway. Portraits of cardinals past stared down at us from the opposite wall. Directly in front of us was Richard J. Cushing, Archbishop of Boston from 1944 to 1970. Kennedy's cardinal—he delivered the younger man's eulogy—and yet as late as the 1950s, Cushing wondered why on earth Catholics would choose to attend a place like Harvard when there were more than enough seats at Catholic colleges to go around. The last towering figure of the insular, immigrant Catholicism in which my parents were raised, his portrait had a square chin, a large, severe nose, and deep vertical creases cut in his face. Even in his lush red cloak and matching three-cornered cardinal's hat, he looked like a guy who might have owned a bar in South Boston—"Southie"— the Irish enclave where he'd been born.

"One time I came up here," Dad remembered, "Cardinal Cushing took me aside. He said, 'Bill, come here, come here . . .'" Dad's voice went gravelly and high at the same time, which surprised me. He is an earnest man, not one for jokes or shtick; I had never heard him try to do a comic voice before. "When I was right up by his side," Dad continued, "he says to me, 'You wanna see my operation?'"

My ears perked to attention, eyes went wide. Growing up, my family stories had been tales of Catholic peculiarity, with oddball clerics standing in for crazy uncles. I still had a taste for it. Not just for the comedy of the unexpected that my parents' memories of eccentric clergy never failed to provide (the priest dressed up as a mother superior one Halloween; the nun who had to be helped out of the rectory after a few too many sips of Tom Collins mix), but for the humanness of all involved: the human clumsiness of the God-minded. The stories I liked best were the ones that showed how anyone putting on the divine was bound to stumble like a toddler scuffing around in his mother's high heels.

"Cushing leads me into that conference room right over there," Dad said, "and beside the same enormous table where we'll talk to the bishop today, he opens his shirt up and says," again that high gravelly voice, "'I'm full of the cancer! They looked around inside me but couldn't get it out!'"

Dad opened the flap of his suit coat, miming it, though now it seemed he was playing it up more to distract himself than to keep me entertained. "All I could think to say was, 'Wow.'

"Another time I came here after I was married to let Cardinal Medeiros know what I was up to." Humberto Medeiros had followed Cushing. In his portrait, he stared down from behind big metal-rimmed glasses, his skin a shade darker than any other man on the wall. Imported from outside the diocese, Medeiros was the wrong man to inherit the worst of Boston's tribalism, the racism that boiled over to violence when black city kids began to be bussed to schools in predominantly white neighborhoods in the 1970s. "Why should I go to Southie?" Cardinal Medeiros infamously remarked when he was asked to make peace in his predecessor's hometown. "To get stoned? Is that what they'd like to see?"

"Medeiros was very interested, listened intently," Dad said. "I reminded him of my work in the inner city, and told him about the ecumenical projects I'd begun. At the end of the conversation, he looked genuinely saddened, and said, 'I wish you'd come back to us, Bill . . .'" Dad laughed lightly. He'd dropped the funny voices. "But I hadn't gone anywhere! 'Look,' I said, 'I'm right here!'" His lips tightened at the memory. "Of course, that's not what he meant. I think he would have preferred if I left my family. That would have been the only way as far as the church was concerned."

Next to Medeiros on the wall was Cardinal Law. After Medeiros died, Law was the great white hope of the archdiocese old guard—the Irish power network of priests, cops, and politicians that for so long had controlled the city and, with the exception of Medeiros's episcopacy, the church. Harvard-educated, quick-witted, Law had been greeted like Kennedy and Cushing rolled into one. Years later, after his resignation, he moved from the grand residence in Brighton to a convent in Maryland. The man who had dreamed of being the first American pope now had his pastoral authority limited to a group of elderly nuns.

"I talked to Cardinal Law a few times, too," Dad said, "about the pensions—all the money the church owes to former priests." I'd heard about my father's latest crusade any number of times but he explained again, talking a bit too loudly for the near-silent house. "Some of those guys paid into the pension fund for twenty years before they left active ministry, and now the church won't let them have it. I told the cardinal we were going to do something about it."

"I'll bet he was glad to see you," I said.

Dad smiled.

At the opposite end of the hall, the light from the chapel shifted, climbing the white walls, and there, in the corner, casting a soft blue glow on the sculpture, the Way of the Cross. Bodies grabbing bodies, men and women wrestling—with what? sex? death? change? They wove around one another like stitches pulled tight, as if the church itself had opened its gown to reveal the scar by which it lived.

Dad's smile faded, and he began wringing his hands. Then he leaned back in his chair again, looked at his watch. How long would we have to wait? He sighed, long and emphatically. I don't know that I'd ever noticed him sighing this way before, but I knew the sound as well as I know my own voice. That long sigh, my one inheritance.

Dad looked at his watch a second time in two minutes, then scanned the portraits again. Power comes, power goes, as fickle as grace. He had made his case to three cardinals. They were all gone. He kept coming back.

"I must be out of my mind," he said. "I really must be out of my mind."

With all the splendors-of-Christendom grandeur implied by its name, and the sense of dread that had come over my father on our way there that day, I had expected the Archbishop's Residence and the surrounding grounds to be much more impressive. Home to both the offices of the spiritual leader of the archdiocese and to St. John's Seminary, the primary training facility for its priests, the Brighton campus functions as the Roman church's administrative headquarters in Boston, and as such served as something like the capital of Catholic America through most of the 20th century, even as it has become its Watergate in the 21st. Compared with the power seats of European Catholicism, it is hopelessly drab: no flying buttresses, no rising spires, no ornamentation of any kind, only spare, squat, practical buildings. The residence itself is just a beige stone cube—albeit a very large beige stone cube—up a low hill from other stone cubes, the visual weight of which made me look for a fallout shelter sign posted in every door. As a whole the complex could almost be seen as a work of architectural prophecy, with the shape and placement of its bunker-like buildings to be read like tea leaves. On this side of the ocean, they say, Catholicism has been built not to soar but to survive.

That my father chose to enter seminary and so to make his home among these colorless buildings for six years seems now as accidental as anything else in life. And yet the fact that my own beginning depends on that choice and all that followed makes it seem necessary, as inevitable as the splash after a rock is dropped.

What was the rock? I had always thought it was God. As a child I marveled at the idea that my father had once been called by a divine voice. That's just how I understood it too: exactly and literally *called*. Saint Paul's fall from his horse on the way to Damascus, the Virgin Mary's chaste acceptance of her fate, the prophet Jonah's flight from his—all were reactions to an actual call, a voice, a vocation. I learned these stories early on and connected them with the events that had made my father a priest. God had called, I thought, and Dad had answered with his life.

But it wasn't really like that. My father's understanding of what it is to be called by God is not the highway to Damascus, but the narrow road to Emmaus, along which, as the story goes, the recently resurrected Jesus bumped into two of his disciples. Disguised somehow, or maybe just unrecognizable after what he had been through—he'd been to hell and back, remember—Jesus pretended he had never heard of himself and used this opportunity to needle the disciples for gossip, to find out what they were saying about him now that he was gone.

We had a painting of the Emmaus scene in the kitchen growing up: Jesus and two friends, presumably after they got where they were going, crowded around a table by a window. Jesus is breaking a small roll that's dark as a bran muffin; on the table in front of them sit a couple of 1st-century coffee mugs. The picture was hung in a painted wooden frame on our yellow kitchen wallpaper. My high school friends liked to call it *The Last Brunch*.

And, actually, that's the point: vocations aren't shaped by heavenly proclamations but earthly influence; not just by portentous Last Suppers or the intricacies of the Latin liturgy, but by breakfast tables and unscripted conversations; the road to Damascus as well as the streets of Lowell, Massachusetts, where Dad grew up.

From those days, my father remembers glass bottles in the basement window, beakers and fruit jars filled with chemicals that glowed like colored light. His father was a mixer of dyes for the textile mills that had built the city, factories that made Lowell's canals run blue with garbage and ink. Agawam Dye Works. Hub Hosiery. I never knew my grandfather, but I know he sometimes took his work home with him, disappearing down the cellar stairs to develop tinting formulas in a makeshift lab. He would have known a thing or two about compounds, about the ways different substances combine to create something new: add red to orange to make the creamy nude of nylon stockings; put too much acetate in your yellow and half the fish in the Merrimack River would bob like corks in water dark as wine. The power and volatility of transformation: my father's father would have known it firsthand. And yet when it came time to explain the birds and the bees to his first-born, the lesson came without a whiff of biology or process, as if there were some areas of experience in which change played no part.

"The most important thing in a man's life," Leo Manseau told his son Bill, "is to remain in a state of grace."

Bill's mother, Jeannette, would not have been in earshot for this man-to-man advice, but she would have agreed wholeheartedly. It was she who marshaled the family into formation every night to pray the rosary on the hard kitchen floor. A nurse, a chemist, and their five children, practical people, they knelt down on scrubbed tile and prayed under a picture of the Sacred Heart of Jesus. They passed plastic beads through their fingers as if they were following a guide wire back to its starting point, never surprised to discover that their prayers connected them to a dying man.

There was a dailiness to faith then that today is found only among fundamentalists: a suburban mysticism formed of the mixture of midcentury conformity and immigrant devotion. Together Leo and Jeannette Manseau had opted for an English-speaking church rather than one of the nearby French parishes many other Quebecois families attended, and then they had moved from one side of the city to another to be more fully a part of it. As children of French Canadians who had relocated to find work in New England, they knew the dangers of living in a culture closed off by language, and they knew their church could be a bridge, a way into the world, not a refuge from it.

There was also the weight of history, of all the Father Manseaus who had come before: one in almost every generation tracing back three hundred years. The genealogists in my family report that the first Manseau in the New World came from France to fight the Iroquois in 1684, but his descendents were more intent on converting the natives than killing them. Even with his antiauthoritarian streak, Dad has always been proud to note that in Quebec, Manseau became a name of bishops. For him this lineage is as grand as tracing our blood back to kings.

No doubt all of this played a role in determining that my father would study to be a priest, and later, what kind of priest he would be, but I wonder if also responsible, maybe more so, were a few fast-passing incidents that now seem to point beyond themselves, the accidental sacraments of childhood: during the war, seeing work crews of German POWs sweeping the sidewalks of downtown Lowell, perspiring through their sturdy uniforms; then, around the same time, working his first job, shoveling driveways for quarters, sweating in the cold until his pants were stiff with ice. When he had saved enough change he went to the corner store and bought nylon stockings for his mother.

Not a grand voice, then, but little lessons picked up along the way: that work for punishment and work for love can look the same sometimes. That echoes of both the sexual and the spiritual can be heard in the simplest functions of family: cold sweat buys nylons for Mother; Father's facts of life are theological and terse. A vocation is conceived not by the dove of the Holy Spirit or the stork that brings babies, but by a commingling of elements, as physical as the church has long wished actual conception was not.

As my father tells the story of his vocation, it was fairly simple: he was a social, outgoing kid, the kind of guy who emceed dances for the CYO, standing at the mike welcoming people by name, comfortable in front of the crowd as the band set up behind him. An early ritual inclination, maybe; a taste for the authority and risk that come with being responsible for other people's experiences. Or maybe he just liked the attention.

More than anything else, though, Bill liked to go off hiking by himself, into the Lowell highlands, the then still-agricultural corner of one of the country's first industrial cities. Away from the crowded house on B Street—three brothers, Dave, Skip, Bob, his sister Barbara—he would build a little fire, toast some bread, make a sandwich, and just hang out in a field all day, hunting for arrowheads.

He was a member of a Boy Scout troop attached to the Baptist church in town, but back then he worried a bit too much about his Protestant troopmates: "I had one friend from a mixed marriage— that was Catholic-Baptist, back then," Dad told me, "and I practically pleaded with him to go to Mass one Sunday. I thought his soul was in grave danger." When the theological stress caused by camping with Baptists proved too much, Bill sought out a priest at his own church and asked his assistance starting up a new Boy Scout troop, one that would meet in a Catholic basement instead of a Protestant one.

Father Thomas Sennott was glad to help. A young, active priest who'd come to the parish a year or so before, he not only cleared the way for Catholic Boy Scouts at Bill's church in Lowell, he asked the young Scout to serve as his personal driver, though Bill was barely old enough to have his license.

The rest is history—Dad's history; my own: One day, they were driving away from the rectory on Stevens Street when Father Tom turned and said matter-of-factly, "Oh by the way, I made an appointment for you to take the seminary entrance exam."

"Oh, well, I . . ." Bill said. He was sixteen, driving a big car, thin wrists connected to a steering wheel as wide as a barrel. Seminary? He'd given it some thought, but he'd given more thought to being a lawyer, or maybe a politician: an emcee on a larger stage, an emcee with more to talk about than the band. But then again he did want to help people, and the only people he knew who did that for a living were Father Tom, and his mother, the nurse. Of course, a man could not go into nursing, so what option did that leave? But then again, what about a family? Was not having one a price worth paying to be in a state of grace? But then again . . . He was sixteen; he wanted to be all of it once. Maybe a priest wasn't so far off.

We had driven to the Archbishop's Residence that day in 2003 in a spitting rain, along the same roads Dad would have taken on his first trip there: south on Route 3 from Lowell, down through the northern suburbs, skirting the top of Cambridge, then dropping into Brighton from the west, going out of our way to stay far from the frustration of Boston driving; the rush hour equivalent of avoiding the occasion of sin.

We pulled through St. John's main gate, past a solitary protestor huddled under an umbrella. His type had been a presence at churches across the city for the duration of the abuse scandal. He sipped from a thermos with steam fogging his glasses, wiping them off to stare into the windows of cars that crossed his one-man picket line. Once we were fully inside the seminary wall, the protestor resumed what seemed to have been his morning's work, marching back and forth across the driveway in a yellow rain slicker. His shoes—heavy maroon work boots—were untied, their tongues flopping in front of the soggy cuffs of his pants. He lifted one foot, dropped it in a puddle, lifted the other, splashed down again. The corners of his cardboard-on-a-broomstick sign—"Accountability!"—were bent like a dog's ears, soft and drooping in the rain.

Dad didn't seem to notice him, focusing instead on the stacked stone pillars of St. John's gate, which he had passed through fifty years before, determined to spend the rest of his life as a priest, an *alter Christus,* as each young man learned to consider himself then. Another Christ.

We parked the car and walked up the hill to the residence, rang the bell, and went inside, where that strange piece of art in the corner caught my eye. While Dad told me his stories of Cushing, Medeiros, Law, I watched the sculpture as if its shape might change. Through the chapel window, light shifted with the rain clouds outside, making the bodies seem to squirm. *Via Crucis:* In most Catholic churches it is depicted as the Stations of the Cross, fourteen images scattered around the walls, or outside in a garden, depicting Jesus' forced march to Golgotha, shouldering the cross over the uneven stones of Jerusalem. First Station: Jesus is Condemned to Death. Second Station: Jesus Carries His Cross. Third Station: Jesus Falls the First Time. The pictures follow him with his torment, the passion play as slide show. Jesus is Stripped—shutter click, advance—Jesus is Nailed—shutter click, advance—Jesus Dies. Yet there in the corner it was happening all at once: all that agony tied in a knot, beginnings and endings wound in one long braid—a braid stretching from the original Way of the Cross suffered by my father's God to the Way of the Cross Dad himself had walked with his life.

Around the corner from where we sat, a door creaked open. There was a rustling, followed by quiet words between a man's voice and that of the secretary who had let us in. Then the bishop appeared. Taller than I'd expected, in a black clerical suit, grinning above his collar, he ate up the floor with his stride. His hand shot forward before Dad was able to rise fully. When their hands met it looked for an instant like Bishop Lennon was helping him to his feet.

"Oh Bishop Lennon," Dad said, his voice excited, as if after all this waiting, he was surprised. "I'm William Manseau."

"Good to meet you."

"And this is my son. I was hoping he could join us—"

Lennon looked pained, confused. Who was I, a bodyguard? A witness?

"I would prefer not," he said.

"—because I think it would be an education for him."

Lennon kept quiet an instant longer, then repeated precisely, note for note, as if he had rewound a tape, "I would prefer not."

His refusal brought on an awkward four-way staring contest: Dad up at the bishop, the bishop down at him, me at the wall, and there on the wall was Cardinal Cushing, the man who had both ordained my father and excommunicated him, beaming at me from under his ecclesiastical pirate hat. Wanna see my operation?

"Well, it's your house," Dad said finally.

The bishop turned on his heels and went back around the corner, presumably to the conference room. Dad followed. The door closed with a soft *shick,* and I was left standing alone in the hall. For all my voyeuristic interest in the arcana of this place—seeing which was, I admit, as much my reason for being there as was keeping my father company—I realized I was where I belonged. What was being discussed on the other side of the door was not a world I or anyone on this side would understand. The two men on the other side were part of a separate, self-contained reality—a mystical reality, and yet one that somehow could be assessed and considered while seated around a conference table, with file folders, with pens. The reason we were there was nothing so mundane as my father's status as an employee of the church—he hadn't worked for the church in thirty-five years—but rather his *ontological state.* As the church sees it, and indeed as my father does as well, what was at issue was the nature of his existence before God. Totally meaningless, unless it is the most meaningful thing you can imagine.

I heard low rumbles behind the door, stood and walked more closely to it, but was unable to make out the words. I heard papers rustle, then a knock on the table, wood on wood. Probably it was the arm of a chair pulled in close to the tabletop, but it sounded like a gavel bringing the court to order. I leaned in and listened a moment longer, standing closer to the door than I would be able to explain. But now I heard nothing.

To save Dad a long walk in the rain, I went back outside to get the car, to move it up from the gate to the small parking lot closer to the residence. From the site through which he'd passed seeking the authority of the priesthood, to the scene of his possible submission of it. Two hundred yards and forty-five years separated the buildings: I walked down the paved hill alongside a field that sloped toward the seminary, the beige brick compound that more than any other place had made my father the man I know. As the hill leveled off, I walked past a life-size statue of Mary, a chalk-white Virgin in weather-worn marble, standing with arms open wide to accept her fate. At least according to the story the church tells itself, it was she who said yes to God and made all this possible. What if she had said no? Was her acceptance the model of Catholic triumph, or of capitulation?

I walked past the solitary protestor, who glared at me from under his yellow hood as I approached the car. Who was he? A man with some connection to this place, obviously; a man aware of the way beige buildings and the men within them affect lives in ways that are not easily undone. Whether or not they truly mediate between heaven and earth, their power remained great enough for my father to make a long drive on a Monday morning to discuss the state of his soul, great enough for this other older man to risk illness and the elements in the name of holding the buildings accountable to the purpose for which they had been built. From the looks of him—the flopping boots, the ill-fitting pants, the deep-cut pain in his cheeks and around his eyes—his connection to this place was one that had left him unsettled, disturbed. Was he a victim of priests? The father of a victim? I didn't want to keep my own father waiting, so I didn't ask.

But still I lingered a moment more, watching him. *Via Crucis:* His footsteps were heavy; his sign sagged over his shoulder. His protest seemed to fall somewhere in the gray area between the stance of a faith that sends a man looking for trouble, and the stoop of a belief that doesn't have enough sense to come in out of the rain. Only then did I slide into the car, realizing finally that he, at least, was wearing a raincoat.

I drove by slowly, around the parking circle and up the hill. With a glance in the rearview mirror I saw the protestor disappear, put out of sight by the sharp incline to the Archbishop's Residence. There one instant, then gone from the glass. Whoever he was, he was another soul tangled in the braid, in this woven pile of bodies and buildings known by that deceptively simple word, *church*. Whether his protest implied love for it or anger or both, he was caught up in it.

And so were we: my father inside negotiating the state of his soul; my mother at home, waiting to learn if her husband was still a priest; and of course myself, a son who would not have been born if not for promises both made and broken.

BRICK AND MORTAR

"Gathering photographs into a family album," Cardinal Bernard Law once wrote, "satisfies the important human need to remember and belong." These words appear at the beginning of Law's preface to *The Archdiocese of Boston: A Pictorial History*, a coffee-table book that, along with *A Day in the Life of Ireland*, lay face up and mostly unopened in my parents' living room when I was in high school. I never questioned why we owned the book; we were, after all, part of the history it tells.

The collection of glossy, black-and-white images is "our family album," the former archbishop goes on to say. "This book helps us, the nearly two million Catholics of this archdiocese, to remember who we are and where we came from."

Writing in 1989, Cardinal Law had no idea that he would one day be shunned by this family for the harm done to it by his negligence. He could not have imagined that in a little over a decade he would be practically chased from the city as priests had been in the earliest days of Catholic Boston's Puritan past, when it was illegal for a Roman cleric to set foot in colonial Massachusetts.

That's where the *Pictorial History* begins. Though the cover shows four of the same confident episcopal portraits that stared down on my father and me from the hallway of the Archbishop's Residence (Law, Medeiros, Cushing, and his predecessor, William Cardinal O'Connell), inside, just under the surface, is the story of a faith at once growing and under siege: page 12 shows a reproduction of Pope Pius VII's brief that, recognizing the Catholic population of New England as large enough to warrant its own bishop, created the Diocese of Boston in 1808. On the opposite page, we see the city's first prelate, Jean Lefeb-vre de Cheverus, who "commanded the respect of many of the town's influential citizens." That this must be noted of a bishop suggests something of how unlikely it would have been for any other member of the Catholic population, and on page 21 we find a newspaper etch-ing that illustrates this fact: the 1834 burning of the Ursuline Convent in Charlestown, the closest thing to a sex scandal the church had in the 19th century. It was sparked when the confessions of "Maria Monk," a woman who supposedly had been held in a convent against her will, became a best seller with its tales of the author's long en-durance of all manner of Catholic impropriety. The book was a sala-cious sham, but when a sickly nun in Charlestown wandered away from the convent grounds and was discovered lost and dazed, it seemed she was Maria Monk come to life. In due course a gang of Protestant workers emptied the convent and set it on fire. In the news-paper etching, flames jump cartoonishly from the convent's windows while the building remains intact. In reality, as the *Pictorial History*'s caption reads, "The damage, in both physical and psychological terms, was almost too great to calculate." The few bricks that could be sal-vaged from the convent's outer wall were later built into the entryway of Boston's cathedral. Since then, every bishop consecrated and every priest ordained has walked through the fire-scarred arch.

   That's the oldest Catholic story there is: abuses built into cathedral walls. Memory may fade, but bricks remain. Family albums set in stone.

The first time Catholics tried to build a church in my mother's corner of Boston, it was burned to the ground. The north side of Dorchester was then home to a small group of Irish immigrants paid low wages to work in the homes and factories of "native" Bostonians, Protestants whose ancestors had crossed the ocean only a generation or two be-fore. To carve out a home in a land that had let them in but didn't seem to want them, Catholics in Dorchester had saved their dimes until they'd gathered enough to pay for a place where they could receive the sacraments closer than the parish in the Lower Mills, a long walk across town. When their hope for a new church went up in smoke before a single candle could be lit or even the slightest of sins absolved, they started saving again.

That the fire was an accident mattered little. It was reminder enough of the Charlestown convent burning that when a sanctuary was finally completed it had the look of a fortress: gray stones stacked like a castle, two crenellated turrets instead of a single bell tower. The new church's thick walls darkened the lines everyone knew had already been drawn. Inside was *us;* outside, *them.* Inside, the ranks of Dorchester's Irish multiplied at such a rate they soon outgrew even the massive St. Peter's, leading the archdiocese to begin a second church less than a mile away.

The idea of a Catholic American was still a contradiction in terms to locals who doubted whether one could be loyal to both president and pope, but inside each new church, that's just what the Irish became: citizens of an alternate universe, complete with Catholic baseball leagues, Catholic Scout troops, quasi-Masonic Catholic men's lodges like the Holy Name Society and the Knights of Columbus, and of course the local branches of the American parochial school system, which would later be deemed a bona fide miracle when the Vatican made one of the system's founders, Mother Elizabeth Ann Seton, the first U.S.-born saint. With a building or two behind them, backed by an army of priests and nuns (the population of both nearly doubled in the first few decades of the 20th century), Catholics in Boston began to feel safe from Protestants and arsonists and anyone else who would do harm to the faith.

By the time Dorchester's second, third, and fourth churches were completed, domestics and ditch diggers of the Irish immigration could finally say aloud the prayer that had long been muttered with the low tones more rightly reserved for the Latin of the Mass. To hell with them.

The burning of the unfinished church had occurred well before my mother's parents found themselves in Dorchester, just off the boat, just before the Depression. By then, Irish Catholics had taken control of the entire city—best seen in the rise of such political families as the Fitzgerald-Kennedy clan—but still the separatist spirit inspired by early attacks remained. While for the boy who would be my father the church was a bridge, a way beyond the old language and the old ways of living, for my mother's family it was more of a wall.

Literally, too: they lived on the bottom floor of a house butting up against the grounds of Dorchester's second parish. The handful of buildings that made up St. Margaret's—rectory, church, two schools, and a convent—hedged Roseclair Street on both sides, the narrow road winding through the parish complex like a hidden valley, kept safe from the world by the red-brick mountains that rose to the sky on either side. St. Margaret's was another line in the defenses that enclosed the city, and its spire was the neighborhood's sentinel, the tallest thing standing at 135 feet, a brick and granite watchtower climbing four stories above the torn tar paper and cracking paint of the wooden triple-deckers below.

The Dohertys lived close enough to St. Margaret's convent that the Sisters of Charity sent over clothes and food from time to time, asking one of the children to take home a bundle whenever the nuns had something to spare. Not that the children ran around in rags, and not that the Sisters had ever seen the state the place was in; in this case, the charity the Sisters were named for was based more on assumptions. The Dohertys were the largest family on the block, five children by the last years of the war, two more on the way. Even with both parents working—Margaret at the laundry washing linens for the downtown hotels; Michael over in Southie, keeping the fires burning at Domino Sugar—they couldn't possibly have enough.

And of course there was the drink, cliché and curse of the Irish. There wasn't a lot of it—"not *all* the time," my mother would now protest—but still if Michael didn't come home in the evening you knew where to find him. When the Sisters sent home their bundles of charity it might have been because they had seen Michael making his way across Boston Street the night before, stopping at the wrong stoop a few doors from home, probably thinking Margaret had gone and changed the locks.

One spring Saturday in 1945, the girl who would be my mother was sitting a few doors from home herself, out on the sidewalk of Rose-clair Street. She was all of four at the time, so her memory of the day is hazy, but let's say she was sitting there watching an inning of the neighborhood game of choice. Ho-ball—short for "half ball," Mom supposes—was a game played with a broken broomstick and a rubber ball that had been cut down the middle, split like a grapefruit, so that it wobbled through the air when you threw it. The ho-ball's shape slowed it down such that if you timed it just right you could hit it on the round side and shoot it off like a bullet. If you hit it on the flat side, it popped straight up and everyone ran forward while the batter plowed through to get to first base. Total chaos. And best of all, when you cut it you'd have two balls instead of one. Play with one half and keep a spare at home in your shoebox, safe for another day.

Swack! A batter hit it on the round side and the ho-ball shot off like a rocket, high as the rooftops and soaring down the block. A dozen neighborhood kids tore off after it, this great ramble of sons of the immigrant Irish: Connollys and Falveys and Walshes and Gavins, every one with a given name like my mother's brothers'—John, Joseph, Francis, Daniel—or one of a few other choices from a menu made up entirely of apostles, archangels, and men who bleed from their palms. The Dorchester streets were full of saints: call one Patrick and you'd be lucky five didn't show up for supper. And of course there were Marys, Marys everywhere: Mary Catherines, Mary Elizabeths, and Mary Annes; Margaret Marys and Mary Margarets; all these city girls named for the Blessed Virgin.

One of them was my mother. She couldn't keep up with the bigger kids chasing down the ho-ball, so for a few minutes she stayed on her curb and watched them as they ran. Wild shouts and dirt kicked up by the clapping soles of their Keds, they moved like a thundercloud down the road. They reached the spot where the ho-ball rolled to a stop and they didn't even pause. The game had changed, they'd get it later.

They were all too busy flying now, arms outstretched like the B-17s they'd seen in the newsreels.

Back in the abandoned ho-ball diamond, Mary Doherty's shadow grew long in the afternoon sun. The sidewalk was empty, the gray concrete cracked. She never felt so tall. Down the road the ho-ball boys were charging at one another, spinning away, barking like machine guns—dogfighting. They moved as a body toward the far corner of the neighborhood. Mary climbed to her feet and wandered off in the other direction, away from Roseclair Street and the brick walls of St. Margaret's, center of the universe.

Mary's mother Margaret had been out on her errands, leaving Michael on the Doherty stoop to watch the babies with one eye, while the other eye kept track of the three older children down the block.

When Margaret came home, she hoisted Joe and Frank onto her hips, and scanned the crowd of boys as it floated past. Before she married, before the weight of toddlers pulled her small frame even closer to the ground, Margaret would save her housekeeping pay three seasons a year until she had enough to travel back across the ocean in the dead of winter, no better time to go home, when there wasn't a bit of work in the whole of Ireland and nothing left to do but dance. In those days when her father took his accordion from its case every soul in Kilgarvan, County Kerry, would make the trek to the Sullivan cottage though it was miles from town, crowding in to clap and jig the cold out of their bones.

But there was no dancing now. Margaret jostled both boys into the crook of one arm, used the other to block the sun, and counted faces—mine, not mine, mine, not mine—looking for her fair-haired daughter behind a scrim of skinny legs. Twenty-five years off the boat, her brogue was still thick as earth.

And where's Mary, then?

Right behind us, one of the boys said.

I'll behind you! Go on now and find her!

A mission at last. The squadron revved up and took off again, running and pedaling like mad toward Columbus Circle, loving the excitement of it, calling out, Mary! Mary! They swerved around hydrants and pedestrians like they were dodging flak on a bombing run. For all the shouting you'd think every meat-rationed kid in Dorchester was out looking for little Mary Doherty.

Mary! Behind St. Margaret's, out and around the rectory, the schoolyard, the church. Mary! Up Mayhew Street, past the granite steps of the Sisters of Charity convent. Mary! Down Dorchester Avenue, quick peek in the window of the Killarney Pub, haunt of all their fathers. Mary! Kicking trash cans over, she could be anywhere.

Finally they all circled back, emergency landing on Roseclair Street.

Mayday!

Mayday!

No Mary.

Margaret called the police, told them her husband had glanced away for just a moment and then Mother of God if their daughter wasn't gone. The children went looking but no. Haven't the police seen anything at all?

Oh sure we seen her. Found her down the drugstore on Boston Street.

Boston Street! Is she still there then?

Nah. She's down here at the station. Had herself a nice ice cream cone.

With that Margaret packed Michael off to the precinct and soon he returned with Mary in tow, eyes wide with ice cream and adventure. She still had a bit of it on her cheek. So did Michael, rubbed off when his scruffy chin rubbed her own. She couldn't stop talking about all the things she'd seen. What a thrill it is to be found when you didn't even know you were lost!

How could she have known? Wherever she had wandered that day, only the slightest glance behind and above would have shown Mary Doherty her exact location on the earth: in the shadow of St. Margaret's Church, the sharp point of its tower everywhere visible, like a knife big enough to cut the sky.

• • •

The world was divided, even a kid knew that. Mary could hear as
much in the air on Roseclair Street: Catholics and Protestants. Ameri-
cans and Japs. Better dead than red. She could see as much in the com-
ings and goings that buzzed around St. Margaret's like flies in the
pantry: The Sisters were the ladies with charity bundles in their arms;
the mothers were the ones with babies. The Fathers were men who
smelled of incense and aftershave; Dad was the one with whiskers that
scratched your chin. Even the ho-ball boys seemed split down the
middle: altar servers and hooligans, depending on where you saw
them. It stood to reason she'd soon be cut in half as well. What else
could explain the strange sight in the step-dancing class her mother
signed her up for: the older girls in tartan skirts and knee socks,
snapped to attention through the shoulders but wild and quick below
the waist, stamping and kicking to the mayhem of a reel?

Soon after Mary began school at St. Margaret's Elementary, she
learned that it all came down to spirit and flesh. Bodies are made of
"noble" parts and "less noble" parts. The head is noble (except when
full of sinful thoughts); the knees are less so (except when knelt upon).
The Sisters said it was a division applicable to every facet of existence:

God and Man
Church and World

She was too young yet for chastity and sex, but that worked too;
white and black as well, though all she knew of the latter was the
piggy bank they kept in a corner of the classroom, where a shrine to
the Immaculate Virgin kept company with the hollow-bodied doll
they called Little Black Sambo. They dropped spare change into a slot
in his plaster head, pennies for the missions, because it was the duty of
the saved to helped the unsaved, sure as lost little girls must be found.
That's the way the divisions worked, one half the hope of the other—

clergy and laity
truth and error

man and woman
grace and sin

Best to find yourself in the left column entirely; if birth happened to lob you an outside pitch, to land you somewhere on the flesh side of the board, well, Miss, you do what you can.

At St. Margaret's School they did not learn that all this comes from St. Augustine, specifically from his youthful dabbling in the notion— officially condemned as a heresy by the church—that the world exists in a constant struggle between the forces of light and darkness. Among his other bright ideas: on the pressing question of whether Adam and Eve could have conceived a child before they ate the forbidden fruit and learned how to sin, Augustine proposed that, yes, it would have been quite easy. Before the Fall, he said, sex would not have been a function of base desire but of holy will. According to Augustine, just as some men "can move their ears, either one at a time, or both together," and others can, "by lightly pressing their stomach, bring up an incredible quantity and variety of things they have swallowed," and others still "have such command of their bowels that they can break wind continuously at pleasure so as to produce the effect of singing," Adam had the ability to will his penis sinlessly to rise. Thus equipped, he could have taken care of business with as little passion as he might've punched a time card at the Garden gate.

The Immaculate Erection: At St. Margaret's Elementary they certainly did not learn that. What did they learn then? Not merely reading, writing, and arithmetic, but, as a school pamphlet from the time puts it, "the love of God, and all that love implies and demands in the way of self-control and obedience to the Ten Commandments and the love and practice of Catholic truth."

In every classroom there was a crucifix above the blackboard, the stars and stripes beside it, flanked by framed photographs of Pope Pius XII, and the new archbishop, Richard James Cushing, local boy made good. On every other wall there were pictures of Gospel scenes and the history of the nation, postcards from parallel promised lands: the Good Samaritan helps a stranger to his feet while Washington crosses the Delaware; Ben Franklin flies a kite while Jesus rides his donkey into town.

In their heavy wool habits and domed wimples that made it seem they were hiding bowls beneath their veils, the Sisters of Charity taught St. Margaret's students to recite prayers at the beginning and ending of each session. Mary learned to sing "sweet hymns in praise of our Lord and his Blessed Mother." She learned from "the Sisters' insistence on the duty of morning and night prayers in the home, the preparation for the regular reception of the sacraments of Confession and Holy Communion, faithful attendance at the Sunday Mass and frequent visits to Our Lord in the Blessed Sacrament in the church before and after school."

She learned especially from the book that explains the basic tenets of the faith in question-and-answer format, the Baltimore Catechism, so named for the site of the 19th-century meeting of American bishops at which it was decided a new manual of the faith should be compiled. This meeting has been mentioned as the true beginning of Catholicism in America: it was here the bishops declared the first duty of the church in the United States would be to provide every Catholic child with a Catholic education. With that mandate, the seeds of the so-called brick-and-mortar phase of the church history were planted: schools were planned, money raised to build them, religious orders founded to oversee their administration. From Europe and Canada, motherhouses dispatched nuns to teach immigrant children and guide as many as possible into convents and seminaries, which in turn produced more priests and sisters, who staffed more schools and churches, which in turn produced more vocations, filling more seminaries and convents, staffing more schools, raising more money, building hospitals, orphanages, rec centers, producing more vocations, building and building and building, ad infinitum—or, as was the mantra of Catholic construction projects back then, *ad majorem Dei gloriam.* For the greater glory of God.

It was the genius of the Baltimore bishops' conference to recognize that if the church was going to make it in a country as vast as America—vast in land, vast in options—it would need to create a veritable vocation factory. Officially parochial schools were declared a miracle for their work educating the children of the immigrant throng, but they were a miracle of continuity as well, incubators of a kind of asexual reproduction, producing in the middle years of the century more aspiring priests and nuns than had ever been seen before, an ecclesiastical baby boom.

All this expansion needed a spiritual blueprint as well as an architectural one. That blueprint was the Baltimore Catechism. Scratch any Catholic over a certain age and you will find splinters of a theological framework built to the dimensions found between its covers.

Mary received her copy of the catechism when she entered the second grade. On its blue and white cover, a wiry Jesus with hair past his shoulders rises through an arched doorway filled with bright light, floating like a comic-book ghost. A lantern swings from a hook beside him, but its glow seems only a reflection of the beams that propel him out the door. Except for a shroud draped diagonally across his genitals, Jesus is naked, risqué in the slope of the garment from left hip to right thigh, the white cloth leaving exposed the lowest part of his abdomen, low enough to show some small patch of pubic darkness were his body below the neck not totally devoid of hair.

This is the book from which she learned the first truths of the faith. It begins at the beginning—*Who made us? God made us. Who is God? God is the Supreme Being, infinitely perfect, who made all things and keeps them in existence*—and it continues through and beyond the end—*At the end of the world the bodies of all men will rise from the earth and be united again with their souls, nevermore to be separated.*

Quite a lot to handle at eight years old. But then that's the point. Every page of the catechism is meant to make it clear: this is serious stuff. It's not just a child's textbook, but a map of the Catholic universe. All that was, is, and will be: baptism to last rites, creation to last judgment, and all of Catholic life in between.

Mary flipped through the pages, looking for the life that would be hers. Every section begins with a pen-and-ink drawing meant to hold the interest of a generation weaned on Lil' Abner and Orphan Annie. Page 6 shows a mother, a father, and their five children, each with rosary in hand, all looking dour though the word PRAYERS floats above them, filling the room with red beams like rays from the sun. Page 14 features a well-manicured hand reaching out of a cloud amid more shafts of holy light. And Lesson No. 3—*What is a supernatural mystery? A supernatural mystery is a truth we cannot fully understand but which we firmly believe because we have God's word for it*—is illustrated by a small boy (an angel actually, wings and all) playing on the beach. Approaching from the left, a robed, bearded figure lugging a massive book points to the ground with his free hand. According to the caption, it is none other than St. Singing-Farts himself, out for a stroll by the sea. Augustine watches the little angel pouring water into the sand and says, "You can never empty the ocean into that hole." Such is the vastness of God compared to the smallness of our comprehension. A supernatural mystery, the picture makes clear, is all the water that won't fit.

Mary keeps looking. On page 33, there's a far less mysterious image: a child shown from the waist up, stripped to the skin, covering his face with both hands. Surrounding him, in the same red ink used for the heavenly prayer beams, a fire rages. Teeth of flame overlap the thin lines of his arms, almost engulfing even the picture's caption: *Mortal sin deserves the everlasting punishment of hell.*

She turns the page. It can't all be as dark as that. Finally she finds an illustration that seems to present all the possibilities: crowded into the foreground before a church with a tower like St. Margaret's, a dozen or so representatives of the world's occupations go about their various business. A farmer guides his plough through a field. A draftsman sits bent at his desk. A worker climbs up from a manhole in the road. In the upper left corner a sailor saunters by. Below him, a chemist holds a beaker to the light. A priest walks with his hand on a small child's shoulder. So many choices for the ho-ball boys. For the girls, though? On the right side of the page a mother walks with her daughter. On the left, a nun walks alone. That's it for females in the picture: the nun, the mother, the small girl in between.

She closes the book at the sight.

I can imagine her squinting incredulously, just as she seems to be doing in the one photograph I have seen of her from those days. It ap-

pears, strangely enough, in the *Archdiocese of Boston: A Pictorial History.*
Right in the middle of the section of images from the church's brick-
and-mortar phase—Cardinal Cushing at the controls of a backhoe;
Cardinal Cushing breaking ground; hospitals, parishes, and schools
rising up wherever he roamed—right in the middle of all that construction is a photograph snapped by an unknown press photographer
during a Holy Name Society parade in 1947, a picture of a family sitting on a Boston street during a nine-hour parade of church organizations and religiously themed floats; a picture of the marathons of
devotion typically undertaken by Catholics of the day. It is also an accidental portrait of the Dohertys of Roseclair Street as they would
have been known by most: my grandmother, Margaret, with the five
children who had by then been born. My grandfather, Michael, is not
in the frame. Margaret is thirty-six, still young in the eyes and in her
Irish excitement. She looks directly at the photographer, the grin on
her face so big it seems she has been waiting for this moment. She
reaches out with her left hand to shake the children to attention—
look, look, look at the camera!—but the kids just keep staring at the
ground. Only Mary glances out like her mother, the same tilt of the
head, but instead of a smile, she squints in the sun.

The harried mother, the distracted children: looking at them you'd
never know that they live in the starkly theological world described by
the catechism, but another photograph of the parade is a reminder.
Among those nine hours of Catholic marching bands, Catholic Scout
troops, Catholic men's and women's clubs, toward the end of the
longest parade in the history of the city of Boston, the "Last Judgment" float comes rolling down the road. It is pictured on the facing
page of the *Pictorial History:* a moving stage twenty feet long, ten feet
wide, creeping along at five miles per hour, covered with white cotton
bunting clumped together in makeshift clouds. Four women stand
around the perimeter, draped in robes, crowned with halos, puffy
wings dipped down to the backs of their knees. They lean back to
blow yard-long plastic horns, heralding the Second Coming with flat
notes that get lost in the din of the bagpipes up the block. At the center of the float, standing before a snow-white cross, Jesus himself

reaches out to a papier-mâché earth. Arms stretched toward an over-sized ball, Christ looks ready to make the catch. According to the caption, it won second prize that year.

In the photograph of the float, a mob five deep spills over the sidewalk behind it, mouths agape at this page of the catechism come to life. On the facing page, if Mary is excited she doesn't show it. She narrows her eyes and peers past the Last Judgment, waiting to see what comes next.

SACRED HEARTS

The letters arrived almost every week, written on stationery from the Fathers of the Sacred Hearts Seminary, printed in the upper left corner with the insignia of the order: a pair of hearts nuzzled up against each other, one stabbed through with a sword, the other bound in a strap of thorns. Latin script—*SS Cordibus Jesu Et Marie Honor et Gloria*—encircled the hearts, identifying them as belonging to Mary and Jesus; twin organs of a mother and a son, held close enough to pump the same blood.

The letters came from Jeannette Manseau's brother, my great-uncle Fred, who at the end of the next decade would vanish from the family without a trace, only to reappear thirty years later as casually as if he'd gone out for a smoke. But that story will have to wait. For the moment all that matters about Fred is that, though as a teenager he had worked at the Dye Works with his brother-in-law Leo, my grandfather, late in the fall of 1940 he set out for a seminary in Fairhaven, Massachusetts, eighty miles south of Lowell, where he began studying for the priesthood.

Before my father, Freddy was the priest in the family, the man whose ministry hung over my father's early years just as his did my own. If in some roundabout way I have my father's vocation to thank for my life, I probably have my great-uncle to thank for my father's vocation. In any event I should add him to the list of those who turned my father the Boy Scout into a man of God: Freddy, my grandparents,

Dad's early mentor, Father Thomas Sennott; all together applying the not-so-subtle pressures of precedent, expectation, and love.

Priests have a way of running in families, you see. The vocation is passed from uncle to nephew; from brother to brother; from father who tried and failed to son who must now tend to unfinished business. Pull a priest out of history, make him a plumber or a doctor or a cowboy instead of a cleric, and the family's ecclesastical lineage just might tumble like a house of cards. Fifty-two pickup and a mess of might-have-beens. A life given to faith can be that fragile, that dependent, as each priest leads to others, reproduction by example and will.

The same goes for their sainted mothers. In the middle of the 20th century the question of women becoming priests had yet to be raised with any seriousness, but the fact that pious mothers more than anyone else were responsible for filling seats in seminaries was common knowledge to the point of being all but officially recognized by the church. Not for nothing were priests known to keep their late mothers' wedding rings in the Communion chalices they received upon ordination. It was a mingling of the sacrifice the woman had made to bring a potential priest into the world (her virginity) and the sacrifice Christ had made to make the priesthood possible (his life). The ring that allowed sex dropped like a seed into the celibate's cup; a small tribute to all those Catholic mothers who generation after generation pumped the blood of vocation into the sacred hearts of their sons; women who sent their boys away to become men of God without a clue as to what the effects of this transformation might be.

All through the war years, in those letters she received from the Fathers of the Sacred Hearts Seminary, Jeannette watched the transformation of her kid brother Freddy into "Brother Bernard." There already was a Brother Frederick in the religious community, so, as was often the case, Jeannette's brother took another name both to avoid confusion and to mark the fact that he would become a new man before his time at the seminary was done.

"Yes, it's Uncle Freddy again," one of his early notes cheerfully and characteristically began, "writing again so that he can annoy you . . .

"Novitiate life is ideal and the rules and regulations are not too difficult. We have a large building four stories high, refectory on the first floor, study hall on the second, chapel on the third, and last, but most welcome at 9 o'clock, the dormitory on the fourth. We rise at 5:30, hear Mass, meditation follows Mass, breakfast etc., up to 9 PM. Our novice master took us on a church visit tour in Fairhaven and at the same time we caught a glimpse of the city. Well, Lowell is not so bad after all . . ."

That was Fred, enjoying his role as wisecracking uncle even while giving the folks back home a glimpse behind the seminary walls. He still had the tone of the boy who'd called himself "The Kid" in Jeannette's high school yearbook, signing his first few letters from the religious life "Pal Freddy" as if all the rest—daily Mass, meditation, the bleeding-heart stationery—was a put-on.

Before too long though, his tone began to change. "I was sorry to learn that you were not feeling well," he wrote later and more ponderously, "but you know the Lord purifies the ones he loves through suffering . . ." In this letter and the others that followed, which he soon was signing *Brother Bernard,* the change seems complete: "Pal Freddy" had become the dispenser of family platitudes. With every note sent home it seemed he became less a brother, more a priest— though not without cracks in the façade: "Say, what I am doing preaching like this?" he wrote toward the end of another pious missive. "Just the same, the war will demand many sacrifices which as yet are to be known, so there is much truth perhaps in the words, Trust in the Lord."

Maybe it was simply that the war had made them all philosophers. Cloistered away as he was from newspapers and newsreels, perhaps Fred's words from seminary were a reminder to Jeannette that her family could rise above even the fighting that everywhere else was inescapable. In such a time, who wouldn't want to believe that they were being purified by their suffering? That their family was meant for higher things?

On visiting days in Fairhaven, Jeannette and Leo brought Brother Bernard supplies he needed: toiletries, a bathrobe, socks, a dollar here and there, none of which seminarians could acquire through other

means. ("It sure would be great if I had a pair of black shoes, size 7,"
he once wrote, "signed, 'the Beggar.'") They also brought the children, Bill and his brother David. Walking the seminary grounds, seeing their uncle and his classmates draped in white cassocks and black
pom-pommed hats, it seemed they had come to another world.

"Say you know I had so many things to tell you visiting day that
seeing you I forgot everything," Freddy wrote when Bill was five years
old. "Great kind of weather for visiting though. Good old Bill and
Dave were right in the pink. Maybe someday they will come here to
stay."

Maybe, Jeannette might have thought. Maybe, and why not? Why
not another priest in the family? The Manseaus soon were on their
way to becoming one of the larger families in the parish—a daughter
followed the two boys, then two more sons after that—but still they
stood apart. Bill was always fighting to belong in the neighborhood,
and sure enough it would be the same for the others. It hadn't been so
in the French parish Jeannette had been raised in on the other side of
town. There, the change in the family's status when Fred left for seminary was immediate and palpable, as if they had suddenly been given
keys to the inner chambers of the church. If one of her own boys were
to become a priest, no longer would she and Leo be puzzled over as
outsiders who had moved their French-Canadian brood into a largely
Irish parish. Then they would simply be Father Manseau's parents, no
other proof of propriety necessary.

Yes. *Another priest in the family.* A thought like a gold ring pinging
into a silver cup. Echoing even when her brother's letters became less
frequent. Echoing louder when they stopped coming at all.

"Please tell Billy how proud I am of him," one of his uncle's last
notes read. Jeannette received it just after her oldest son announced
his intention to follow in her brother's footsteps. The family wouldn't
hear from Fred again for thirty years, and Jeannette would never know
what had happened to him. In fact it was not until Jeannette died, in
the early 1980s, that my father learned what dark secret had driven his
uncle away. An elderly priest from Freddy's order made a surprise appearance at Jeannette's funeral and told the tale: Brother Bernard had

fallen in love. As was the custom of the church at the time, the superiors of his order had demanded he move five hundred miles from anyone who had ever known he had been ordained. To avoid scandal, they said. A married priest was the worst kind they could imagine.

By the time he reached high school, Bill Manseau had been an altar boy for six years. Never a remarkable student or athlete, he was, it turned out, a top-notch sacramental mood setter; an accomplished maker of the "smells and bells" of Catholic worship. He was always first to volunteer for service at weddings, funerals, and early morning Mass, welcoming any opportunity to face the congregation, to light the candles before the priest and deacons approached the altar at the beginning of the liturgy, to carry the cross high above his head when leading the procession at the end.

Leo and Jeannette Manseau knew their son well enough to suppose this level of participation was due in part to the fact that Bill had a hard time saying no. He was so eager to please most of the time. His mother, his teachers, why should it be different with priests? And the fringe benefits—weddings put a little money in his pocket, funerals often got him out of school—probably had something to do with it too.

But that didn't explain it away: Bill also seemed genuinely to enjoy it. He was a boy partial to uniforms. I have one picture of him in the brown shirt and tie of the Young Officers Corps; in the tinted photo he is blond and pink-cheeked. The costumes, the secret oaths and incantations—*Introibo ad altare Dei*, the priest says. I will go to the altar of God. *Ad Deum qui laetificat juventutem meam*, the acolyte replies. To God the joy of my youth—it was as if a vocation to the priesthood would be a natural extension of his time in the Boy Scouts, which even more than church had shaped his life until then. The Scout manual in fact had been the true catechism of his childhood, life's rulebook since before he was old enough to join. Leo had seen him study it in the weeks leading up to his initiation to the Scouts ("Crossing the Bridge of Light," they called it) as if he were preparing for an inquisition.

Now it seemed Bill had decided it was time to take St. Paul's advice and put away childish things. "Be prepared," was the Scout's credo, and Bill was prepared to fulfill the unspoken duty of every Catholic household, to trade his Scout's neckerchief for a Roman collar, his beloved Scouting manual for a breviary.

All of that was fine with Leo. That his eldest would be the one to do so was not a surprise. And they did by then have three other sons to carry on the family name. But still, certain details of Bill's apparent vocation were troubling.

The problem wasn't the priesthood—it was one particular priest. As far as Leo was concerned, Bill was spending far too much time with Father Tom, the parish priest who had helped Bill start a Scout troop of his own, and then had drafted him as a driver. Between school, Scout meetings, and this new job, the boy was rarely home. Leo didn't always know where his son was, but it was a safe bet who he was with.

"Doctor's orders, Leo," I imagine Jeannette Manseau reminding him. Just home from the second shift at the state hospital, still in her crisp white nurse's uniform, it would have been difficult to argue when she made the issue medical. Difficult too to argue with such a disarming face. I know her only through photographs and a few flickering frames of 8-millimeter film, but I don't doubt it when my father tells me that his mother was often mistaken for his sister. "The man has hypertension," she'd say in Father Tom's defense. "Better for us all if he's kept from behind the wheel."

Maybe so, Leo would say. But still it made him uneasy. It was only Bill's loyalty—again that eagerness to please—that allowed the priest the freedom and mobility he had enjoyed before his diagnosis. It seemed a lot of pressure to put on the boy. Not to mention the hours involved, the lack of a regular schedule, the priest's sudden need to be here or there. For someone who shouldn't drive, Leo would have been justified in thinking, Father Tom sure got around.

"It's quite flattering, if you ask me," Jeannette would say. "Shouldn't we be proud he chose Bill over anyone else?"

Maybe so, Leo said, maybe so.

•　　•　　•

The Manseaus lived around the corner from the rectory, close enough that Father Tom could drive himself without much trouble. Maybe the doctor wouldn't like it, but the quarter mile down B Street took barely two minutes, and he wasn't a complete invalid, after all. A sick man will remind himself of that however he can.

Not a week went by when he didn't turn up visiting with Jeannette in the kitchen for an afternoon, drinking coffee with legs crossed under his cassock like a neighborhood housewife come to borrow salt. An older housewife, maybe. He had gone silver at the temples; his eyes sagged behind his glasses. No longer a young man, though at forty-one certainly he was too young to need a driver. He'd been aged by his health troubles. They'd given him an ashen look, as if his skin had grayed with his hair.

And yet he never failed to brighten when Bill appeared. When in the company of any of the teenagers from the parish whom he was steering toward the seminary—"Father Sennott's Boys," they were called—he still had that unsettling youthfulness of priests; the perpetually boyish quality they maintain until they are suddenly too old not to act it.

In the Manseau kitchen those afternoons, it would have been difficult to say what was an act and what was not. Bill had come to count Father Tom as a friend, but that he was a priest was more or less all Leo and Jeannette knew of him, and that was enough. The collar lets a man in the door sometimes, finds him a seat at the table with his life hidden in the folds of his cassock. Everyone played their parts: the priest and the parents no less than the Sacred Heart image that hung on the wall above the kitchen table, the rosary beads they handled when they knelt down on the kitchen floor. Catholic parents hosting the priest. All these icons, drinking coffee.

Later, Bill would hear from another altar boy rumors of Father Tom's time as a chaplain during the war. He would hear the story of a young man going from seminary to his first church and then off to the South Pacific. Not until after Bill had decided to attend seminary himself would he hear how his mentor had danced at night with a navy nurse and thought of leaving his vocation behind. A wartime dream. Then the bomb dropped and he returned to the States, back to the life of a parish priest; back to being a man whose closest human contact was with boys he cared for as if they were his own. As close as Bill felt to his mentor, as much time as they spent together, he hadn't heard any of this from him directly. There are things icons don't say.

Another cup, Father?

Don't mind if I do.

More than once Bill walked in the back door from school and found Father Tom waiting there, and just as the priest could not help but brighten in his presence, something in Bill inevitably changed as well. If Leo and Jeannette could not see it, Bill would make it plain in a letter to his parents that year, written when they mistakenly worried that Bill meant to end his position as Father Tom's chauffeur. Bill couldn't believe, he wrote, that his parents could have "so low an opinion of me . . . How could they think that I have deserted my beloved Father Tom. Him, whom I love more than anyone, except my family, in the world?"

Despite these strong feelings, because of them, maybe, when Bill arrived home to find himself in the middle of a conversation between his priest and his mother, it was a feeling as much of ambush as delight. The ambiguity of being chosen. The conspiracy of mothers and priests.

"Well here he is!" one of them would say, as if Bill's arrival at 3:15 on a school day was a surprise, and then the real reason for Father Tom's impromptu visit would emerge. Sick or no, he was always spry enough to drag Bill off here or there before he'd hung his coat.

Thanks as always, Jeannette.

Our pleasure, Father.

And then the priest and his driver would head out the door.

Bill escorted Father Tom on local errands, mostly. Some were no different from anyone else's everyday tasks—the pharmacy, the post office—but others were distinctly the responsibilities of a priest. Bill would drive Father Tom to St. Joseph's Hospital for the anointing of the sick; to older parishioners' homes to check in on shut-ins.

There were longer trips as well, and that might have been where Leo's misgivings began. Several times that year, Bill had headed off in the priest's sedan to the Cape, or into Boston. Once they went as far as New York City, late in the winter of 1953. Father Tom took Bill and one other altar server from the parish—another of Father Sennott's Boys— to see St. Patrick's Cathedral, a bit of Old World gothic grandeur in the new world, a foreign sight to the thoroughly American Catholicism Bill had known; a glimpse at the vastness of church. They mailed off a note to Bill's parents the evening they arrived, each writing a line in his own hand on the gilt letterhead of the Barbizon Plaza Hotel:

"Hi!" Father Tom began. "At least we arrived. How we'll get back is another question . . ."

"As far as I'm concerned," the other boy wrote, "we need never go back, up to the wild north!"

"Me too!" Bill added, and that was the end of the letter.

A regular Friars Club, they were. Well enough for Bill and the other boy, but one would hope Father Tom would be the adult of the bunch. No doubt they sent the note as soon as they reached the city to allay the usual fears: Bill behind the wheel for his first long car drive *(would they have an accident?)*; their boy on his own in the big city *(would they find a place to stay?)*. But what of the unusual fears? Bill's letter the next day did little to lessen Leo's concern:

A good, good hello! We arrived yesterday evening at 7:30 PM. We then dined out and went to bed about 11:30. This morning Father Tom said Mass at St. Pat's. We then watched a parade. After this we decided we were hungry so we went to an automat for breakfast. We returned to our rooms, hung around for a while and decided to go to the Empire State Building. We were there for about two hours before we finally got out, it being quite crowded. We then drove around the city for a while before we had lunch. After this we returned to our rooms, where the good Father ordered me to bed . . . Please say hello to all the kids for me.

Innocent enough, maybe. But how much time should a teenage boy spend with a grown man not in the family? After all, they had really not known this priest very long—he'd come to the parish only the year before. Or perhaps Leo's suspicions arose because he feared he was being slowly closed out of Bill's life. Was his son already becoming part of the realm of priests, just as Pal Freddy had become Brother Bernard? The family forgotten for the sake of this secret world?

Oh Leo, don't be silly, Jeannette Manseau would say when her husband hinted at his concerns. What secret world? We've known priests all our lives.

But it *was* a secret world. That was the excitement of it, as far as Bill was concerned. He had learned from watching Father Tom that a priest's life was hidden and in plain view, his collar like the shade drawn on a nighttime window, a light shining inside. Bill knew he wanted to help people for a living, to be that light, but that was only part of it. There was also something to the specialness of the priesthood, the talisman the collar became. Let's see any of Bill's other friends show up unannounced at the Manseau door and be treated as well. In his mother's kitchen and in every restaurant Bill had been to in the priest's company, there was always a space waiting for Father Tom.

Priests had power to say and do things no one else could, and not just in the church. Bill's father had told him the most important thing in a man's life is to remain in a state of grace. Only Father Tom gave him advice how actually to do so. He understood the pressures, the desires a man faced. He told Bill the only sure way to keep from touching yourself as you drift off to sleep at night was to wrap a rosary around your hand, putting the crucifix right in your palm. Clutching it, you could think of life's true intention, of the blood that had bought you from the necessity of sin. Failing that, a crucifix in the palm offered the added deterrent that it would not make for comfortable self-abuse. Only a man in a collar could say things like that.

There were practical considerations, too. The collar meant a man didn't have any financial wants: just look at Father Tom's big car. He had a driver; in the rectory there was a housekeeper, a cook, a secretary—it was closer to the good life than anyone Bill knew. What did the man lack? The collar meant Bill would have no bouts with unemployment, as his father had had. The mills may die, the canals emptied and Lowell left like a body drained of blood, but the church would always be there, Bill thought. It was the one thing in life that was unchanging, reliable. The collar secured a man's place within it, and at the wheel of the priest's car, Bill knew there was one waiting for him.

One night Bill was out late into the evening. The afternoon had been full of errands, and then Father Tom had taken him to dinner. A little reward for a job well done. It had been a long drive for a school night, down to Sheehan's, the church supply shop in Boston, where all manner of clerical accessories could be obtained, everything from scapulars and communion wafers by the boxful to carved wooden pews and life-sized plaster statues of patron saints.

As an altar boy Bill had already been privileged to see the sacristy of the church, to don his acolyte's robe in the room behind the altar just as the priests did. Now, at Father Tom's side, he saw how far the workings of the church extended. To see the vestments, stoles, and chasubles hanging at Sheehan's as if they were part of the fall line at Filene's was to see the reach of the Catholic world. Every garment destined for a priest, every priest destined for a parish, a universe of connections.

Now they sat in the car on B Street, just chatting in the dark. Bill didn't know it at the time but his parents were waiting inside. Maybe they were watching from the window. The car idling, the door not opening. He only heard of his parents' conversation years later, after he'd become a priest, after he'd left.

This is too much, Leo said. A grown man and a teenage boy.

Never mind, Leo, Jeannette said. The man is sickly and he needs help.

But the way they sit out there in the car—

Bill is his *driver*. Where else should they sit?

Outside, the two friends sat and said goodnight. As would often happen, talk turned to Bill's coming graduation, to his plans for the summer, and finally to the trip to the archdiocese seminary that would follow.

Father Tom had been ordained eighteen years before, and had fond memories of the early days of his life as a priest. Maybe he couldn't help but see Bill as his younger self, the son that might have been. In so many ways they were joined. In the morning they would perform Mass together. That ritual by which the rift between spirit and flesh could be healed. I will go to the altar of God, Father Tom would say. To God, the joy of my youth, Bill would reply. For now, though, all they said in the dark of the car was—

Thank you for dinner, Father.

My pleasure, Bill.

And then Father Tom reached across the bench seat. My pleasure, Bill, as he pulled him close. The cold of the car, the slip of the vinyl seat beneath his slacks. The shame of this feeling. What does he see? The boy's blond hair rolling up from his forehead, shining with pomade. Beneath the boy's jacket, a pink oxford shirt, making the blush of his cheeks seem the red of fire. A softness to him, apple cheeks. Still staring down on the dashboard at controls he only lately understands. Blue eyes so pleased to be of use. The cool between them visible in the incense their breath makes when it hits the air. It fogs the windows, you could write on the glass. He pulls Bill to him and holds his hand, kisses him, squeezes his arm like it is a final goodbye.

When my father first mentioned Father Tom to me, it was the memory of his mother inviting the priest for coffee that came most easily to him. As it happened, we were drinking coffee at the same table that had been in his mother's kitchen a half century ago—she's been dead more than twenty years and it has stood in my parents' kitchen ever since. At first, he spoke only of his love for this man, the great change Father Tom's attention had made in his young life. But in the telling, the love seemed to exhaust itself, leaving a space filled with long silences and half-formed sentences. "I suppose it should be acknowledged," Dad said, "that it was not an entirely healthy relationship." He paused as he poured cream into his coffee, white into black, as if watching the struggle between his dueling perceptions of the man who helped make him who he was.

"He was an honorable man and so it never went further than those awkward moments in the car." He stirred and stirred, staring down at the cup. "There was never any explicit sexual touching, or talking." Dad put down his spoon. "Of course in later years I realized." He took a short sip. "When I was a teenage boy and here was this person holding my hand, an arm around me, kissing my lips, I was sexually aroused."

Taking a long breath, he tried to put it in context: "If you were to go and talk with a lot of priests, I think you'd find that when they were kids some priest in their parish had befriended them and had initiated them sexually. Or something close to it—like me. There wasn't anything overt, but clearly I was being introduced to a very specific culture that supported the intimacy needs of priests. Even if you are oriented not to pay attention to the self, as a priest is, the self has needs. They need to be attended to psychologically, and if they're not, they will be in some other way.

"The difference between Father Tom and some of these other guys," Dad said, "is that he was very careful not to step over the line."

For the moment, that was all he cared to say about his mentor, and not much more can be known. I do have a picture of Father Tom, though. I found it tucked away inside the envelope from the Barbizon Plaza Hotel in New York, kept most likely by my father's mother; kept just as she saved all those letters from Pal Freddy/Brother Bernard: keepsakes of the men who made her son a priest.

In the picture, Father Tom stands stone still wearing his cassock, his white collar. What more can be said, he looks like a priest: the only flesh visible is that of his head and his hands. He has a fresh haircut, tight above the ears. He is jowly beneath the chin, but not round-faced. He holds his hands in half fists, as if he is bracing himself for the photograph, as if the flash might knock him down. There is a slight glint off his glasses. Some large part of his individual identity is purposefully obscured. But in those half fists—those fingers that held a blond boy's hand too long; those same fingers that held a navy nurse, dancing until the war ended and the old rules meant something again—in those fists he seems to know what Bill could not yet understand in those cold nights in the car: not even the collar lets you stand alone.

Where else should they sit? Leo Manseau would say. In the living room? The kitchen?

Maybe they want their privacy, Jeannette would answer.

Leo stared out the window, the headlights from the priest's sedan lighting the curb, the telephone pole, the neighbor's lawn.

Finally the driver's side door swung open, and there was his son, hands in his pockets, loping up the driveway. Bill would leave for seminary in just a few months. Maybe his training had already begun.

And for goodness sake, Leo, Jeannette said, Father Tom is his *priest*. If Bill can't talk to him, who can he talk to?

ACCORDING TO
THY WILL

Faith asks for trust in the unseen; institutions demand ledgers. For all its secrecy, its closed-door meetings and sanctified silence, the church excels at holding on to evidence. No sooner had the first tomb turned up empty than early Christians began filling clay pots with parchment, stocking reliquaries with saints' fingernails and splinters of wood, lining catacombs with the husks of the martyrs. A macabre efficiency, but also a pragmatic one: if God's new promise was to persist once the man it became was gone, memory would have to become material. As Christians became further removed from the miracles they proclaimed, the church expanded its archival purview, packing parish basements with sacramental records—baptism and marriage certificates, hard-copy databases of confirmations, ordinations, and deaths—as if this had been the purpose of its temples all along. For twenty centuries all manner of documents have been tucked away in a vast bureaucracy of grace. The word made paperwork.

It is thanks to the church's scrupulous record keeping, for example, that I know that on a Tuesday in February 1957, the pastor of St. Bridget's Catholic Church in Maynard, Massachusetts, sat down at his rectory desk to compose a letter that made my life possible.

"Dear Monsignor," Reverend William O'Brien wrote, "I spoke to you over two years ago about giving Father Creighton a change from here for the spiritual welfare of the parish and the peace of all concerned. Since that time, things have happened for which I do not accept any responsibility. I am still awaiting your pleasure in the matter."

William O'Brien is now dead, and as far as I know no member of my family ever knew him. But I have a copy of his letter in front of me, a third- or fourth-generation photocopy from the looks of it, a copy of a copy of a copy, showing not just his words but the scratch and curl of his pen, shaky as a distressed seismograph. Despite being directed several rungs up the ladder of the hierarchy, the note is written in a dashed-off hand that underscores the urgency and irritation of its tone. The sentences bow like wet wood as they cross the page, and the words run past the margins, shrinking to keep from spilling off the edge. That strange word choice, *pleasure*—"I am still awaiting your *pleasure* in the matter"—is almost illegible.

Given the significance this hastily composed note would later have for the girl who would be my mother, I study it now as I would a sonogram of my conceived yet unborn self, a text from my prehistory. I keep it along with a few others pinned to a cork bulletin board beside my desk. When I look at it now, almost half a century after it was written, I imagine Father O'Brien sitting back, looking over the note one last time before slipping it into its envelope, already posted with a ten-cent stamp. His letter, he would have to admit, looks like what it is: an afterthought of self-concern; a life preserver tossed into the wake of whatever incidents are meant by that ominous phrase, "things have happened." But what else can he do? He is straddling the church's fault line here: an *alter Christus* who seems to be the devil's own.

Father O'Brien rubs his left temple, taps his pen on the desk. He is a graduate of St. John's, and so he may be a bit nervous, sending such a petulant complaint back to the place that made him.

No more stalling, though. In the envelope it goes, the kind of letter written when enough is enough. He addresses it to the Archbishop's Residence, Brighton, Massachusetts, attention Monsignor Lawrence J. Riley, assistant to Cardinal Richard Cushing.

A year later, on February 19, 1958, the pastor of another parish on the outskirts of Boston, St. Raphael's in West Medford, sat down and wrote the same archdiocesan official about the same troublesome priest. I have this letter as well, and it appears to have been composed with far greater peace of mind.

Dear Monsignor Riley:

I wish to thank you and through you, the Archbishop, for transferring Father Creighton from St. Raphael's. He was becoming to me an intolerable burden, I am sorry to say. Perhaps some other pastor can bring out the best in him. I just could not. I guess that I lack pastoral power of direction or need to take a course in Psychiatry. At any rate, I am grateful for your favor in this instance.

With every good wish to you, I am,

Sincerely in Christ,

Joseph P. Murphy

In the course of a year, Father Gerard Creighton had been removed from one church, positioned in another, and then removed again. The reasons implied for the transfers mentioned in these two letters are intriguing but vague. Elsewhere in his file—one of the career-spanning dossiers the Archdiocese of Boston keeps on all members of its clergy—words like "homicidal" and "sick" appear. He would be similarly moved eleven times through his first ten years as a priest, three times in 1960 alone, averaging less than a year per parish—sometimes just two or three months—while the ideal length of priestly assignment was thought to be six years or more. Most of the transfers follow the same pattern: complaints are made, remade, and soon a letter is sent from the Archbishop's Residence:

February 11, 1958

Reverend Gerard Creighton

St. Raphael's Rectory

38 Boston Avenue

Medford, Massachusetts

I write to inform you that you are hereby transferred from Assistant in

St. Raphael's Parish, Medford, to Assistant in Saint Margaret's Parish, Dorchester effective February 18, 1958.

Kindly inform Rt. Rev. Lawrence J Riley, S.T.D., LL.D., Secretary to the Archbishop, of the receipt of this communication.

I am confident you will have a zealous and fruitful ministry in your new assignment. If I can be of any assistance to you at any time, please do not hesitate to contact me.

Invoking God's blessing upon you and your work, I remain,

> *Devotedly yours in Christ,*
> *Richard J. Cushing*
> *Archbishop of Boston*

With the exception of the name of the parish, the letter is always exactly the same: whether the move was to Sacred Heart in Lynn or Sacred Heart in South Natick, the archbishop was ever confident of the zealous and fruitful ministry that would follow Father Creighton's transfer. And whether it was St. Bridget's or St. Raphael's that would benefit from this zealous ministry, the archbishop never failed to invoke God's blessing. No matter the complaint that had been made, he remained "devotedly yours."

Another letter, written on the same day as Father Murphy's thank-you note, and likely sent from the very same West Medford rectory, charts the next stop on an "intolerable" priest's long tour of parishes in and around Boston, in his own words:

Dear Monsignor:

Received a letter from the Archbishop that I have been transferred to St. Margaret's Parish, Dorchester effective Feb. 18, 1958.

I was deeply moved when I received this notice as in saying Mass for my father yesterday, the feast of Our Lady of Lourdes, I prayed that if he were in heaven with St. Bernadette he would look out for my welfare, and I feel sure he has.

> *Sincerely yours in Christ,*
> *(Rev) Gerard E. Creighton*

• • •

By winter of 1958, the season Father Creighton arrived at St. Margaret's in Dorchester, Mary Doherty had made up her mind. Of the two paths through life presented to her—the way of the flesh on one hand, the way of the spirit on the other—she would be a Sister of Charity, like the nuns who had initiated her to the mysteries of the Baltimore Catechism at St. Margaret's Elementary, like the nuns who then were teaching her typing and bookkeeping in her senior year at St. Margaret's girls' high school, Monsignor Ryan Memorial, just around the corner from the Doherty house on Roseclair Street.

MRM, as they called it, was named for the parish's first pastor, who had arrived in the neighborhood in 1893, when the intersection of Columbia Road and Dorchester Avenue was nothing but an overgrown cow field. The half-dozen church buildings that soon loomed over these streets had all been built on the Reverend William Ryan's watch, last of all those which he called the parish's "crowning work": two schools almost identical in design, three-story brick boxes with so many windows spread across their façades they seemed held together less by mortar than by glass.

Even before the schools had been completed, Father Ryan had persuaded the Sisters of Charity of Halifax, the Canadian branch of the teaching order started by Mother Elizabeth Ann Seton, to send a contingent of nuns to Dorchester for the purpose of educating the children of St. Margaret's. No sooner had he given the Sisters authority over the schools, however, than he set about casually undermining it. In the usual ankle-length cassock of the day and the red pom-pommed hat that went with his ecclesiastical rank, the lanky monsignor would happen by a line of students one Sister or another had just organized by height. "Sister, Mother Superior would like a word," he would say, and as soon as Sister Justin or Sister Fenbar or Sister John Martha had gone, he would rearrange the children as he saw fit, a tall one here, a short one there, making a jagged mountain range in navy skirts and knee socks, jumbling Sister's small attempt at order and then scooting away the moment she returned to the scene of the crime.

No harm done, of course, except that no matter how many times the monsignor pulled this prank, Sister's cheeks would burn crimson under her veil. What's black and white and red all over? Sister Alphonsus when Father Ryan is around, enraged to be reminded once again that even if she should one day run the best school in the diocese she would remain, by reason of the clergyman's ordination alone, a theologically second-class citizen. Bride of Christ, footstool to His emissary.

Is it any wonder a generation of parochial school students remember the women who taught them as caricatures of discipline, penguin-frocked despots quick to snap a ruler at any bare knuckle in sight? If they did lash out at their students occasionally, no doubt it had something to do with the fact that the more likely targets for their pent-up anger were categorically out of reach. Such was the one-sided rivalry between priests and nuns: within the universe of the Catholic Church, to chafe under the authority of a pastor or even a junior cleric was a bit like being jealous of God—and if it was an amiable, elderly, well-meaning God, somehow it was all the worse. Monsignor Ryan was the first priest Mary Doherty knew, and so on some level at least it must have seemed to her that goading the Sisters into a state of paralyzed frustration was one of the sacred duties that came with the collar.

All through her previous three years at MRM, Mary had spent enough time with the nuns to see both the good and the bad. They were not just her teachers but her basketball coaches and choir directors. When she was young she liked to meet them by the door of the convent to carry their books to the school. As she got older, they became her confidants, her friends. Her favorite teacher, Sister Helen Thomas, was not a fire-breathing spinster of a Sister but a pretty young woman with kind eyes and a quick smile. Wonder of wonders, she almost made the habit look comfortable. So, while by the winter of 1958 Mary did not believe that to become a Sister of Charity would be, as Monsignor Ryan himself wrote of life within St. Margaret's Convent, "Paradise begun," still the life did seem attractive.

It's not hard to imagine why. Seven children lived under Michael and Margaret Doherty's roof by then: Mary, the five boys, and a sister, Rita. Crowded into the first floor of the rented house on Roseclair Street, the family slept crammed into every corner.

As for the Sisters, on the other hand, though none was allowed to go anywhere by herself, as far as Mary could tell they still enjoyed some level of autonomy. The very fact that they had no absent or alcoholic husbands to make excuses for, no seven children to feed and fret over and lose in the streets, this was as close to liberated as many a poor Catholic girl could hope for. Even if she had only seen the nun's life from the outside, Mary had seen the alternative from the inside and felt no pull to it. If it had to come down to the devil you know versus the devil you don't, at least the one she didn't know would come with a change of scenery.

If age were measured in life experience rather than years, by then she would still have been that little girl who wandered away to see what was around the corner. The next time she wandered, though, she wouldn't be alone. Come the fall, Mary would travel with a half dozen other MRM girls to the Sisters of Charity novitiate in Halifax, wherever that was, as a similar number of local girls had done the year before and the year before that. Well over a hundred girls from the neighborhood had gone off to Halifax since the founding of St. Margaret's schools, filling each graduating class's yearbook with pictures of chalky-white seventeen-year-olds boarding convent-bound trains at North Station. Freckled arms in white gloves, traveling hats pulled tight over hairdos that soon would be cropped to the skin to fit beneath their veils, they waved goodbye like they were off for the sort of holiday none of them had ever dreamed of. And in some ways they were. What came next remained a mystery. The Sisters had been a daily part of Mary's life as long as she could remember, but after she boarded that train and watched through the window as it chugged out of the city, into the unimaginable New England countryside and beyond, she didn't know what to expect. All she knew was that after September her life would never be the same.

Some of it, she hoped, would be familiar. By then Mary had made a second home of St. Margaret's, letting the liturgical year with its schedule of saints' feasts and days of holy obligation order her life. Those were years of novenas and daily communion taken only on the tongue; years when children who didn't know the Reformation from reform school collected indulgences like autographs. Mary in fact was gifted at accumulating both—her book of Red Sox signatures was her pride and joy. On any Saturday when she wasn't down at Fenway Park in her red knee-highs, loitering by the back gate to catch a glimpse of Teddy Williams or Jimmy Pearsall, she would more than likely be in the basement chapel at St. Margaret's, leading a novena to the Blessed Mother, though never so lost in devotion to forget that every prayer in the missal was followed by an indication of how much time would be taken off her stay in purgatory for each mindful recitation. An Act of Contrition was worth three years; "Hail, Holy Queen" was good for five; and the Angelus—

> V. *The angel of the Lord declared unto Mary.*
> R. *And she conceived of the Holy Ghost.*
> V. *Behold the handmaid of the Lord.*
> R. *Be it done to me according to thy will . . .*

—that was ten years right there, and you could say it in under twenty seconds, once your lips got limber. Quite a racket, these indulgences. You didn't even need to be in church to receive them. The use of certain pious exclamations when a curse might otherwise come to mind also had a measurable benefit:

"My Jesus, mercy!" (300 days)
"Mother of mercy, pray for us!" (300 days)
"Most Sacred Heart of Jesus, have mercy on us!" (500 days)

Every moment of every day was an opportunity to quicken one's pace toward the eternal reward.

By this accounting, the salvific gain derived from taking part in the May procession the parish held every year was almost incalculable. That was when all the school kids lined up in their Sunday best in the small patch of green beside St. Margaret's and one lucky girl was selected to place a crown of flowers on the alabaster head of the Virgin.

Mary never was chosen for the honor, but with her name the same as the Queen of Heaven's, the excitement of such days felt almost as if she herself had been crowned.

Through all these devotions, she'd grown from that squinting blond child watching the Holy Name Society parade to a wide-eyed teenager, her hair now dark and cropped short, mirror image of a girl she'd seen inside a promotional brochure for one of the sisterhoods: On the booklet's cover a girl looks skyward with the stars and stripes rippling behind her, a small gold cross resting against her chest. "Valiant women," the caption above her reads, "I can be one!" Inside, there was an explanation of who such women were: "The best candidate for the religious life is the healthy, modern American girl . . ."

As far as she was concerned, that's just what Mary was. She would always love the Irish jigs and reels her mother had taught her, but these days she was devoted more to their American equivalents: the quick footwork of a charge to the basket with the ball keeping time; the heart-pounding rhythm of a stolen sprint from first to second as the pitcher turned to throw her out.

In one of the few pictures I have of my mother's high school years, from the 1958 MRM yearbook, she sits at the center of a V of her basketball teammates, holding the ball and wearing a grin so wide you can see every one of her teeth. Joy like a rock dropped in water: the ripples spread through to her eyes and from there seem to light the room around her. That's how all the games made Mary feel.

That the Sisters of Charity were her mentors on the court and in the field as well as in the classrooms where she'd first learned her prayers seemed no accident—the games made her feel special, and church provided a similar feeling. If she chose to give her life to it, maybe she'd feel special all the time. As the sisterhood's brochure went on to say, "The Religious lives more purely, falls more rarely, rises more promptly, walks more prudently, is refreshed with graces more frequently, rests more securely, dies more peacefully, is purified more quickly, and is rewarded more abundantly." More, more, more: that's what Mary had to look forward to in the winter of 1958.

• • •

And then the new priest arrived.

Immediately there seemed to be something different about him. He was young, first of all, and strong-looking, not at all like Monsignor Ryan, remembered by Mary as a stooped, elderly presence from the days before her First Communion, or the current pastor Father Farrell, round-faced and soft and said to be given to drink. In a photograph of Father Gerard Creighton taken at the time of his graduation from St. John's in Brighton (class of '51), his broad shoulders and dark hair swooped up in a square-topped pompadour combine to give him the look of a big man on campus. In the picture he wears his new clerical suit with wide shoulders and a smirk that says he's got it all figured out. Fresh from seminary, the new priest looked like a jock messing around in a Roman collar.

When he unpacked his bags at St. Margaret's rectory seven years later, he looked much the same, still boyish at thirty-three years old—the age of Jesus, appropriately enough, since one church teaching Mary could not forget was that a priest was a stand-in for the Lord himself. She didn't know the words *alter Christus,* but she remembered what she'd learned of priests in the lessons of her youth:

What are the effects of ordination to the priesthood?

The effects of ordination to the priesthood are: first, an increase in sanctifying grace; second, sacramental grace, through which the priest has constant help in his sacred ministry; third, a character, lasting forever, which is a special sharing in the priesthood of Christ and which gives the priest special supernatural powers.

In her catechism, priests were never portrayed as the ruddy-cheeked ministers Mary had known until then. They were always handsome and slim-faced, not a wrinkle or a rheumy eye in sight. Sometimes they were pictured as none other than Jesus, naked and gaunt on the catechism's cover, inside transformed into square-jawed young men dressed in the vestments she'd seen every Sunday of her life. In Father Creighton, it seemed the parish finally had a priest who fit the part.

Not too long before, Gerry Creighton had been a city kid too; one with an impeccable Irish Catholic pedigree: his father had been a cop in Southie, and his mother had once worked as personal secretary to James Michael Curley, longtime mayor and "rascal king" of Boston. Such credentials should've given Creighton easy access to the lower rungs of the political-religious power ladder ruled by the likes of Curley and Cardinal Cushing, but still he had had a bumpy start of trying to become a priest. After a lackluster beginning at the minor seminary in Jamaica Plain, which initially barred his entry to St. John's, he'd set off to another seminary in Baltimore, and then another in upstate New York. There, things seemed to improve, but to remain in New York was out of the question. He wanted only to be a priest of the Archdiocese of Boston; anything else, whether it was service in a religious order or with another diocese, would take him far from his parents, and he felt he had to take care of them.

Eventually he made it back to Boston, where—after he was told by seminary officials that his earlier performance "would not be held against him"—he was ordained by Cardinal Cushing in the spring of 1951. But then came the inevitable shock to a young priest's system: after the alone-in-a-crowd solitude of seminary came a kind of roving isolation, almost more alienating because it followed you wherever you could go. The collar cut both ways—providing instant respectability, but also a permanent sense of difference, as if after giving your life to the church no other relationships were possible.

Father Creighton's assignments to parishes in and around Boston followed one after the other, six months here, eight months there, bumped like a pinball between parishes of the diocese; asked to serve a vital role in people's lives yet never really knowing any of them, and never being known. Such was the fate of the *alter Christus*. As a prayer popular among priests of the time had it:

> *Jesus from His childhood had the deadliest*
> *Of enemies,*
> *Yet He went on.*
> *Jesus was ignored and passed over*
> *For thirty years,*
> *Yet He went on.*
> *Jesus was not quite understood even by*
> *His Mother,*
> *Yet He went on.*
> *Jesus had the very worst of interpretations*
> *Put upon His very kindest actions.*
> *Yet He went on . . .*

On and on Jesus goes for sixty more lines: He was sneered at by the great. He was worn to death by labor. He was treated by His friends with galling familiarity. Yet He went on.

And so did Gerry Creighton: April 1951, assigned to St. Thomas Aquinas, Bridgewater; January 1952, transferred to Sacred Heart Parish, West Lynn; June 1952, transferred to Sacred Heart Parish, Natick. Yet he went on. In his first decade as a priest he would be transferred twelve times. After his father died he didn't care why they moved him so long as he remained close enough to tend to his mother. He thought of it like the army, he said. He did what he was told.

As the youngest curate at St. Margaret's, and on account of his youthful interests and demeanor, Father Creighton was assigned to supervise the parish's youth ministry and Monsignor Ryan Memorial. He learned soon enough to keep his distance from the school—apparently the nuns at MRM had become more feisty since Father Ryan's day; when he saw the mother superior coming he would run the other way. That left most of his time devoted to the altar boys (who would later write a letter to Cardinal Cushing praising Father Creighton as "the best priest we ever had") and the CYO.

That's how he met Mary. Active with the youth group, a planner of record hops and activities, there were more than a few girls like Mary

Doherty at St. Margaret's in those years, pious young things with heavy-drinking fathers and a gaggle of brothers at home, girls who were in the church so often you wondered if they were hiding out. Up to a point they had all pretty much blended together for Father Creighton; there had been so many CYOs by then, so many church softball leagues, so many carsful of children carted off to the beach.

One evening that spring, though, Mary said something that impressed him. He had piled a few of the older kids into his car for a short ride out through Fields Corner to Neponset with its strip of waterfront. As he would recall it, five or six of them sat there on the rocks across from the yacht club. Water flapped on the rocks and against the whitewashed bottoms of the anchored boats, the other kids went about their talk, and then out of the blue Mary told him that she thought the right thing to give Jesus Christ was your life.

That moment and those words would be what Father Creighton would claim to remember best about Mary forty years later. "I thought they were wonderful words," he would say. She was a nice girl, very religious, from a good Catholic family; how could he not see something of himself in her?

No surprise then that when Margaret Doherty stopped him after Mass one day to talk to him about her daughter, he offered a sympathetic ear. Mary was all set to join the Sisters of Charity, she told him. Of course she was happy her oldest girl wanted the religious life, but Halifax was a long way off, wasn't it.

Father Creighton figured he knew the situation well enough. He had an aunt who was a Sister in the city, and when his grandfather had died, it was a great comfort to his grandmother to have a nun in the family who was close by, someone she could see once in a while. Margaret's husband was still alive, but Father Creighton had seen the size of the Doherty clan, had seen how Margaret seemed to mind seven children single-handedly. He supposed she could use all the help she could get, and he took it upon himself to do something about it.

The next time he saw Mary he asked her, So what do you want to go way off to Halifax for anyway?

Well it's like I told you, she answered. To give my life to Jesus.

You think you need to go up to Nova Scotia to do that? What's wrong with giving your life to Jesus right here?

But that's where the novitiate is.

That one, maybe. There are others, you know.

Others?

Mary hadn't given a thought to other religious orders. All the girls in the parish who wanted to be nuns went to Halifax. Every nun she had ever known had been trained there, in fact. Why would she go anywhere else? Maybe it was flattering that Father Creighton took such an interest, but he had only been there a few months by then; she had known the Sisters of Charity all her life.

Sure there are others, he told her. His aunt for example was a CSJ, a Sister of St. Joseph. Their novitiate was just over in Framingham, an hour's ride from Dorchester.

That's a long drive without a car, Mary said.

Hey no problem, he could take her sometime, he said, and then told her the Sisters of Charity and the Sisters of St. Joseph were two different ball games. With nuns, there's a distinction between being a missionary and being a diocesan just like there is in the priesthood. He'd never wanted to be a missionary, he explained. His mother needed him so he always wanted to stay right there. The Sisters of Charity meanwhile had branches all over the place: Canada, the Islands. Jeez, they're liable to send a girl anywhere.

They are?

Maybe you should go and see my aunt and have a conversation with her, he said. See if you'd like to be a Sister of St. Joseph. If you're giving your life to do this you should know the details.

But I've already been accepted, Mary told him. Sister Helen Thomas is my sponsor.

Never mind that, he said. He'd talk to her. He'd take care of it.

And so he did. Much to Mary's surprise, she did not hear more from Sister Helen Thomas about her vocation after that. Years later, she would learn what happened. Soon after speaking to Mary about the Sisters of St. Joseph, Father Creighton went looking for Sister Helen

Thomas in her classroom at Monsignor Ryan Memorial. The nun was sitting at her desk, doing paperwork, and then the priest stormed in. Mary Doherty has changed her mind, he told her. Stay away from her. Sister was naturally very upset; first to have heard of Mary's change of heart in this way, moreover to be treated so harshly by a cleric of the parish she served. But what could she do about it? Like the Sisters before her who had to put up with Monsignor Ryan's shenanigans— Brides of Christ, footstools to His emissaries—she accepted Father Creighton's gruff intervention as another cross to bear.

Why would a young priest take such an interest in what kind of nun a schoolgirl became? It might have had something to do with the personal gratification involved in shaping a vocation. It wasn't just Catholic mothers who craved association with the next generation of the ordained or professed; anyone who came in contact with young people in the church was susceptible to this vanity. If prayers could buy you time off from purgatory, just think of the benefit of winning another soul for service to the church. Mary had heard one Sister or another bragging up and down that Mary's brother Johnny was going to be a priest, and she, this Sister or that, was just the one who would make him so. He never even thought of entering seminary, but from the way the Sisters carried on, it became plain enough that to them a priest was the plum, the best reward any parochial school teacher could hope for. Sending a student off to be a nun was its own kind of prize: often a girl entering religious life would take the name of the Father or Sister who put her on the path, like a living patron saint. Wouldn't it be nice, my mother remembers Father Creighton saying to her, if she became Sister Gerard when she took the veil?

So perhaps there was an element of ego fulfillment in all this, a man's reinforcement of the choices he had made, a celibate's one shot at legacy. But it's likely it also had something to do with his own ultimate lack of control—all those transfers by then, church after church after church—a priest's limited ability to direct his own life. He did what he was told because the pastors did what they were told and the bishops did what they were told. He did what he was told because the church of the day was a neatly ordered universe. To such a man of

such a church, it might have seemed that if a priest couldn't raise a finger of warning now and then—*Stay away, Sister; she's going where I
say*—it would all fall apart.

Mary had no idea at the time how Father Creighton had treated her
favorite teacher. Had she known, it is unlikely she would have spent as
much time as she did with him through the months that followed. It
would have been hard to avoid him, though. He seemed always to be
around.

The CYO used the basement of St. Margaret's Elementary as its rec
center, and in the evenings after school, kids from the parish would go
there to get the place ready for their weekly record hops, affixing decorations to the walls, using the reel-to-reel recorder Father Creighton
had bought for them to make long-playing tapes from their favorite
records. Sometimes they'd all be there taping and Father would drop
by to check on things, then he'd pull Mary aside to talk. Other times
Mary would be taping alone and he wouldn't need to pull her aside;
they'd talk right there among the scattered 45s.

Even off the church grounds he was always popping up unexpect-
edly. On her seventeenth birthday, early in May, Mary was walking up
Roseclair Street when back behind her she heard her name, shouted
out like she had left something at home. Only when she turned
around did she see that the shout was coming not from the Doherty
stoop but from a familiar dark figure, fast approaching on the sidewalk. Mary! he called, Mary Doherty!

It was the voice of a man in a black suit and a smile she could see a
block away. He had something in his hand, waving it over his head.
Mary Doherty! He approached so quickly she could make it out an instant later: a baseball glove. He held it up in the air like a flag of sur-
render.

Mary Doherty!

She couldn't help but be embarrassed, a little unsettled by the sight.
This priest was practically chasing her down the street, causing such a
spectacle she wanted to cross to the other side. She didn't, though;
just couldn't seem to move from that spot.

Happy birthday, he said when he caught up to her. I figured you could use one.

With the school year ending, the CYO was always taking trips here and there outside the neighborhood. They would go down to Nantasket and Father Creighton would buy them tickets to Paragon Park, or they'd go over to Wollaston Beach and he'd treat them all to ice cream. One Saturday he told Mary the pastor had three tickets to the Red Sox game, would she like to go along? Would I, she said, then went and sat there for the afternoon with Father Creighton and Father Farrell. Just Mary in the middle, no other kids around. Maybe a girl couldn't be a priest, but she could still feel chosen.

On hot days that summer they'd go off to another regular spot called Houghton's Pond, an evergreen-ringed swimming hole that was only twenty minutes away and yet seemed so far from the city they could've been farm boys and country girls, playing in warm water green with pine needles and frogs. They waded out into the pond and the whole day long Father Creighton would lift and throw the willing ones, heave them through the air so they splashed down laughing. They'd be in the priest's hands and then flying high and then crashing into the water: held, thrown, submerged, a rush of transformation. The freedom of it, to be tossed effortlessly into the air, practically a sacrament to kids whose own fathers could barely hold themselves up sometimes; to hear the whoosh of water as it covered their heads, to feel that moment of confusion when the rules of the world were suddenly undone. No wonder they'd been baptized in it: the way that water changes lives.

When the playing wound down some of the kids would lie on blankets on the muddy beach while the others stayed in the water, either wading to their waists or floating on their backs, staring at the sky. Mary was a floater. Father Creighton was a wader. Beneath the surface, hands would grab and slide and touch, and Mary would be very still, floating as if she were nothing but a long patch of pine needles, a dark spot on the pond.

•   •   •

That's the way the months went: other weekends, other trips. Sometimes they'd all go, sometimes just Mary and Father Creighton. Those
times, on the way back they would stop in at another of Dorchester's
parishes, St. William's, or else make a detour downtown and go to the
Arch Street Shrine. It would be almost evening by then; they'd stayed
away from St. Margaret's so long they'd missed Saturday confession.
Father Creighton would go in first, have a quick talk with a priest he
knew there, then he'd send in Mary. *Bless me Father for I have sinned,* she
would say, and the priest would absolve her quickly, as if he had heard
it all before.

On Friday nights all the kids gathered in the school basement for the
CYO dance. Father Creighton would always be there, the perpetual
chaperone, and Mary would never miss it, like the first lady of the
CYO. One night he called Mary into the boiler room to talk about her
vocation and it just didn't feel right. Oily air; the scalding metal of the
furnace. All the kids were there, on the other side of the door, dancing
as if everything was right in the world. She wanted to go back to the
crowd, didn't know what they'd think, told him they shouldn't talk
like this anymore.

   Hey now, he said. You're going to be a Sister of St. Joseph. We can
talk whenever we like.

   But it's not right, she told him. The heat of the boiler made the
smallness of the room unbearable. The church school needed enough
heat for four floors of classrooms; here was its source. The boiler
hummed and clanged in the darkness, the record hop buzzed beyond
the door, but those were the only sounds. He stood there in his cassock and she had nothing more to say.

   Well you're going off to the convent anyway, the priest said finally.
So just as well.

As that summer came to an end, Mary was nursing a toothache. With
everything going on, she hadn't made a fuss about it. Now, though,
the pain was getting to be too much to ignore.

Bad timing. Any health troubles at that point could delay her entrance to the novitiate. Her letters of recommendation were all in order ("The young lady possesses the intellectual, physical and mental qualities so necessary for a good religious," Father Creighton wrote, "and comes from an excellent Catholic family"), but still there was the required medical checkup to get through, and a toothache might cause a problem.

She mentioned it to Father Creighton, told him she was concerned that if her tooth prevented her from entering with the rest of the girls going in that year, she might have to wait until the following fall.

What was she expecting him to say? Perhaps there was still a part of her that would've liked to be told, Oh that's not so bad; it'd be nice to have you around another year. Perhaps it would've made her feel special for just a moment if he had frowned and said, Oh that's terrible, but then gave that smirk of his and added, But look on the bright side.

Perhaps there was a bit of disappointment, then, when all he said was, You should try a dentist I know. He had a friend who was a dentist over at Upham's Corner. He'd talk to him, he said. He'd take care of it.

And perhaps because she wanted still to believe, despite it all, that Father Creighton had her best interests at heart, perhaps that was why she did what she was told.

You're the girl Father Creighton sent?

Yes.

Well, let's have a look.

She tilts her head back, opens her mouth wide.

Mm-hmm. Mm-hmm. Well, they might just have to come out.

They?

Oh not all of them, he says. Just the ones on top.

No, no, she says. It's only one tooth. This one. Here.

Look they all need work, he says. Quickest way to deal with them—the whine of a drill in another room; the swirl of the rinsing dish beside her padded chair; the way that water changes lives—is to take them all out.

But—

Don't worry, though, he says. We'll get you off to the convent in no time.

Of course such a procedure couldn't be done in his small walk-up office. The dentist recommended that Mary check into Carney Hospital for oral surgery, avoiding any future dental trouble before it could begin. No teeth, no problem, his prescription seemed to be.

Because the extraction required a general anesthetic, she stayed overnight after the operation, lying in bed with a dozen holes in the top of her mouth. All that remained now between Mary and the life she had chosen was a routine medical exam, a checklist of possible problems a would-be nun might bring with her behind the convent walls. "Eyes: 20/20; Ears: OK; Teeth: being repaired," her doctor wrote. "This girl has a congenital heart with a loud murmur . . . it is a ventricle defect; it has never produced any symptoms . . . I believe this girl as far as her heart is concerned will be able to carry on normal activity for many, many years, and may well outlive other girls her age who have normal hearts."

The Carney, like a growing number of hospitals around the country, was run by the Daughters of Charity, so before the lights clicked off for the night, and again when the sun found her window the next morning, nursing Sisters in their milk-white habits came in and checked on her—*I hear you're off to the novitiate?* they said. *Good for you!*—and then Father Creighton dropped in for a visit as well. She remembers how he stopped in for a chat but she didn't have anything to say to him. She remembers that she wasn't able to talk much anyway, what with gauze and blood where words would be.

That's all right, just rest, he said, and slid his hand through the space between them, even here. You'll be fine, you'll be fine, he assured her. You'll be off to the Sisters and then you'll be fine.

Pinned to my corkboard with letters charting Father Creighton's movements through the Archdiocese of Boston in the late 1950s, is another document from the same era. It's a page from the *Record American,* early fall, 1958. Across the top in boldface letters it reads,

"Dedicates Life to Glory of God." Beneath the words, there is a black-and-white still frame of a Catholic dream come true: the day a daughter leaves for the convent. It is a scene captured in the living room of the Doherty house on Roseclair Street. A priest stands with one hand raised at the starting point of a sign of the cross. The family kneels around him. Mother and father, brothers and sisters, priest and photographer: there are ten people in the frame, so there must be at least eleven packed into the tiny room. Michael and Margaret Doherty beam at their eldest daughter. The other children look instead to the priest, embodiment of the forces that will take their sister away. There is a puzzlement on some of their faces; one of the Doherty boys looks angry, glowering at the man lording over them, *who the hell does this guy think he is,* while little Rita tilts her head back to wonder at Father Creighton as if he was the Lord himself, her hands folded in prayer much like a child on a page of the catechism.

Mary also looks up at the priest. Dressed in the simple black dress of a postulant to the Sisters of St. Joseph, in a few hours she will enter the convent he chose for her, embarking on the path from which the rest of her life will follow. As I know now, it was a detour whose course he set. And yet he stands there as if he has nothing to do with this family, just a man in a uniform come to do his job.

Father Creighton holds his hand frozen before him, in the direct line of vision from her eyes to his, as if there was only this blessing between them now. He scrapes a cross in the air, Father, Son, and Holy Ghost, while Mary tries to smile with the new teeth in her mouth.

Part Two

FORMATION

BENEDICAMUS DOMINO

"Well, I'm still a priest."

Dad had practically bounded out of the Archbishop's Residence, down the rain-wet steps, across the puddled walkway and into the waiting car. His meeting with Bishop Lennon had lasted a little more than an hour, and now, sitting behind the wheel of his Ford Taurus, he seemed a new man. Though I expected him to be drained by the experience, he let out a hoot of satisfaction followed by a sigh of pleased relief, "Isn't that something!"

The last time I'd heard such spontaneous exultation from him might have been twenty years before, when he took my brother, sister, and me to see the PG-rated *Raiders of the Lost Ark;* whenever Indiana Jones escaped certain death beneath a rolling boulder or in a hail of poisoned arrows, Dad would make the kind of noise you might hear on a fast but not too frightening roller coaster: *woo-hoo-hoo!* Back then it surprised me every time with its innocent joy. It was the same noise he made now.

"Woo-hoo!" he hooted again. "Isn't that *something?*"

He grinned as if I should agree that, yes, it was indeed something; as if I had stayed with my ear to the conference room door and had heard all that was said inside. In fact, I'd witnessed only the greetings and the goodbyes that bookended the meeting. I'd seen Dad go off with Bishop Lennon deferentially, addressing him by his ecclesiastical title like a junior officer to a general: "Yes, Bishop. Very good to meet you." And then I'd seen him come back boisterous and casual, even calling the bishop by name. "Talk to you soon, Dick," he'd said collegially as we left the residence. "I know how busy you must be these days. Thanks for your time."

It was clear that something had happened from the closing of the conference room door to its reopening. After pondering the *Via Crucis* for most of the previous hour, I couldn't help but think of the big door's closing as a tomb being sealed, the room within some kind of crypt in which my father's life as a priest would be interred. Outside, though, seeing that Dad's spirits had obviously been lifted, it seemed the stone had been rolled away. He had jogged to the car and climbed into the driver's seat like a man reborn.

The rain, which had been drizzling down when I went to get the car, started splashing hard on the roof and windshield as soon as we slammed our doors. Through the passenger-side window, I watched the brick campus of the seminary and archdiocese offices disappear as the glass blurred with half-dollar-sized drops, blown horizontal by the sudden wind. I waited for Dad to tell me what happened that made him so joyful, but after his initial cheers of relief, he sat silent for a moment, looking back toward the residence with an amazed and grateful gaze, his face beaming despite the gloomy afternoon.

"So what happened in there?" I asked finally.

Dad turned toward me looking younger than he had a few hours before, the color returned to his cheeks. "My petition for laicization has been denied!" he said.

Laicization is the process by which a priest becomes a layman, a member of the laity. It was what Dad had come here for—or so I thought.

"And that's a good thing?" I asked.

"Well, no," he nodded, backtracking a bit. "Not technically, no. Technically I suppose what I asked for has not been granted." He acknowledged the fact with some reluctance, like something he begrudgingly must admit, though his expression made clear that what he had asked for was not what he had wanted after all.

"You know what that means?" he asked.

"It means that—"

"It means I'm still a priest!" Dad whooped again. "Son of a gun," he said, "I'm *still* a *priest.*" This last thought he repeated like he'd found a new mantra, as if there was a mystery hidden in the words.

Still a priest: that, of course, was the point of it. Dad had gone there that day not to give up his status as a Roman Catholic cleric, but to fight for it. On our way down to Brighton, he'd explained that he had not followed the usual route of a priest asking to be "regularized," to be returned to good standing in the church after committing the canonical crime of breaking the celibate's vow. He had not expressed, penitently and in writing, that he was never fit to be a priest in the first place, that the responsibilities of the discipline, the lifestyle, and the service to the church were in fact too great for him, that he wasn't up to the challenge, that he was generally unfit and a failure. All of that is de rigueur when dealing with church procedurals. Because the church believes itself to be eternal and infallible, in its view if it deigned to make a man a priest forever, there must be something terribly wrong with him if what that means changes over time. As Dad saw it, the way priests who wish to be married are made to denigrate themselves for their decision is part of the problem. And so, instead of taking the prescribed path toward resignation, he had set terms. He wanted to make it clear to the church that he felt strongly that he had done nothing wrong; that he had neither made a mistake in seeking ordination nor in choosing to be married. He wanted to state as publicly and formally as possible that he believed it was in fact his vocation to be a married priest; if he was called by God for anything, he felt, he was called by God for this. Months before, he had written a letter stating as much and mailed it off to the archdiocese; they had never seen such a thing, didn't know what to make of it, and so had forwarded it on to Rome. Today's meeting, then, had been part of that old trickle-down of church authority: Bishop Lennon telling my father precisely what he had been told to tell him. To have been summarily defrocked on the spot was not out of the realm of possibility. And so, whatever were the details of the apparently less extreme response he had heard from the bishop, it was easy to understand why to my father the meeting seemed something of a victory.

"This calls for a celebration," Dad said. "I feel like we ought to have a drink or something."

Dad was then and always has been the furthest thing imaginable from a whiskey priest. Twenty years before, when his mother died and he had realized, as many do upon the death of a parent, that he was not as close as he'd like to be with his siblings, I remember he'd made an effort to be one of the guys around his brothers by bringing lite beer to a family barbecue. He probably had half of one can that day, but drinking it wasn't the point. It was the ritual.

"Let's see; it's 4:30," he said. "It will take us forty minutes to get back to Tewksbury. Mom has a workshop at the school; maybe she could join us after she gets out. Let's call her."

I dialed Dad's cell phone for him, asked for my mother at the school and after a quick hello handed the phone over.

"We're going out to celebrate," Dad told her. "We're still sitting here in front of the bishop's house so I'll tell you more when we get back. Yes, it's good news! Okay, see you soon." He held the phone away from his face and stared at it, puzzling over the screen and the buttons before handing it back to me.

"So what actually happened in there?" I asked again as I turned the phone off. "What did the bishop have to say?"

"Ah," he said, then unzipped the top of his soft-sided briefcase, tucking it between his chest and the steering wheel. He reached inside and produced a document folio, which he clicked open to show me a letter printed with the seal of the Archdiocese of Boston.

"This insignia makes it seem like a local matter, but the substance of the letter comes from on high," Dad said, reading over three neat paragraphs for what was undoubtedly the fourth or fifth time.

"It comes at the directive of Cardinal Arinze at the Vatican." Dad said the name like the cardinal was what a churchman of his generation would expect, some plump Italian ecclesiastical bureaucrat, rolling the r's and accenting the final syllable: Cardinal *Arrrrinze.* As we would later learn, Arinze in fact is a face of the changing church: the most powerful of African bishops, known for his conservatism and his tennis game. When John Paul II took ill later that year, a church-savvy online bookmaker listed Arinze among ten men likely to be the next pope. Dad didn't know this then, but still his eyebrows arched behind his glasses. It wasn't the name that impressed him; it was the address.

"The *Vatican*," he repeated. "They say they will not regularize my status unless I give up CORPUS, the Society of Sts. Peter and Thomas, and the International Vicarate of the Good Shepherd." He lowered the letter and looked back out the window. "Son of a gun. From the Vatican. You know what that means?"

I shook my head; I did not.

"It means they know about us!" he grinned. "It means they know about the work of these organizations I've been part of through the years! They know and they're worried. Your mother always gives me the business about all these things not being real—"

That was certainly true; disputes about the time my father spent creating and working for this group or that are the family arguments I remember best from my childhood. The way Dad started new religious organizations was a good reminder that the early church was sustained more or less by one guy and a box of letterhead: St. Paul sending off his epistles—if he'd had a wife she would have thought he was nuts. My mother was similarly unimpressed; as far as she was concerned, much of my father's work was an idealist's fantasy.

"—but this proves it!" Dad said, gripping the letter like evidence. "All those groups: the Vatican knows about them!"

"What does the Vatican know about them?" I asked.

"That they *exist*!" he cheered, then looked back down to the letter, studying it now as if it was Scripture itself. In a way it was: when you're trying to get the attention of a possibly indifferent, eternal entity, a single *thou shalt not* goes a long way to letting you know you are not being ignored—or worse, not noticed at all.

"So you know you're doing the right thing because they don't want you to do it?"

Dad's eyes brightened behind his glasses. Had he not been so excited, he might have pointed out that this was a life's work he was talking about here, and so, no, it wasn't as simple as that. Just now though, still idling in the bishop's driveway, he was too caught up in the moment for his usual precision.

"*Exactly,*" he said.

When my father entered seminary a half century ago, he had no intention of becoming anything other than exactly what the church wanted him to be, exactly what his bishop and the priest-professors of the seminary would make him. Trouble was, the kind of priest the church wanted and the kind it created were not always the same.

By 1953, the year Bill Manseau left Lowell to begin his training for the priesthood, the best and the brightest young Catholic men around Boston more often ended up not at St. John's but directly across Commonwealth Avenue, studying literature or law with the Jesuits at Boston College, or out in Worcester, sixty miles west, at the College of the Holy Cross. As Cardinal Cushing lamented, more and more men with each passing year didn't bother with Catholic schools at all, opting for other local institutions: Harvard, Boston University, Northeastern, schools where many Catholic students, at least according to Cushing, "had lost both their Americanism and their faith."

Cushing's generation of churchmen had reason to be insular: even as Catholics gained acceptance in, and then control of, formerly Protestant strongholds like Boston, many of the smartest Catholic kids were more interested in pursuing secular careers than in serving their church.

If the church was headed for a shortage of those on the ecclesiastical track, however, you never would have known it from pulling into St. John's driveway back then. In its heyday, the archdiocese seminary was overpopulated, filled past capacity with young men much like my father: B+ students with devout mothers, not many stars among them, not many options either. They were working-class boys raised in working-class parishes, their surnames overwhelming Irish, with handfuls of Italian, Polish, and French-Canadian names thrown in. And yet they were boys whose models for priestliness were clerics of a thoroughly American Catholicism, as athletic and anti-intellectual as a pep rally. My father remembers priests who played football in their cassocks; others famous for rushing through the liturgy in twelve minutes flat; and of course there was his own mentor, Father Tom, den mother to the Catholic Scouts of Lowell. These priests were the products of the training each new crop of boys received in seminary, and they reflected well what one would find at St John's and in the rectory life that would follow: a culture of jocks and "gents," as they were called, priests more interested in a round of golf and a good cigar than any deeper questions of faith.

To be sure, some of the boys entering each year did so with a true sense of religious mission; for others, the guaranteed comfort of the lifestyle was a sufficient lure; for more than a few, the choice had seemed inevitable, barely a choice at all, for as long as they could remember.

Whatever were their individual reasons, as a group the boys who entered "the Sem" with my father were products of a ghetto culture that had flourished within the walls. The vocation factories created by the Baltimore bishops' conference had proved so effective at sending the teenage boys of Catholic Boston down the path to the priesthood that from the beginning of the 1950s to the end the Brighton campus nearly tripled its size. Two extra dormitories were built, and nearby Cardinal Cushing established a minor seminary in his predecessor's name. The minor seminary was a kind of preparatory school for the boys who went straight from high school to their ecclesiastical training, as my father did, and it was useful both for making room at St. John's and for weeding out the halfhearted. With so many seeking admission to the ranks of Boston's clergy, the archdiocese could afford to be selective—or at least pretend to be. In truth, pretty much anyone who could pay the five-hundred-dollar tuition was in.

Ultimately, all this growth would prove to be a high point preceding the rapid decline of the decades to follow. In 1953, though, with seminarians numbering in the hundreds and no end in sight to the flood of aspiring priests, it was impossible not to be optimistic. Whether it was seen from the new residence halls at St. John's, or from the beige block of Cardinal Cushing's palatial residence, or by a pink-cheeked seventeen-year-old fresh from Lowell High School, newly arrived at the Cardinal O'Connell Seminary, the future of the church looked bright.

Even so, Bill spent the first few days of his new life under a cloud. As much as both the seminary and the archdiocese had grown in the past few years, the world of priests and would-be priests remained very small. No matter that upon entering seminary he was supposed to put his old concerns behind him—"to put away childish things," as St. Paul would have advised—word had reached him at home even as he packed his bags: Father Tom was dead.

His mentor had died the morning he left for seminary, dropped over at age forty-one due to complications of the high blood pressure that had led him to have Bill as his driver, and the news was devastating. Father Tom more than anyone else was responsible for Bill's decision to enter St. John's, and now he was gone. Far from lifting the burden and responsibility he'd known as the priest's protégé—that shadow of inescapable chosenness that had covered him at the wheel of the sick man's car—he now felt it more than ever. Suddenly he had not only a mother's hopes and a father's piety to answer to, but the legacy of a beloved priest who had died too soon. What's more, with this death there was literally a grail waiting at the end of his quest for the future Father Manseau: he was told Father Tom's eucharistic chalice—a priest's prized possession, in which by tradition a cleric's mother's wedding ring could be kept—would be Bill's upon ordination. The late priest's only two living relations—a widowed aunt and a brother, Monsignor Sennott—each told Bill that he had been Father Tom's favorite; that, in fact, Tom had thought of Bill as a son. Yet that the chalice was an inheritance fraught with Freudian implications was something Bill would not realize for years. At the time he would have been far more likely to think of it scripturally: "Take this cup away from me," was Christ's famous plea to his father in heaven on the eve of his crucifixion. "But not my will, but yours be done." Now, as it was for Jesus so it was for Bill: ready or not, the cup of the priesthood would be thrust into his hands.

That the start of a vocation could have a tint of death to it is not a surprise. Like boot camp, seminary is intended to unmake and remake a man; with the central story of the faith being what it is, this process cannot but call to mind Jesus' days spent in the tomb. Inside the wrought-iron entryway, the sign read *Cardinal O'Connell Seminary* but if they looked fast over the well-groomed lawn and the somber building behind it, the boys might have wondered if they'd come to be buried. Such was the shudder of finality as they approached the gate.

It was especially so for my father. He was preoccupied for the first day or so with the question of whether he should go to Father Tom's funeral. "I talked with the priests there, and when they advised against it, I decided not to go," he told me recently. "Later I came to regret that decision. But I don't think they would have allowed it anyway."

He wrote home the day after he arrived:

Sept 22, 1953 8:20 AM
Cardinal O'Connell Seminary
Dear Mom, Dad, and kids,

We just finished breakfast and our morning walk. Boy, it was cold. Well, so far everything has gone off alright. Gee whiz, I can't get within a foot from the bed without getting lint all over my cassock. Later on, please send me a whisk broom.

I still can't get used to the idea that Father Tom is dead. I know that he is, but I still can't believe it. Please pray hard so that the ache will go away and I can get down to business.

I slept like a log last night and the bell this morning nearly knocked me out of bed.

This initial shock of confusion and loss was followed by a more gradual letting go. His only contact with his family came when, once a week, Leo Manseau made the hour-long drive from Lowell to Jamaica Plain. He didn't come to visit—seminarians weren't allowed visitors—but to drop off a bundle of freshly washed socks and underwear, along with provisions one couldn't get in the seminary's dining hall. Seventeen-year-old Bill would watch from inside a darkened doorway for his father to arrive and leave the bundles on the front steps, and only after the car had driven off would he step out of the shadows and collect the goodies, which were almost always the same: a roast beef sandwhich and a couple of milk shakes, one for Bill and another for some lucky classmate—not necessarily a friend, since seminarians weren't technically allowed those either.

In his laundry bag Bill would never fail to tuck a note for his parents. "Greetings from not so far, but o so very far away," he once wrote. With four younger siblings crowding the house on B Street, replies came far less often than he would have liked.

You must be quite busy at home, but out of five people who claim they know how to write it doesn't seem as if anyone does. You have the family, I have four walls, a ceiling and a floor. O, yes, and a window, door, and mirror.

The loneliness, the separation from family and their world, was part of the process. In fact, it was part of the Rule, the slim green volume that outlined all the regulations and restrictions of seminary life. "No seminarian shall receive visits from outsiders," the Rule's 63rd commandment declared, "either within the Seminary buildings or on the Seminary grounds." The 69th: "Absolute silence shall be maintained at all times, even during the periods of recreation, in the corridors, toilets and showers immediately adjacent to students' rooms. No one shall speak at the door of another seminarian without explicit permission." The 78th: "It is forbidden to introduce into the Seminary, or to read, or to keep in one's room, any newspaper, magazine or periodical, with the exception of the official publications of the Archdiocese of Boston. . . ."

It was a procedure like tuning an instrument, taking the loose strands of a boy's life and tightening them until they played on a common scale, suspicious of every outside influence. "By the way, they read our mail sometimes," Bill wrote another time in those first few weeks. "It's in canon law, I guess."

Such rules of isolation and control were supposed to make the boys who entered seminary into men wholly of the church, holding them to the advice of the Gospel of Matthew: "Everyone who has left houses or brothers or sisters or father or mother or children or farms for My name's sake, will receive many times as much, and will inherit eternal life. . . ." But the rules created an atmosphere as much like summer camp as a hermitage, prolonging among the seminarians a timid adolescent's approach to authority. Rules weren't to be questioned or challenged but to be publicly affirmed and privately worked around.

In the first two summers, for example, Bill went home and guiltily but no less eagerly transgressed by going on dates whenever he could, trying out the life he was giving up—and scandalizing the girls when they learned he was a seminarian. Once he was in the front seat of a car with a girl, kissing awkwardly with the steering wheel in his lap. Then they stopped and started talking, laughing and enjoying each other's company. "This is a whole lot better than that other stuff," he said.

"Looking back on that now," Dad told me, "I think I grew up a bit then." Grew up a bit maybe, and also became more of a priest in a number of ways. From the start the question of celibacy for him had been less about sex and more about family, about not marrying and not having children. It had seemed to him a price worth paying, and parked in the car with that summertime sweetheart, he was able to reaffirm that this was so by convincing himself that if he could have one part of intimacy it would be enough. But it seems to me now that the other way he became more of a priest that night had to do with the division of his interior life. As seminarians they learned to live two lives: one sanctified, one unsanctioned, concealing the usual longings of men barely past adolescence beneath the heavy cloth of their cassocks.

If this was true at the minor seminary, it was even more so when the boys, two years older and wiser, and perhaps two years more jaded by the system, arrived at St. John's for a curriculum of four semesters of philosophy followed by eight of theology.

Through all this, they learned very little about the reasons behind the peculiarities of the life they had chosen for themselves. And nothing was more peculiar about the life than celibacy, which at once defined them and was never discussed. They were taught simply that they were celibate because Christ was celibate. They were taught that unlike such moral issues such as murder or theft, in anything involving sex there was considered to be no *parvitas materiae*—no smallness of matter. It was the one area of experience in which the church saw no gray, and celibacy was the one sure way to stay on the right side of the black and white divide.

In fact, there was nothing but gray. The history of celibacy is far more interesting than the church led the young adherents to believe. Whatever conflicted with the claim that the church's attitude toward sex was the same as it had been since the beginning was conveniently passed over.

The willful blindness started with Scripture. In the Gospels, for example, not only is it never stated that Jesus was celibate, it is explicitly and repeatedly mentioned that his disciples were not. What's more, in order to maintain the illusion that celibacy was practiced by the founders of the faith, they had to ignore James, the brother of Jesus, for if Mary was supposed to be ever-virgin, and Jesus was the only virgin birth, who the hell was this guy? Similarly, they ignored much of the writings of Paul—his letter to the Corinthians, for example: "Do we not have the right to be accompanied by a wife, as the other apostles of the Lord?" And certainly this, from his letter to Timothy: "A bishop then must be blameless, married but once . . . He should rule well his own household, keeping his children under control and perfectly respectful . . ."

They also ignored history. Though seminarians grew up reciting a profession of faith called the Nicene Creed, they never learned that when the Council of Nicaea was held, in the year 325, the majority of priests and many bishops were married. They never learned that, at this same council at which the creed was adopted, when the question of celibacy was raised it was decided it should be left to each priest's sense of vocation, to his personal choice. They did not learn that more than a dozen popes had fathered children. They did not learn that it was not until the Second Lateran Council, 1139, that marriage became forbidden for clergy, and even then the issue was less about sex than about property. Too many priests were passing their churches down to their sons.

Worst of all, given the lifelong sacrifice the church asked of these young men, seminary education avoided complexity. As long as the church has existed, it has been moved and shaped by the conflict and complement of the physical and the spiritual. The earliest Christians who chose to swear off marriage did so because they believed what their murdered teacher had told them: that the Kingdom of Heaven was at hand. With Christ due back any day now to redeem the world, you can understand how sex might seem beside the point. Whatever else it is, celibacy is the legacy of that early yearning. Down through the centuries, though, hope for the world turned into hatred of it. Christians dreaming of revelation became seminarians hiding in the shadows when their fathers came to pick up the laundry.

Of course, no one questioned it, not then. Cardinal Cushing's official motto was *Ut Cognoscant Te*, "That they may know You," but the unofficial credo of the seminary he controlled was hinted at in the advice heard by any seminarian who sought to distinguish himself. Keep your head down, they used to warn each other at St. John's, or you'll get it cut off.

To help them keep their heads down, they followed a tightly regimented schedule, starting each morning with a 5:40 bang on every seminarian's door and a call of *"Benedicamus Domino!"* Let us bless the Lord. *"Deo Gratias,"* came the groggy reply from every darkened dorm room. Thanks be to God.

The rooms were small: a desk, a bed, a chest-high bureau; barely enough room for even two men to stand at once, but that wasn't a concern—they weren't allowed inside one another's rooms, not even a foot over the threshold. This was officially in the name of maintaining a quasi-monastic environment, but it may have also had something to do with the fact that even then, in the late '50s, there had been rumors of sexual encounters between St. John's third-year seminarians, "Theologians," and the first- and second-year students, "Philosophers," to whom the older boys had formerly been assigned as spiritual mentors. Details about these incidents were hard to come by, but still it was a fact that Theologians were not allowed under any circumstances into the Philosophers' buildings. (The Rule's 3rd commandment: "The Theology Community shall be completely distinct from the Philosophy Community . . . A line running south to north from the garage . . . will mark the boundary between the two communities. Theologians will remain to the west, Philosophers to the east of this line.") Likewise, after each morning's call of *Benedicamus Domino!* there'd be no nudge from a classmate to get you up on time, only a bang on the door, a fist that declared it was time to pray.

From then on the day ticked by in intervals of twenty, forty-five, sixty minutes: 6:00 Morning Prayer and Meditation. 6:30 Community Mass, followed by Thanksgiving Mass. At 7:15: Care of Rooms. 7:35: Breakfast. 8:10: Retire to Rooms, and then classes until dinner. From the seminary course catalog, 1958:

Special Dogma 205: *De Creante et Elevante*
A study of the creation and formation of the world. The Angels. The nature and origin of man; his elevation, his supernatural and preternatural gifts. Original Sin, its nature and consequences.

Moral Theology 305: *De fortitudine. De Abstinentia et Sobrietate. De Virtutibus Theologicis*
The functions of fortitude in a man's moral life. Abstinence as an act of mortification. Ecclesiastical legislation on fasting and abstinence. Sobriety; the sin of drunkenness. The infused virtues of faith, hope, and charity.

Moral Theology 306: *De Castitate et de Usu Matrimonii*
The virtue of chastity. The practice of chastity. The virtue of chastity in relation to married life.

After dinner, it was more of the same—1:10 Class, 2:05 Class, 3:05 Recreation, 4:30 Study, 5:40 Spiritual Reading—a routine designed to maintain order, to focus efforts on both the stated and unstated goals of seminary life. The stated goal was the transformation of teenage boys into other Christs, mediators between God and God's people. The goal left unstated was nonetheless more apparent: the making of company men, cookie-cutter priests, baked for six years. 6:00 Supper. 7:00 Study. 9:30 Night Prayers. 10:00 Lights Out.

BETHANY

The Congregation of the Sisters of St. Joseph occupied a tidy, tree-hidden estate in Framingham, Massachusetts, forty-five minutes west of Boston, on eighty acres donated to the order early in the century. At the top of a mile-long driveway winding up a steep grassy hill, the Sisters used the red-brick mansion that crowned the property as their novitiate, its first floor carved into a warren of classrooms, chapels, and common areas, its once-opulent upper levels remade as spartan living quarters for two hundred or so young women on their way to making solemn vows.

They called their hilltop sanctuary Bethany, named for the biblical home of the sisters Martha and Mary, who according to the Gospel of Luke once received Jesus and his disciples as guests at their table. As the story goes, Mary sat and listened to the master's teachings while Martha rushed around the kitchen preparing the meal. Catholic tradition has it that the sisters are symbols of the two heights to which women may aspire: prayer and service. Jesus told Mary she'd chosen the better part, prayer, but the Sisters of St. Joseph, perhaps not wanting to decide between the two, chose to name their novitiate for the place where both ideals were shown to the world.

It was a fitting name for another reason as well: the biblical Bethany was also home to Martha and Mary's brother Lazarus, whom Jesus called forth from the tomb. For the Sisters of St. Joseph, Bethany Hill was the beginning of the religious life as well as its end. Adjoining the novitiate, they had erected a church in which novices took the habit and became full members of the community; connected to that stood the infirmary, used as needed when novices fell ill, but intended primarily for the care of elderly nuns. Having "died to the world" when they arrived at Bethany as teenagers, the Sisters of St. Joseph hoped, after forty or fifty years spent away running the schools, hospitals, and charities of the archdiocese's brick-and-mortar building boom, to return to Bethany to die again.

That's a part of the Lazarus story that goes unmentioned in Scripture, that inevitable second death, and it was not a fact advertised in the Sisters of St. Joseph brochure. Probably it would have been slightly off-putting to the seventeen-year-olds who arrived every fall. Fresh to a new stage in their lives, who would want to be shown the place they were likely to end them?

Advertised or not, though, it would not have surprised the girls who arrived in the fall of 1958. One September Sunday that year, the scene at Bethany resembled nothing so much as a funeral: a line of dark cars snaking up the driveway at midday; a slow procession of families reaching the end of quiet rides from the city and the surrounding towns. They converged on the convent in Oldsmobiles, Edsels, Buicks, big American automobiles that filled the width of the gravel road. In every front seat a man and a woman sat in their Sunday best; in every backseat, a brown-haired girl in what could have been a widow's dress—an ankle-length gown the color of bicycle grease, with a stiff white collar like that of a pilgrim—stared through the window toward the rust-colored fortress just now visible through the trees.

Each girl arriving at Bethany that day had her own tale of how she got there, of course. Climbing up toward the novitiate were eighty stories of beneficiaries or victims, depending on how you view the outcome, of the circumstances that could send a teenage girl into the convent. Some had sisters in the order; some had alcoholic fathers and a reason to leave home; some wanted to further their education and saw no other way. A few felt called by God. For all these individual histories, they also, together, told a single story: they were part of a moment in the history of the faith and the nation, the high point of the religious involvement of women within the structure of the American Catholic Church. All through the preceding half century, the population of nuns in the Archdiocese of Boston had been growing every year, and never at such a rate as in my mother's first seventeen years, the early '40s through the late '50s. In that period the number of Sisters in and around Boston climbed from 4,000 to almost 6,000, jumping from three times to five times the number of priests and seminarians combined. As at St. John's in Brighton, plans were under way at Bethany for the construction of an enormous new dormitory, as if the flow of the young into the religious life would never end. And there was no reason to believe it would. Around the country there were similar numbers reflected in identical scenes: arriving in processions at convents in every diocese in America were girls who, though they never knew it and were never told, were more responsible than anyone else for the growth, life, and prosperity of their church.

One by one the cars crested the hill and found places beneath the evergreens that ringed the parking circle. Doors creaked open and pale girls in black dresses began to gather before the novitiate's double doors, open on this late summer day to make the new recruits feel welcome. A nice gesture, but the convent as a whole had the opposite effect: the grandeur of this place, the rich bulk of the buildings, the wide green field that sloped down the hill to the road below; the sight of it made these city girls gape and wonder. Could this really be where they would live for the next three years?

Some of them had been brought not just by parents but it seemed by entire families: brothers in suits with clip-on ties, sisters in ribboned dresses with white cotton gloves, a grandmother or two, each with a black lace handkerchief on her head. The younger ones milled about with the mothers near the crowd of girls, while, back at the cars, each father hoisted on his shoulder his daughter's one permitted piece of luggage, a small steamer trunk roughly the size of a child's coffin. By the time eighty of these dark cases had been carried across the parking circle and laid together in the grass, they seemed like evidence of some great tragedy, neat rows of black boxes, each labeled with a single name.

In truth they held little more than linen. A few weeks before, the eighty girls who arrived that day at Bethany had received a list from the novice mistress, Sister Elizavetta, telling them what to bring and what not to bring. Among the former: toiletries, bed sheets, towels. Among the latter: underwear.

Yes, they had been instructed specifically not to bring underwear. It would be provided, they were informed. Strange, especially given all the other private items they were asked to bring; that this was a recent change in policy somehow made it stranger still.

In years previous, Sister Elizavetta had instructed the incoming girls exactly what kind of undergarments to purchase and pack into their trunks. Certain items remained on the list: black stockings; a corset from Eva Wyatt's specialty store; one dozen boxes of Kotex and an elastic sanitary belt.

If these unmentionables could be mentioned, why not the underwear? They had heard a story. At some point, it was said, before the item had fallen off the list, a party had been thrown for a girl entering the community, and her younger sister had taken photographs of the required undergarments. In due course they had made their way into the hands of every girl considering the religious life. Difficult to tell much about a piece of clothing from a four-inch-wide, black and white photograph, but the images were sufficiently mysterious that they struck wonder and fear in all who beheld them, and apparently led not a few to reconsider their vocations. Thereafter, the underwear had been kept under wraps.

None of the girls arriving that day had seen either the underwear itself or the photographic evidence, but a few, those with older sisters in the community especially, had been warned. They were seventeen-year-olds in the late '50s, bobby-soxers, teeny-boppers. As they waited with their families for their new lives to begin, they were as anxious about that as about anything. Never mind prayer, never mind service, never mind dumb old Lazarus rising from the grave. For weeks now the first question the word *Bethany* inspired in most of the future Sisters of St. Joseph was, *When am I going to see this underwear everyone is talking about?*

•   •   •

The other girls' giggling did not lighten Mary Doherty's mood. Many of them knew each other already, and that only made her feel more out of place. She could tell by the way they tittered and talked that they'd come from the same parishes or else from one of the diocese's several CSJ-run high schools. Some of the girls even seemed to know the nuns who would be their new teachers, or at least were known to them. Mary couldn't help but think that had she gone off to the Sisters of Charity with the others from St. Margaret's, she'd be one of the insiders, too. Standing in front of the novitiate in Halifax, she would look to her right and there would be Rosemary, her teammate from the Monsignor Ryan Memorial basketball team; she would look to her left and there would be Frances and Maureen, girls with whom she haunted the bleachers at Fenway. All around her would be faces from back home. No doubt the nuns at that other novitiate would have spoken to Sister Helen Thomas about who was coming up from Dorchester. *Oh we've heard good things about you, Mary Doherty,* they would say. *This is where you belong.* But here that wasn't so. How had she ended up in a place where she didn't know a soul, she wondered. And then she remembered, and she felt even worse.

She'd arrived at Bethany that morning not with her whole family but with just her mother Margaret and her Uncle Pat. Mary's father, Michael, thought she should go to work instead of disappearing into the convent, so he was not on the scene. The duties normally undertaken by a father at such an occasion had fallen to Pat, as they often did, for no other reason than that he owned the car.

Whenever the Dohertys needed to get somewhere it was Pat they would call, and he was usually happy to oblige. Often as not the trip would be to an event that promised to occupy him as well, such as when Mary or her sister Rita needed to be in Hingham for a stepdancing competition. Pat would drive the girls and their mother down, then he would play the accordion for the dancing. Naturally there would be a drink or two or more depending on how long the dance would go, and the whole way home Margaret would chant a litany from the passenger seat: Pat, Pat, Pat, on the right side now, Pat, keep on the right now, Pat, the right.

This day, though, there had been no accordion in the car and there would likely be no dancing, so they arrived without incident. Like all the other men, Pat had carried the black trunk across the gravel driveway to the novitiate door. Like all the other mothers, Margaret had walked with her daughter to the edge of the crowd, where they passed a half hour milling about and saying goodbye until the novitiate's bell rang. Low, loud, and persistent, the bell bonged and bonged from the tower atop the convent chapel as all the mothers, fathers, brothers, and sisters piled back into their cars and rolled down the hill. Then, like all the other girls, Mary was on her own.

Once the families had gone, the novice mistress was in charge. She called the new girls together with the other Sisters into the community room, where all nonliturgical gatherings took place.

Sister Elizavetta had a frown like an upside-down smile, a perfect half circle she made with thin lips drawn tight at the slightest sign of disapproval. She showed it even then as she stood before the community, reminding the newest of them what was in store for the months and years to come.

Today began their time as postulants, she told them. By tradition, the postulancy was the period during which aspirants to religious life petitioned to be accepted into the community. In the earliest days of Christian monasticism, at least according to a few apocryphal stories, a postulant was a young man who hiked up to the monastery door, banged to be let in, and then waited outside for hours, days, weeks, proving his devotion through his ability to endure the elements until he was admitted. In the Middle Ages, a postulant was more likely to be the unmarriable daughter of a nobleman, and the beginning of her time in the convent was less about devotion and more about settling the terms of the dowry her family would pay to the church to keep her locked away. In the Catholic Church of the 1950s, however, the postulancy was closer to a test run, a six-month trial membership in the community, during which the girls with cold feet could call it quits and head home without too much danger to their reputations or their souls.

Because the church is as mindful as the wildest of pagans of the symbolism of the seasons, the postulants would not have the true start of their lives as nuns until spring. In six months time, the novice mistress explained, they would formally begin their novitiate.

To Mary's dismay she learned that, just as the nuns at Monsignor Ryan Memorial had separated their students into those on an academic track and those taking "commercial" courses, during the novitiate the novice mistress would determine which Sisters would study, teach, and eventually assume governance of the community, and which would be bound for the more mundane work of keeping the order fed and in clean linens, and making sure they knelt only on well-scrubbed floors. It was Martha and Mary all over again, only this time the choice seemed not to be between two heights of devotion, but between one height and the bottom of the barrel.

It was the fear of many a postulant that she would be sent to the kitchen. The kitchen girls followed different schedules than their Sisters, rose earlier, took their meals separately, and were made to keep long hours with no company deep in the bowels of the building. Those unlucky few often seemed to lose their wits in the piles of potato peels, becoming jealous guardians of the slightest provision, even the stale jelly sandwiches served at collation. It was often said that a novice sent to the kitchen was never the same, having only long years of isolation and little reward to look forward to. Everyone dreaded the possibility, and Mary was no different. When it came time to take aptitude tests, as they did in those first few days—check 5 if you enjoy an activity, 1 if you don't—Mary checked the box marked 1 for every question with even the faintest whiff of cleaning products or cooking grease.

Not that it was by any means in her control. Sister Elizavetta explained to them the rule of obedience: the will of the superiors was the will of God. In other words, what she gave you is what you got, and there should be no grumbling about it. Every slight you received was a cross to bear, and wasn't it the cross they were there for?

Some crosses weighed more than others, though, and who got which cross seemed a matter as predetermined as the stain of original sin. Even on that first day at Bethany, there was already a process of selection and separation under way.

The girls from the two CSJ academies—Fontbonne and the Mount, posh prep schools for the daughters of lace-curtain Catholics who might as well have been Protestants, their money and roots ran so deep—were immediately at the top of the list. Behind them were the girls whose sponsors were well-regarded Sisters in the order, and behind them were the few odd girls who for whatever reason ended up at Bethany without much previous connection to the community.

Because her application had been sent in so late and because she'd come from a Sisters of Charity parish, Mary was third to last in rank, just ahead of a girl whose father wasn't even Catholic. Her name was Judy, and though she had come there that day in the backseat like everyone else, Judy told Mary how her father had talked nonstop in the front seat as if he alone saw the strangeness in all this. Some fathers walk their daughters down the aisle, he kept saying, but oh no, I've got to bring mine to the nuns with this big trunk in the back.

Despite Mary's late entry and Judy's parents' mixed marriage, the CSJs were glad to have them both. That not everyone can be first in line is a lesson they would learn at every point in their formation.

While Elizavetta stood at the front of the Sisters explaining all this, around the community room sat models of what the postulants had to look forward to. At each transition—postulant to novice, novice to Simple Vows, Simple Vows to Solemn Vows—there would be a change of dress to accompany their deepening devotion to the order and the church, each to be endured as that long-ago would-be monk endured the elements.

The postulants themselves sat in their little black dresses, each girl's pale neck sprouting awkwardly from the matronly gown. Mary's hair was cut short, tight above the collar and around the ears, as it had been all through high school, but other girls let it fall down to just above their shoulders. It was their last remaining vanity, and they would not keep it much longer.

Behind the postulants were slightly older girls, the novices, who had entered the previous year. They wore thick black habits and white veils, which they would trade in for the full black veil after a period of two years.

Sister Elizavetta and a few of the other Sisters who acted as the teachers of the novitiate were the only professed nuns in the room, their bodies entirely hidden in yards of black serge. A stiff white wimple wrapped their throats to the chin. When a professed Sister pulled her hands up into her sleeves, only an oval of flesh barely larger than a kitchen saucer remained in view.

These levels of concealment were quite a surprise. Mary and the other postulants had thought of their entry into the religious life as an instantaneous and fully transformative process, but in fact it was gradual, a years-long accretion of layers. If the black cloth of the habit was the ground in which they would die to the world, they were even asked to dig their own graves: every free moment of the day, the postulants were informed, would be devoted to crafting their habit and veil, cutting it from whole cloth and piecing it together. Like Bethany itself, the habit, which they would start to sew in the first days of their postulancy and then, as far they knew, would never take off, represented the beginning of religious life and its end. Or so Sister Elizavetta explained. Symbolism was one thing, but just to look at the habit she wore was to be certain of something else: it was going to scratch like hell.

When the first day's lessons were done, the postulants made their way up to the dormitory, spiraling up the wide stairwell in their black dresses just as earlier in dark cars they and their families had climbed Bethany Hill. At the top, they entered a hallway and from there a long room, two of its walls filled with windows that looked out on one side toward the driveway that had brought them here, and on the other to the field and trees that sloped down to a cemetery by the road. The room was big enough for eighty beds, each with a white curtain draped around it that made the place look like a sick ward. Like everything else in their new world, the beds were assigned and organized by rank, so Mary's was near the very end.

She located her place, a closet of stiff white curtain on a metal frame, barely big enough for its contents: a small bureau, a towel rack, and a narrow bed. So this was home.

Beyond the curtains she heard the silence of eighty girls taking it all in. And then there was a collective gasp, as a large number of those girls simultaneously made the same discovery. It sounded as if each had been startled, grabbed from behind. Then there was laughter, the surprised cluckings of a dozen tongues, sighs of resignation. In the next partition, Judy huffed with disbelief.

Mary looked down, and then she saw it too, folded and waiting for her at the foot of the bed: the underwear.

When she picked it up to inspect it, it made her think of pictures she had seen of John L. Sullivan, the old boxer from the days when fighters still wore full body suits. She'd hate to sweat much in this thing, though. It was coarse and stiff, like half of a burlap sack, with a drawstring waistband that held it snugly just below the ribs. It was to be worn with black tights and a corset, below a long-sleeved lumber-jack's thermal top, over which a straight-line, cupless bra would be strapped. Mary wondered, Was this what they could not see beneath the older Sisters' habits in the community room? Was this the sort of thing worn closest to the skin by every nun she had ever known? The gasps around the room were more than shock. The gasps were won-der, sheer wonder at the mystery they had just begun.

It was more simple than that to Mary. Their new underthings seemed not so different from the new life they had chosen. Uncom-fortable, maybe, but a good place to hide.

It could have been the quiet. It could have been the dark. It could have been the lack of privacy that made them long even for the crowded triple-deckers they'd left behind. It could have been Sister Elizavetta's pursed lips in that mean smile. It could have been the simple fact of being seventeen and far from home, alone with the realization that the religious life might be much further from paradise than they had imagined. Maybe it was some combination of these, or all of them to-gether. Whatever it was, something in the lessons, beginnings, and goodbyes of that first day led to the crying of that first night.

After dinner and prayer, the bell rang for the Major Silence. Once the lights had gone out, though, Mary soon heard the void around her fill with stifled sobs and the creaking of narrow mattresses, with the unfamiliar noises of strangers breathing at her side. Then—twice, three times, hard to tell as the night wore on—she heard the tap of footsteps and the groan of the dormitory door. An hour or so later, there was the murmur of idling engines, the slamming of metal trunks, the crunch of tires in the gravel.

It wasn't until the morning that the sounds had meaning. Mary woke to see several beds empty, dressed with sheets and blankets but undisturbed. Not a word would be spoken about it, but a handful of girls had gone before she could learn their names. All that remained of them was their new underwear, left where they had found it, for everyone to see.

RADICALIZED

In their theology years, seminarians at St. John's were assigned a number of extracurricular offices based on ability and inclination, all with titles that tended to make much of entirely ordinary tasks. Among the two dozen or so varieties of class officers, there were the Sacristans, who lit candles and kept the vestments tidy for the twice-daily liturgies; the Infirmarians, who helped out in the seminary's small medical facility; the Multigraphers, who did the carbon-copying; and the Directors of Waiters, who made sure all meals were served in a timely and organized way. The Excitator was the fellow in charge of banging on doors each morning, and on every floor of the dormitories could be found holders of the highest office, the Prefects, whose permission seminarians required to leave their rooms after lights-out, even to use the jakes. Other offices were filled only from time to time, such as the Masters of Ceremonies and the Masters of Games, which were assigned by another office holder, the Regulator, who kept the tightly controlled occasions of recreation running smoothly. When an event called for documentation, there were even seminarians given responsibilities as official Photographers and Cinematographers. It was an economy of service with a twofold purpose: assurance that things would get done when they needed doing, and a subtle reminder of the lesson seminarians learned at every turn—a life in the church is a life of roles; a life of order.

Bill Manseau was pleased to be offered the office of Librarian. Even if the work would be on the dull side, the benefits—a quiet place to read; a regular schedule—might make it worthwhile. Still, when he took the position, he never imagined a part-time job could change his life.

Two or three afternoons each week, Bill walked from Theology House to the Creagh Library, an overgrown cinder block of a building just north of the seminary gate. Inside, he would climb down two flights of metal stairs to a concrete bunker basement. Had he worked upstairs in the same building, among the shelves of 19th-century lectionaries and medieval theological treatises, the job might not have made much of an impact on the way he thought about his vocation, about what it should mean to be a priest. Sorting and shelving the same tomes of Aquinas and canon law he regularly encountered in his course work, he might have completed his studies without much ado the following year, and then gone off, as most of the newly ordained did, to pass his days in a parish not too different from the one in which he had been raised. Instead, he worked in the periodicals room, and that made all the difference.

It was a strange place to be radicalized—the institutional ocher of the walls, the scrubbed tile floor—but that is exactly what happened. As closed off from the world as the Creagh basement seemed, it was there, in the lowest level of the library, that Bill Manseau was granted a view of the church that extended beyond the ghetto walls of American Catholicism. What he saw was the future as it appeared in an unlikely crystal ball: the pages of European theological journals, filled with the first jottings of a reform movement that had been brewing in seminaries and universities across the Atlantic. St. John's received several of these unassuming journals, though Bill couldn't imagine why. It seemed no one ever bothered to read them; he only happened to do so by accident.

All that was required of him as Periodicals Librarian was to sort the various journals as they came in each week and then to place them on the shelves in their plastic bins. From time to time a volume would fall open and, curious Boy Scout that he was, Bill couldn't help but glance inside. It was here he first read names likes Hans Küng, Yves Congar,

Edward Schillebeeckx, Pierre Jounel, Jean Danielou—Swiss, Dutch, and French theologians who, far from the intellectually indifferent climate of the church Bill had known all his life, were quietly working to bring the faith into the modern world.

The Swiss and Dutch theologians he could explore only when they were translated or written about in English, but armed with his parents' native tongue, he could puzzle out in the original the meaning of the works of the Jesuit Danielou and the French diocesan priest Jounel, professors at the Institut Catholique and the Institut Supérieur de Liturgie respectively, and he couldn't believe what he found. The French-speaking priests he'd known when he was growing up in Lowell had lived in a ghetto within a ghetto, doomed to crumbling parishes full of Quebecois grandmothers unable or unwilling to learn the language of their new land. The clerics in such places had always seemed like throwbacks, relics of the Old World. Not so the Frenchmen in these journals. No artifacts here, they were the avant-garde.

"It is quite certain," Father Jounel wrote, "that in hearing the call of the Apostle on that first Sunday in Lent: 'Behold now is the acceptable time, behold, now is the day of salvation' (2 Cor. 6:2), we have no temptation to transport ourselves back nineteen hundred years; it is *today* that we are invited to begin our paschal ascent into Jerusalem, to enter into combat with Satan . . . In that same way, then, when on Palm Sunday we take part in the procession after the singing of the Gospel which announces the triumphal entry of Jesus into Jerusalem, or when, at the evening Mass on Holy Thursday, the celebrant reproduces the Gospel scene by washing the feet of twelve of his brethren, this is not an evocation of the past, it is not a play—it is *today*."

In my father's copy of that text from a talk given by Father Jounel, the last sentence is underlined, as is every appearance of the italicized word young Bill took not as only context but command: *today*. Here were Catholics—priests, no less—who proposed a way of understanding the faith that was radically different from anything he had encountered before. Up until then he knew only the church that would not admit its own history, opting for simplified explanations of its most closely held practices and beliefs; the church that flinched at the chal-

lenges of the day. What a wonder to find another side of the faith in
the basement of an institutional library. You can't always judge a temple by its stones.

Tucked into a book of his from the time I found recently two slips
of paper that show the intellectual and spiritual distance my father
traveled in a short time, due in large part to his encounter with the
writings of this groundbreaking new theology. The first is a holy card
decorated with blue flowers and two slender, praying hands. The text
on the card is called "A Boy's Prayer."

> *I pray, whatever wrong I do,*
> *I'll never say what is not true;*
> *Be willing at my task each day*
> *And always honest in my play.*
>
> *Make me unselfish with my joys,*
> *And generous to the other boys;*
> *And kind and helpful to the old,*
> *And prompt to do what I am told.*
>
> *Bless everyone I love, and teach*
> *Me how to help and comfort each;*
> *Give me the strength right living brings,*
> *And make me good in little things.*

Bill kept the card nostalgically, a reminder of the surety of the bed-
time prayers he'd said on B Street in Lowell; of the security he'd felt
when the family recited the rosary on the kitchen floor. But really
hadn't that been the extent of his faith and his ambition until then?
Simply to be a comfort and help? In fact, this Boy's Prayer expressed
the prevailing hope of the American church: merely to be "good in little things."

With his new understanding of the faith, though, that kind of hope
seemed insufficient. Since his altar boy days, he had been reenacting
the formative events of the church—the incarnation, the miracles, the

resurrection—through the theater of the Mass, the highly scripted drama in which, as a priest, he would soon have a starring role. But what if, as Jounel said, it wasn't just a play? What could that mean? If all the mystery and power of faith were happening *today*—how could being "good in little things" possibly be enough?

At some point during his time working in the library basement, thinking such thoughts and stealing glances at the European journals, Bill wrote on a slip of paper just the size of his juvenile prayer card and slipped it into the same book:

"Whenever the Christian Mystery of Salvation, the Good News, is 'proclaimed' in a merely juridic, skeletal recitation of component truth, grace is squandered—the fullness is hidden, the beauty of love is obscured. Response is in proportion to stimulus. The Christian message is: Joy is Incarnate. Grace is incarnate. God depends on man."

Response is in proportion to stimulus—perhaps up until then he had only hoped to be good in little things because he faced only little challenges, little pursuits. No more, as far as he was concerned. Keep your head down or you'll get it cut off, they told each other at St. John's. But if you didn't stick your neck out to take a look around from time to time, what was the use of having a head at all? The distance between one slip of paper and another is no less than the growth of a boy, who until then had been acted upon, becoming a man who has decided it is necessary to act; a boy shedding the vocation that had been given to him, thrust upon him, by his mother and his priest; a man learning how to make his vocation his own.

Bill found this lesson reinforced in another unlikely place. Though a great deal of time in the daily horarium was reserved for course work, there was never any doubt that the seminarians' education took a secondary role to their gradual assimilation into the culture of priests. "A seminary loses its essential orientation if its program is directed primarily toward scholastic goals," Cardinal Cushing told the seminarians once and it was not a surprise to hear as much. Mediocrity, pretense, and sham, were the words often used to describe the education offered at St. John's, a not-too-subtle play on the initials of the rector at the time, Right Reverend Matthew P. Stapleton. Some of the professors weren't even trained as teachers, they were just priests brought in to fill the space while the cardinal's office decided where they should be assigned. Many of them would stand there reading the textbook to the class. The more conscientious among them took care to stay one chapter ahead.

The stories of ill-equipped and possibly disturbed professors are endless. There was one priest who taught a course on empirical psychology. He was a large man, his plastic collar bunched like a belt around his throat, and though he was given to rough, labored breathing, it didn't stop him from droning nonstop about a subject he seemed to know next to nothing about. For every psychological abnormality and mental illness on the syllabus, he used a member of his family as a long-winded example. When their reading for the week discussed senility, he talked on and on about his mother. When they got to epilepsy, he delivered a monologue about his brother, who was painting his family's house one day and had a seizure while he was up on the ladder. No one could guess what on earth this had to do with being a priest, but still they found it useful information. If they ever wanted to see the place where Father Abnormality grew up, they figured they could just drive around until they saw the yellow house with a brown stripe down the middle.

Naturally, though this was an overview course intended to give seminarians insight into all aspects of human psychology they might deal with as priests, no mention at all was made of sexual development. Had there been need, though, Father Abnormality could've found anecdotal evidence readily at hand. He himself was famous for a speech he gave to students when they reached their diaconate year, near the end of their training. "Gentlemen," he breathed, "there will be days, oh yes, there will be days," *breath,* "when you will feel your whole body has become one elongated—" *breath* "penis—" *breath* "surging . . . surging . . . to penetrate—" *breath* "the vagina—" *long breath* "of some . . . young . . . woman!"

The stunned crowd of twenty-three-year-olds sat gaping like they were watching a stag film. Not that there was anything appealing about the fat priest's sermon. It was just the closest any of them had been to the huffing uncertainty of first-time sex.

Given the poor quality of much of the education offered to Boston's future priests, it was quite a surprise to actually learn something from time to time. One bright spot among the seminary's often dim course offerings was a Scripture class taught by a professor by the name of Phil King, who arrived as St. John's shortly before Bill's ordination. Bill was too far along in his studies to take King's class himself, but it wasn't long before he'd heard that something different and very much needed had arrived. It was from Father King's approach to the subject that Bill first came to a new way of thinking about Scripture, which in fact was a new way of thinking about faith.

For centuries—since the Reformation, when Martin Luther declared that, *Sola Scriptura*, Scripture alone held the key to understanding God's revelation—the Bible had been considered more or less a Protestant book. Catholics already had their eternal and unchanging entity on which to lean for stability: the church itself, which, in their conception, had always existed in some cosmic way, making it far older and more authoritative than the Bible. Sure they might cherry-pick sections here and there for the liturgy, but that was basically stealing lumber from the house next door to build a porch for your own. For Catholics, tradition was the bridge between the faithful and the object of their faith, the sacrifice of Jesus. And tradition was personified in the office of the pope—that's why they call him the supreme pontiff, the bridge that surpassed all others.

Yet in that year Bill and every other Catholic around the world had seen this idea of tradition dealt a blow—a deathblow, in fact. The death of Pope Pius XII in October 1958, just as Bill was discovering his European journals, so shook the church that suddenly it seemed anything was possible, even at St. John s. Pius was the pope that a generation of Catholics had known all their lives. He was a symbol of an understanding of the faith that Bill just then was beginning to outgrow. That Pius could die was another lesson: the church Bill had been raised to believe was eternal was not immune to history, or to change.

The new pope, John XXIII, was originally elected as a cushion warmer for St. Peter's throne, a placeholder intended to hold office only until someone more *papabile* could be found. Having difficulty reaching a consensus on Pius's successor, the College of Cardinals picked an old, simple man by the name of Angelo Roncalli, who, they supposed, would not live long enough to do any damage to the church, and whom, in the meantime, it would be easy enough to control. But perhaps Roncalli too had been doing some reading in a basement library. In the first months of his papacy, he would, as John XXIII, set to work trying to give "new hope," as a contemporary account put it, to a modern world plunged into "agitation and anxiety." It soon became clear that the church led by Pius XII and what was to come under John XXIII would be as different as the devout pleading of the *Boy's Prayer* and the last words Bill jotted down on that scrap of paper in the periodicals library: "God depends on man." From one pope to the next, Bill's faith had gone from feeling needful to knowing he was needed. When Pope John called for a council of bishops to help bring the church into the modern age—into that italic, commanding *today* Bill had underlined so emphatically—it suggested that Bill was not alone, that Catholics all over the world were growing up too, realizing it was time, to paraphrase another Catholic John about to ascend to the throne, to ask not what their faith could do for them, but what they could do for their faith.

That's where Phil King's Scripture class came in. Like celibacy, the new life they had all chosen for themselves, it turned out that St. John's seminarians knew next to nothing about the Bible, even though it was the book responsible for the choice they had made. To most of them, it was merely an anthology of half-remembered ancient history, stories taken more or less at face value, with about as much critical thinking as would be applied to a Saturday matinee. Catholic families, after all, knelt and prayed the rosary together, they did not read passages from Scripture—they certainly did not memorize it chapter and verse, as Bill had learned Protestants did in his short time among the Baptist Boy Scouts in Lowell.

Seminarians encountered the Bible, in other words, as they en-

countered the world: as a taken-for-granted element of God's creation. That it must make sense was a matter of faith, even if it was in-
scrutable on the surface. But what if such a book required more
thought than that for its meaning to become clear? That was the question first posed in Scripture class. "Biblical truth is to be grasped only
in its full context," another of those European theologians wrote
(again, helpfully underlined, this time in an essay called "God Has
Spoken Human Language," by Reverend Hans Urs von Balthasar). "In
each word the whole is echoed; each word sends us back to the whole.
But the particular text may have been conveyed to us through successive and different experiences." What this meant, essentially, was the
Bible was a two-way street. The modern world could be used to understand Scripture just as Scripture is used to understand the modern
world. They didn't realize it then, but they were learning a process of
biblical interpretation, of critical religious thinking, that would not
keep them at their desks or in their pulpits, but would send them out
into the streets—where, as Bill came to see it, the only true significance of a sacred text could be found.

These encounters—first with the avant-garde of Catholic theology
and then with a new approach to the book that started it all—brought
about what can only be called a conversion, though to all appearances
his faith remained unaltered. In fact, the tenets of his belief had not
changed at all, but their meaning had changed dramatically.

There was still the same trinity there had always been, but no
longer did Bill's faith rest in pleasing the Father, or in the false humility of identification with the Son. Now he was taken up entirely by
God's third and most volatile aspect. "The Father always speaks his
Word through the *Spirit*," he wrote that year in his theology thesis. It
is only through living a life devoted to the Holy Spirit, he wrote, that
one could be "Christofied": "God's salvific work for man and all creation is not something external to him. It is not a production, it is a
personal endeavor."

It wasn't just rhetoric: soon he became so obsessed with this personal endeavor that everything else became secondary. Losing sleep,
forgetting to eat, he developed a facial tic when overstressed. Bill's

family doctor ordered him to rest and even prescribed use, for one hour a week, of a beach chair and a radio, granting him special exemption from the Seminary Rule's 57th and 66th commandments respectively.

Before long some of his classmates were calling him "Ivory Tower Bill" for the way he tried to stick to his research and remain above the fray of seminary life. But he didn't care. He had found the Spirit, and with it a new sense of his role in the church.

Sitting at his desk, alone before lights-out, he was filled with gratitude. "Thank you, Lord," he said, believing for the first time that God might have a plan for him. "Thank you. Thank you. Thank you." Facial tic aside, perhaps this was what his father had meant by living always in a state of grace.

It's no coincidence that a new idea of faith should bring with it a new idea of friendship. Until then, Bill had had a rather utilitarian approach to making friends at seminary. When he wanted to learn about putting on a production for St. John's yearly talent show, he set about becoming acquainted with a fellow who had experience staging plays; when he decided he wanted to direct the show himself, he befriended the Regulator, whose responsibility it was to select the director. All of these friendships, he later realized, were about his own gratification.

According to the Seminary Rule, that's more or less as it should have been. Officially, the closest to friendship you got at St. John's was a twice-weekly walk with another seminarian, pairings subject to the approval of the administration, which frowned upon "particular friendship," the church's fraught term for connections that under any other circumstances would be seen as quite normal. The rules against particular friendship basically forbade any kind of regular conversation with or attention paid to this classmate or that. If they were all other Christs then they all were equal; what need could there be to single out one fellow or another as a friend?

There is, though, that other hunger, the need for some sort of intimacy in a life. Because of it, even the highly regulated recreation of the weekly "walks" became charged with a kind of sexless eroticism.

They were teenage boys acting like teenage boys of the day, keeping black books to schedule their walks with one another as if they were dates at the drive-in. One note Bill received hints at the complications, the potential for hurt feelings and adolescent jealousy fostered by the seminary's fear of friendship.

Dear Bill,

George M. informed me tonight that you would like to have a walk with me Monday night. As much as I would like to I'm afraid that I'll have to decline your kind offer because Roger B. asked me Saturday night for a walk and I accepted. Today Bob S. asked me for a walk Wednesday night and again I accepted. It's not that I'm so popular it's just that I was just asked and all at the same time. Other times I don't have a walk.

If it's alright with you we could have a walk at the first inter-house activity that might come up after Wednesday. If nothing comes up before St Pat's night we probably could get together then, Okay? Thank you very much.

Gratefully,
Dick M.

When I first asked my father if he saw any homoeroticism in all of this, he reacted defensively, "No, no, maybe there were some things like that more recently at St. John's—but not when I was there, no." Later, however, he said he had been thinking about it and in fact could remember one time when a fellow seminarian made a pass at him, and there was often talk about the few pairings of men who too often walked together.

Another time, when he was out for a rare walk in the city, he and a classmate went into Sheehan's church supply store downtown. They weren't supposed to go into any stores, but they figured Sheehan's was okay. They met an older priest, and of course he recognized them as seminarians. He asked them what priests they knew. Proud of his association with his late mentor, Bill said, Father Tom Sennott.

"Oh," the older priest said, and a sly smile drew across his face. "The priest who gave boys money."

Bill didn't know what he was talking about, but still he had an awful feeling. He felt the color drain out of him and he didn't know what to say. There was the implication of an improper relationship, and there was also the hint that he was not the only one to have enjoyed the priest's attention. He had felt such specialness in Father Tom's company, Bill had never considered the possibility that, to the older man, he had been as unique as one weekly walking partner among many. How many Philosophers and Theologians at the Sem had been similarly chosen?

Listed in the back of the course catalogs from my father's time at St. John's are names of his fellow seminarians. There are among them several names that years later would become infamous, such as John Geoghan, class of 1963, whose case would set off the clergy abuse scandal. To the boys at St. John's he was the little imp of a man who always seemed either too young or too happy with that high squeaky voice of his. And there is Paul Shanley, class of 1960, who would become the most notorious priest-pedophile of his generation by speaking in favor of sexual relationships between adult men and adolescents, and later by being convicted of child rape. In my father's time at St. John's, he has told me, if he had to pick one man among all the seminarians who would be a great priest it would have been Shanley. Going further back to older course catalogs, there are more names—more than one hundred others—all who spent six years at the Brighton campus, all who would later be accused of sexual abuse. Ultimately 7 percent of the men who attended St. John's with my father would be implicated.

Much has been written about celibacy's role in the abuse scandal, but very little has been said about the possible effects of this symptom of celibate culture: the seminary's attitude toward basic relationships, the distrust of which might have been just as damaging to those who persevered at St. John's as the denial of their sexual impulses. In the name of preventing particular friendships, the seminary system seems to have done its best to create a clerical class filled with men who never learned that other people are more than objects from which something may be obtained.

Of course, most learned despite the obstacles seminary life put in the way, and matured in the face of the combined effects of the exalted sense of self and the crippled ability to engage in adult, mutual relationships that the seminary provided.

Bill learned with the help of one of the radicals in Phil King's scripture class, a first-year theology student from Watertown, Dominic George Spagnolia, whom everyone called Spag. Shorter than Bill, a little pudgy, a wit, not just a wisecracker, he was decidedly not part of the jock-and-gent culture of the seminary. Perhaps because their friendship was based on a shared introduction to such exciting new territory, Bill's connection to Spag was immediately more vital and engaged than any he had known before. He seemed to Bill far more focused than the other seminarians, far more interested in the intellectual pursuits Bill himself had recently discovered.

What Bill didn't know then, and would not know for years—not until after they'd both taken the lessons they'd learned from Phil King and become radical priests in the streets of Boston; not until after one of them had left the priesthood—was that Spag studied as hard as he did because if he didn't keep his nose in a book he knew his eyes might wander. Though he was considered a "regular guy" by his classmates, he had known ever since his aunt's boyfriend stumbled drunk into his bed one night years before, that he was not. In seminary-speak, "not a regular guy" was a handy euphemism for something they didn't even have words for. In such an environment, to keep being a regular guy, Spag had learned to live with blinders on. To be two things at once.

Perhaps Bill was drawn to him because he was learning something similar. He did not have the same problem Spag had—the aching, restless nights because of the temptations all around him—but he could see even then that there was an inherent contradiction in the life he had chosen. To be a priest, he now knew, was to be called into the world, to live his faith as a reality *today*. And yet, could he truly be in the world if, as a priest, he was necessarily separate from it?

His new way of thinking had brought with it more questions than he had ever had before, but it also brought his hopes for the priest-

hood into focus. Sitting in his room one night as he prepared for ordination, all he could do was stare out over the beige buildings of the
Brighton campus, jotting down his thoughts while he scanned the
open air for something he had not found in the buildings below.

"I would like to walk out of this open window and walk straight
into the sky and hug God," he wrote.

I would like to leap from my body—to leave myself—and race
along and through the puffs of white clouds this evening. I
would run and run and run until I found the terrifyingly tremen-
dous God, who is my Father, My Brother, and my Existence-
Giver. I would like to meet this God who loves me, this fantastic
God who became like me because He wanted to.

O Great God how I wish I could reach out and tear the clouds
away and see you. God the Father, Father of all real things, you
are terrible, huge. Yet loving and small, and tender and loving.

God, how could you do it? How could you love us—me—animals—birds—flowers? How could you love such little things?
You are not little, but you have become little.

What, then, is love if it did that to you?

What is love?

After eight years of seminary—eight years of separation from his
family, eight years of scheduled walks and regulated friendships, eight
years of loneliness, eight years of mediocrity, pretense, and sham—he
was ready to find out.

BRIDES OF CHRIST

It must have seemed like some kind of joke: a girl on her way to lifelong virginity marching down the aisle in a bright white dress, as if on the eve of a honeymoon.

The day before, Mary Doherty had taken off her black postulant's chemise for the final time, and that morning donned an ankle-length wedding gown. The first dress she'd been given was yellowed and shabby (further proof, as far as she was concerned, that Sister Elizavetta had it in for her) but then another gown became available and she stepped happily into what she believed would be the last feminine clothing she would ever wear: low on the neck, form-fitting under her arms, light and puffy from the waist to the floor. It even had a lacy veil.

She and the other girls who had arrived at Bethany the previous fall wore such costumes on that spring afternoon because the "brides of Christ" business was no figure of speech. As the church saw it, the day they took the habit was in fact a wedding—a wedding in which sixty-nine brides were joined to a single, absent groom, but a wedding nonetheless.

I have a photograph of the occasion: three tiers of dark-haired girls crowded around a cross of white chrysanthemums. They all are smiling, though those in the first row stand awkwardly in their gowns, hands cupped against their corseted waists. The dresses had been worn before, but they weren't family heirlooms. In Catholic Boston, devout newlyweds would donate their gowns for just this purpose.

The postulants put on the ill-fitting dresses knowing they'd been worn not too long before at actual weddings, by girls their own age or a little older; girls like them who had been raised collecting tin for the war effort, to whom turning a slightly used dress over to the Sisters seemed the most natural thing in the world.

In the photograph, three faces stare down from behind the assembled novices; left to right they are the episcopal portrait of Cardinal Cushing in an opulent white fur; a small statue of the CSJ's patron, St. Joseph, husband of the Blessed Virgin; and the late Pope Pius XII, who had died several months before. The date is March 19, 1959, six months into Mary Doherty's life as a sister and five months into the pontificate of Pope John XXIII.

That a portrait of the new pope had not yet arrived is a telling detail. Just as the teaching Sisters in the parishes were second-class citizens compared to the priests, so too were the church's convents considered less important than its seminaries. So while in that same season the cardinal himself made regular appearances before Bill Manseau and his classmates at St. John's in Brighton, the nuns at Bethany made do with out-of-date images and occasional visits from auxiliary bishops. The Sisters of St. Joseph, along with every other women's religious order, were an afterthought of the all-male hierarchy. To be out of loop even concerning something as important as giving "Good Pope John" his due was not all that surprising.

The irony is that this was a time when the schools, parishes, hospitals, and charities that then defined American Catholicism were entirely dependent on convents and the women trained within them. That was the double meaning on display whenever a new group took the habit: renunciation for the individual; renunciation's opposite, the wealth of labor and devotion each vow represented, for the community which held the individual in such little regard.

Nevertheless, it was a big day in the life of a young nun. Despite the strangeness of it, the ceremony in which she became a bride of Christ showed to Mary all that was best of the vocation she had chosen. By her vows, she was joined not just to Jesus but to all these nuns, many of whom would be her friends for life. Who else could know what it meant to leave your family as a girl, instantly to become seen as a holy woman? Who else but God and these new Sisters could understand how little Mary Doherty from Dorchester had changed, and at the same time how much?

In all that shining white, with gauzy veils draped down their backs like wings, they could just as easily have been a chorus of angels as a gang of city kids turned professed nuns. They even took new names suggesting as much: spiritual aliases drawn from the canon of saints. Mary had only just learned one set of names when a whole new role call was required for the same people. Some were easy to remember: Maureen Farrell became Sister Mary Florence; two girls named Peggy became two nuns called Marie (Sister Marie Stephanie and Sister Marie Ursula); Judy, Mary's friend at the back of the ranks, was now known as Richard Therese, like the cardinal himself joined to the Little Flower, St. Thérèse of Lisieux. Other names were trickier: Christine Sullivan was named for St. Alexis, whoever that was; and Roberta Ristucia, who could've become Sister Robert without too much trouble, instead became Sister John Clare.

Mary's new name had been an easy choice: she would be *Thomas* for Sister Helen Thomas, the Charity Sister who had been so good to her at St. Margaret's; and *Patrick*, not for her uncle but for the savior and scourge of Ireland, a good man to call upon when snakes need driving out. She would be *Sister Thomas Patrick;* and though later she would cringe at having chosen two male names, as if the habit alone would not sufficiently obscure the girl who had been Mary Doherty, on that day it felt right. On that day, she was dressed, named, and looked upon as if heaven was her next destination.

She might have even believed it herself, especially when she received what she considered a far greater blessing than either her new gown or her new name. Her mother had come to Framingham for the ceremony and, in the short time the newest Sisters of St. Joseph were allowed to visit with their families, Mary learned that the most fervent and frequent of her prayers of the last six months had been answered: Father Creighton had been transferred from St. Margaret's.

Until she heard this happy news, the mere thought of visiting the church in which she'd been baptized filled her with dread. To run into him on Roseclair Street, to hear his voice intone the Mass, to see his hands hold the Eucharist . . . it would be better never to go home again than to bear such possibilities.

But now he was gone—transferred to another parish after barely a year. Where or why she didn't care to know. Gone, was the point; the simple fact of it made her feel the hardships of her new life were worthwhile. Was it a coincidence that she made her vows on the day she heard the news? Or were poverty, chastity, and obedience the cost of answered prayers? Either way, on that day she could only feel grateful. With a dark spot removed from her past, with no more fear of what waited in the future, on that day she was able to say, "It was like God reached down and put things right."

The next day, though, it was back to the routine.

As long as she had been at Bethany, it had been waking that was worst. When it was still dark in the dormitory, the first bell rang out telling the Sisters it was time to rise, time to pray. At that moment—when the bell, the dark, and the convent cold combined to form a single sensation, a chill both in the air and in her bones—that's when Mary would remember. Every morning, just as her eyes opened and her yawning tongue found the holes in her gums where her teeth should be, she felt a jolt of fear at being seen and covered her mouth with her hands.

On the bureau beside her bed lay a small prayer card she kept as one of her few personal belongings. On the front there was a dark illustration of a short-haired girl with coal-pit eyes reaching up to remove a mask that was an exact replica of her own face. The girl on the card looked eerily like Mary herself, which might strike one as vanity if not for the text on the back—a poem called "Masquerade," written by an anonymous Sister of Saint Joseph, about "the masks that man voluntarily wears"

> with mouldering mind and crannied heart
> He plays on life's stage an insidious part—

Cloaked with placidity and a forced smile,
Hiding pretense, his deceit, and his guile.

Personal decorations and tastes were frowned upon in the dormitory—there was no room made for her tattered photograph of
Michael and Margaret Doherty sitting together on a hillside in Kilgarvan; no allowance made for the *Irish Hour* radio show she had listened
to weekly on Roseclair Street—but this one card seemed sufficiently
general and appropriately Catholic that Sister Elizavetta let it pass. She
might not have, had she known how closely Mary identified with it—
with the "placidity," the "forced smile," even the "deceit" and "guile."
    Every morning she would rush to the bathroom with her chin
tucked into her throat, her night bonnet tied tight over her cropped
hair and her freckled cheeks, not pausing even to look another girl in
the eye until she had reached the bathroom. There she would claim a
sink against the far wall and turn her back to her Sisters to hide the
fact that she brushed dentures instead of her own teeth. Returning to
her curtain to finish dressing, only Mary knew how the petition with
which the poem ended was, for her, a private plea:

O God, this do I beg; this do I ask:
Help me so live that I need no mask.

No matter how often she prayed this, she lived in fear of being found
out. Though she came to regard her replacement teeth as what she
would later call "a badge of shame," a reminder to her and an indica-
tor to all of the secret that kept her separate from the other girls, she
dreaded the possibility of being seeing without them.
    After the ringing of the bell the Sisters had twenty-five minutes to
get to the chapel for prayer and meditation. Even with their wardrobe
predetermined, there was always something of a mad dash about it: all
those girls needing the sinks, showers, and toilets in the common
washroom, and then the ten minutes or so required to properly assemble the habit and veil. So many wraps and coverings: the underwear, the stockings, the corset, the pockets (detached from the rest of

the uniform, worn on a belt, a bit like a holster), and finally, the habit drawn over it all. The accumulated layers were like strata of earth over an ancient civilization.

On their heads too there was concealing to be done. Since the day they took the veil, when they awoke it was with hair cropped almost to the skin beneath their nightcaps. As usual there were a variety of reasons, not just theological and symbolic, but practical: beneath the unbreathing cloth of their veils, hair any longer than an inch or two would start to smell like something dead in a matter of days. You could smell it on the girls who thought of leaving, who grew their hair in to ease their transition back to the world of hairdos and hats. There was no washing it in such instances—a veil made wet by damp locks underneath was a dead giveaway—so though they thought their plans secret, you could smell the intention days before a single strand snuck down into view.

With so many garments to arrange and fasten in place, and with no conversation allowed in the dormitory, the first sounds of morning were only of sixty-nine habits folding and unfolding, and the occasional muttered curses of drowsy girls clumsy with pins. The silence could be overwhelming, oppressive, but to Mary the quickness and the quiet of the morning routine were welcome. Like the dark cloth of the habit, like the shadowy half-light of the church, silence could be a good place to hide.

At times it seemed there was no end to the hiding. They hid under their habits, and they hid within their routines. During the daily round of prayer, chores, and classes, much attention was paid to the numbing repetition of regulations, as if the unruly interior lives of teenagers could be subdued by relentless, tedious engagement.

Each morning after breakfast, one by one the novices would ask Sister Elizavetta the same set of permissions:

Please may I rise, wash, dress, use prayer books, take meals, attend to my charge, go to school, study, teach, take recreation, change, wash, and mend my clothing when necessary, pick up pins and needles, use the discipline, and any other permissions that I cannot conveniently ask.

Every day for three years the novices recited this same mundane litany, lest a single act be undertaken without the approval of their superior. The "daily permissions" became such a part of them that they could say it in their sleep—forty years later, my mother can still recite it on command.

Throughout the day they were expected to master the Maxims of Perfection, instructions on how to live a productive and harmonious life within the community. Sister Elizavetta announced that every novice who hoped to remain a Sister of St. Joseph must obey all ninety-nine of these aphorisms, and moreover she must memorize them to show they had been taken to heart.

As if designed to undermine the nuns' awareness of their importance within the life of the church, the maxims were obsessed with impossible ideals and the inevitable failings and denigrations of self that arose from trying to realize them.

Let it be the general rule of your life to be perfect, as your Father in Heaven is perfect . . .

Be persuaded of this truth, that you scarcely do anything but put obstacles in the way of Divine Grace.

Glory in contempt, and receive confusion, not only with patience, but with joy and thanks. In confusion and scorn courageous souls find treasures of grace, merit, and celestial benedictions.

Regret that the world thinks of you, if any one entertains affection for you. Believe this truth, that its thoughts and affections are uselessly bestowed on persons who so little merit them.

These sentiments were given physical expression in a practice that was simply called "the discipline." I first learned of it having lunch one day with my mother and two other former Sisters of St. Joseph—two of her "convent buddies," as she calls them.

"Did you tell him about the discipline?" one of them asked.

"Oh, no, no," my mother answered.

"You've got to tell him about the discipline," the other former Sister said.

"When I told my husband he thought we were just nuts."

"I never told mine. I knew he would too!"

"Well," my mother said, turning to me, "the discipline, it was—"

"I know, let me show you!" the first former Sister grabbed the pen out of my hand and proceeded to draw on her napkin a half-dollar-sized circle with sharp spikes shooting out on all sides, like an angry sun.

"Bigger," the other former Sister said. "They were bigger and sharper, I'm sure of it!" She took the pen from her friend and enlarged the spikes until they were larger than the ring that joined them.

"And the chain, don't forget the chain!"

She added a long curving line with a small square handle at the end, then slid the napkin across the table. It looked like a medieval torture device, which, I realized, it probably was. Even as late as the 1950s, certain otherworldly elements of Catholic life had survived in American convents as if the New World had never been discovered. The habit was one, the Latin of the liturgy was another. One less often talked about—and one far more embarrassing for the modern women who left it behind—was the discipline.

Once a week the novices at Bethany would return to their curtain-enclosed cells and, shouting prayers in the dark, they would whip themselves with a spiked metal ring on a chain, "the discipline."

"No one could see you so I just swung it against the bed, *whump, whump, whump*," the first former Sister said. "It sounded just the same as if I was hitting myself!"

My mother made a face as if such subterfuge had never occurred to her, not even with forty years to think about it.

"Mother of God, I swung that thing like I was in a competition!" she laughed. "I wanted so badly to be good."

•   •   •

It must have paid off. When their work assignments came in that year, Mary was relieved to learn she had not been sentenced to the kitchen. Instead, she would be a teacher, like Sister Helen Thomas and all the other Sisters at St. Margaret's who helped her family through the years. In the long run the assignment meant she and the other lucky girls would spend their summers away from Bethany and whatever parishes they were assigned to, earning a two-year teaching degree in about ten years' time. In the short term, though, it didn't make much difference. Becoming a teaching Sister meant they would take a few more classes, but mostly the time remaining in the novitiate would be occupied with the same old chores.

There was the endless sewing, of course, and various clerical make-work, all of which at least did have some practical end, even if it was obvious that this end was entirely unnecessary. Other tasks, though, stretched their conception of what it was to live a religious life beyond all reason.

In the marbleized entryway of the novitiate, for example, the novices were sometimes made to flatten the tiles, a process in which a dozen or so sisters in their heavy nunnish shoes would tramp up and down across the floor for an hour at a time, apparently for no other purpose than to keep the floor in its place. If Galileo could be doubted by the church, why not gravity? They stamped and marched and dug their heels into the tiles, making sure every square inch of floor was met by the thick sole of each nun's shoe. Stomp, stomp. Pound, grind. March, march, march, and swish, swish, swish as a dozen black habits lifted dust from the floor. All the while they would sing the novice's mantra:

> *Oh dear*
> *Bread and beer*
> *If I were married*
> *I wouldn't be here*

Given all the accumulated unpleasantness of convent life, it's little surprise that the Sisters lived for their infrequent contacts with the outside world.

On visiting days, they loved to smell people. One Sunday each month, the novices waited upstairs in the dormitory and carefully peeked out the window, down to the walkway below. Through the trees they could see the spot where the driveway crested the hill and when the first car arrived someone would say it, "I smell *people,*" and the other girls could not help but giggle with the excitement of it. First one car, then another, then a third . . . With each shining bumper one of the novices let out a yip of recognition, claiming it as her own.

Mary's family was rarely able to make the trip, so for her such Sundays were bittersweet. She had come to enjoy the nun's life on normal days in the novitiate. She welcomed the routine and its ongoing alternation between work and prayer. When she prayed she did so as fervently as she ever had back at St. Margaret's, and when she worked, at her studies especially, she found she had skills and abilities she never imagined before. Just recently she had written a paper on the theme of peace, for which she interviewed a few of the older Sisters in the infirmary to learn what the word meant to them after decades in the veil. Talking with them, hearing the hard-won wisdom of nuns of the previous generation, she'd discovered that learning and expressing what she'd learned came easily. Within the community it was easy to feel the equal of all her Sisters, and the feeling was freeing. On visiting days, though, as she watched one novice after another run to meet whoever had come for her, Mary felt the difference between herself and the others all over again. She knew her family couldn't drive to see her for the simple reason that they didn't have a car, but still the pain of it, the loneliness of looking out the window knowing no shining bumper would be hers, reminded her of the darker feelings that set her apart. That was the tangle of emotions hiding in the folds of this life devoted to the pursuit of perfection: while first there would be the thrill of seeing her friends so happy, then there would come the feeling of loss triggered by standing alone at the top of the stairs.

Most visiting days, though, the infectious joy of so many in the community could only win out. One Sister or another would grab Mary by the hand and pull her along to the festivities below.

Soon the chapel, emptied of chairs and kneelers, filled with mothers and fathers, sisters and brothers, just as it had on the day the girls arrived. Some families always had a gift or two with them—not the kinds of things novices were permitted to bring back to the dormitory, so they were often enjoyed on the spot. The chapel's hardwood floor brightened with baubles and toys and the girls couldn't help themselves. Most of them were eighteen or nineteen years old by then, but still they crouched and stared, assuming the height and expression of toddlers as they took turns winding up a plastic duck and clapped with glee as it waddled across the table.

The way they basked in the light of this window of attention, it was as if they could store it up and use it another day. Once the visit was over and the girls went back upstairs, the windup dolls and other playthings would be swept away and never seen again. Like the affection of their families, they knew well enough to enjoy the toys while they could. As soon as their families were gone, the Sisters realized they couldn't take any of that feeling back into their everyday lives.

Not that they didn't try. The more daring novices smuggled candy bars and other contraband up to their beds, tucking bundles of treats into the folds of their sleeves, then walking in clumps of three or four back to the dormitory so that in the flowing fabric of their habits a few small mementos of their contact with families could be preserved.

One visiting day, Sister John Clare's father, who owned a drugstore, brought a whole boxful of sweets. Into a canvas laundry bag they went, and into her habit went the bag. That night, the girls gathered around in the dark as she dug through the sack and called out its contents: *Who wants a Hershey bar? Who wants a sucker?*

Bars and disks of candy flew through the air, spiraling above the bed curtains like a sky full of Sputniks, finding who ever was brave enough to shout out a preference despite the Major Silence.

Sister John Clare stuck her head in the sack to see what else she could find.

Okay, who wants a Mallomar? she asked.

This time, though, no one said a word.

No one wants a Mallomar?

By the time Sister John Clare looked up she saw curtains hanging undisturbed around all the Sisters' beds. Then, across the dormitory, she saw Sister Elizavetta. The mistress of novices stood in the doorway, staring down and frowning so severely the curve of her lips could be seen in the dark. Without a word Elizavetta shot out a finger and hooked it through the air.

The next morning, the other Sisters saw how Sister John Clare would pay for their sins. As the novices left chapel, they nearly tripped over a shrouded figure kneeling outside the door. Her hands were pulled up into her habit's sleeves, her head bowed so low that her veil fell to the polished floor in front of her.

"Sisters please have the charity to pray for me," she said, the oft-heard formula of contrition. Whatever the infraction, this would be part of the penance: over and over again as each Sister floated past the rule-breaker would plead, "Sisters please have the charity to pray for me." It was the spoken equivalent of writing a punishment on the chalkboard. "Sisters please have the charity to pray for me . . . Sisters please have the charity to pray for me . . . Sisters please have the charity to pray for me . . ." One hundred times or more for as many days as the offense warranted.

They couldn't see her face but it was easy enough to know who it was. With her head in her veil she sounded just as she had when searching for treasure in the bottom of her canvas sack. Head buried, voice muffled—seeing her there could only make the other girls wonder where all that candy had gone.

As much as they looked forward to their Sunday visiting days, through all the years Mary Doherty lived on Bethany Hill, the day the novices most wished they had contact with the outside world fell on a Wednesday.

To be Irish and Catholic and in Boston in the Year of Our Lord 1960 was to care about one thing, one man, above all else. It was not Jesus. It was not the pope. It wasn't even Cardinal Cushing. In the convent as everywhere else around the city and in the church, it was Kennedy.

JFK was to them the alpha and omega, the beginning and the end. Prescient in this alone, the nuns knew years before his martyrdom that he was like Jesus, a man safe to love. Their own handsome, virile *alter Christus.* Of course, it wasn't just the nuns who claimed him as their own—it was the whole church. Soon after the election Cardinal Cushing himself would claim that he and Joseph Kennedy had planned the campaign at a conference at the chancery offices in Brighton. Today that would seem a clergyman's overdeveloped sense of self-importance. But then? Well, Cushing was Cushing, so it might be true. With his imprimatur, even the novices at Bethany were free to dream of JFK.

Free to dream of him, that is, but still not free to vote, or to follow the election as closely as they would have liked. Though there was a television and a radio somewhere in the convent, it was only the luckiest of the novices whose chores took them within ear- or eye-shot of either appliance. For all the others, there was only hearsay, secondhand information that might have been true when it was first spoken but was totally unreliable by the time it had gone through the telephone-game of convent rumors.

So imagine the frustration in November of that year when these young women who had dedicated their lives to the faith were kept in the dark on perhaps the biggest night in the history of the American church. Despite the fact that the nation's Catholics awaited the outcome, for the Sisters of St. Joseph, the evening of Tuesday, November 7, 1960, was just another silent night, and the Wednesday morning after, they were sure, would still find them wondering. They would learn the result of the election only when Sister Elizavetta was good and ready to tell them.

By then, two years of convent life had had on some of the novices the opposite effect of its intention. Though they'd arrived at Bethany as pious youngsters willing to wait and wait until the supervisors deigned to allow them to "pick up pins and needles" and tend to other daily tasks, two years and a thousand permissions later, patience was in shorter supply. As far as many of the girls were concerned, waiting for approval was out of the question when it seemed that sufficient justification could be found in simple common sense. And never was the issue more clear than when it came time to learn the fate of the man who could be the nation's first Catholic president. Whether or not the novice mistress found such news disruptive to the life of the community, the novices simply had to know as soon as possible.

But how would they find out? Sister Marie Ursula had a plan. That week she was one of the unlucky Sisters cast down into the kitchen to do the bulk of the cooking for the entire community. For all the drudgery of the work, though, it did have one benefit. Only the Sisters with kitchen duty had contact with the outside world. Every morning the milkman would arrive with enough glass bottles for one hundred nuns. Of course she wasn't supposed to interact with him any longer than necessary, no idle chatter. (Maxim No. 42: *Be always serious in your intercourse with strangers,* was one of the first many of the Sisters had been able to commit to memory.) But at that hour who on earth would know?

So it was that, the night before, Sister Marie Ursula informed the novices she would find out from the milkman the outcome of the election and then would let them all know.

Would they have to wait the whole day, then? another novice wondered. They couldn't stand the suspense of it.

No, no, Sister Marie Ursula said. There's a way to let you know first thing, soon as I do.

But we'll all be in chapel by then, how could we know?

The bell, Sister Marie Ursula said.

The Angelus?

What else?

In addition to her cooking duties, it fell to Sister Marie Ursula to ring the Angelus bell every morning at sunrise, marking the end of the Sisters' silent meditation. It was a solemn way to begin the day, and that was the point, to focus the mind on God's truest intention for it. It was meant for no other purpose.

Nonetheless it was decided. If JFK should lose, God help us, Sister Marie Ursula would ring the Angelus as slow and mournfully as ever, marking the start of just another dark day for the Irish, another cross for the church to bear. If he should win, though, saints be praised, she would bong-bong-bong the fastest Angelus they ever heard.

So it was that the Sisters of St. Joseph appropriately celebrated the election of the first Boston, Irish, Catholic president, a president like them, making a ruckus under the watchful eye of the mistress of novices and Holy Mother Church.

When the Angelus rang out that morning the novices erupted right there in the chapel. Laughing and cheering and sitting on their veils so they wouldn't jump up off their kneelers.

Sister Elizavetta made her upside-down smile and would surely have them all kneeling and penitently chanting *Sisters please have the charity to pray for me* before the morning was out. But let it come. It was a new decade and a new president and within a matter of months they'd be off into the world, doing the good work they were trained for.

As the Angelus rang on that morning they couldn't know how soon their world would change. But still they could feel the excitement of it. The Angelus bonged on and on with possibility.

So let Elizavetta frown. She'd be cheering too, if only she'd known the meaning of the bells.

Part Three

REFORMATION

PROPHETS OF DOOM

Not long after my father's meeting with Bishop Lennon in the spring of 2003, Rome announced that a new archbishop had been chosen to take his place. The appointment of the Franciscan Sean O'Malley as leader of the most aggrieved branch of the Catholic Church in America changed the local face of the ecclesiastical hierarchy from stern to soft, arrogant to apologetic, as the office once held by the clean-shaven clerical businessman Cardinal Bernard Law, and then temporarily by the by-the-book middle-manager Lennon, was filled by a jovial bearded friar. After enduring almost two years of having its public perception shaped by priests-gone-wild, it was as if someone at the Vatican finally thought to pick up a phone and order a "good priest" from central casting. O'Malley arrived in Boston ready for his close-up; no tailored suit, no Roman collar, just a humble brown robe tied off with a rope.

The press ate it up. For ten years, O'Malley had been the church's go-to man where sex abuse was concerned. He'd come to Boston from the scandal-shaken Diocese of Palm Beach, Florida, where not one but two former bishops had resigned after admitting to molesting boys. Before Palm Beach, he had headed the Fall River Diocese on Massachusetts' south shore. It was there that what was to become the unifying theme of his various episcopacies first revealed itself.

In a story recounted in the *New York Times,* among other places, Bishop Sean, as they knew him in Fall River, showed up unannounced one night at a meeting of victims of the notorious abuser-priest Father James Porter. Lawyers for the victims' group had shut out all press and were prepared to turn any church representatives away. They were taken aback, however, when the good Franciscan arrived at their door.

"Oh no, Bishop, you shouldn't come in here without your lawyers," one of the attorneys present is said to have advised. But O'Malley was undeterred. "I just want to listen," he insisted, and listen he did. For Sean O'Malley, newspaper coverage of his every move had been rough drafts of hagiography ever since.

After his appointment, the bishop was all but sainted even by the *Boston Globe,* which had first broken the story of Cardinal Law's ongoing cover-up of abuse by priests, quickly won a Pulitzer for its tireless coverage, and then churned out an insta-book well before the scandal was over. Having proved with Law's resignation that the pen is mightier than papal appointment, the *Globe* then seemed to view O'Malley as the archbishop the press built. Its editors made no effort to conceal the joy they took in their creation. On July 2, 2002, the day after it was announced that O'Malley would take over, the *Globe* ran what was probably the largest front-page photograph in any daily paper since September 12, 2001. Nothing nearly so dramatic as burning buildings, of course: it was just a press conference still frame of the brown-robed bishop, grinning through his beard, his arms spread wide, both palms stretched open. Above the picture, a hopeful headline: O'MALLEY OFFERS PLEA, PLEDGE. Below, the endearing back-story: "New leader's life marked by intellect, sense of mission." Sandwiched between these paeans, the picture was twelve inches wide. Any larger, it would've needed a centerfold.

That so venerable a watchdog as the *Globe* was all too ready to take the O'Malley bait suggests that in that season the Catholic Church pulled off its most impressive public relations coup since the Gospels turned a murdered rabbi into a king.

But who could blame the *Globe* for biting? Bait, after all, tastes good. It's the hook you've got to watch out for. Professional church watchers were more staid in their response. "You can't help but be struck by the contrast between Cardinal Law's formality and Bishop O'Malley's personable, warm nature," Stephen Pope, of Boston College's theology department, said. But: "There could be something misleading in that—my impression is that Bishop O'Malley's theology for the church is exactly the same as Cardinal Law's."

In other words, though the new bishop meant a change of rhetoric and a change of fashion were at hand, for real change, deep change, Catholics in Boston would likely have to wait. Under O'Malley, it would be apologies and payments to victims and then back to business as usual, back to a church ruled by the systemic sexual dysfunction that started this mess in the first place. Reformations aren't always what they seem.

It was just at that time that Dad and I went down to Boston College ourselves. Not long after we'd left the Archbishop's Residence a few months before, Dad had spoken to one of the archdiocese's canon lawyers, Reverend Mark O'Connell, an expert in the internal legal system of the church, about the discussion he'd had with Bishop Lennon. Father O'Connell informed Dad he had interpreted the meeting, and the Vatican-provoked letter Lennon had passed on to him, a bit too optimistically. Yes, the canon lawyer explained, the church did still consider him a priest, but that did not mean they approved of it. In fact, notifying him that they were aware of his work as a married priest was the first step toward taking action against him. Dad's inquiry into what would be involved in resigning his clerical status had set in motion an ancient ecclesiastical process that would now lead to a tribunal of church-appointed judges who would decide his fate. Call in the Grand Inquisitor. They were putting him on trial.

O'Connell's advice to Dad: get yourself a lawyer. A canon lawyer. Church trials are set up so you can't in fact win—because, as the hierarchy sees it, the church can't be wrong (really)—but nonetheless he should have someone on his side with experience in these kinds of things. After a few phone calls and e-mails, he found his man. From the acclaim of every priest and former priest Dad asked, he found there was just one person he needed to get on his side: Father John McIntyre, a crusading Jesuit who had stood up to the church before, writing a number of unpopular papers on optional celibacy for priests. From the awed descriptions of him Dad had heard, he was a rock-flinging David to Rome's lumbering Goliath.

He was not what we expected. Dressed in beige slacks and a white linen shirt, socked feet stuck into sandals, he doddered up to us in the entryway of BC's clergy residence. Before he even nodded a greeting, he pointed out the restrooms, saying, "There's one over there," and then, with all the speed you'd expect from a man of his years (at least eighty, from the looks of him), he shuffled his feet to turn and point in the other direction. "And," he said, "there's one over there." He shuffled his feet again, turning back to face us. "If you should happen to have need."

With that, he led us, slowly, into a small conference room just off the hallway. As we sat, my father asked if he'd had time to review his case.

"Oh, yes," McIntyre said. "Oh, yes." And then he sat quietly in that way that can make you wonder about an elderly person's presence. Oh, yes, he was there with us, but where was he really? In that long moment of silence I began to wonder if someone had sent my father down the wrong path—and, for that matter, if there was even a right path at all. Nowadays Catholic churches tend to be filled with blue-haired ladies; maybe experts in the laws of the church were a dying breed as well. Maybe the best we could do was this possibly senile old man. If this was our David, I thought, Goliath is going to eat Dad for lunch.

But then McIntyre spoke. "It all seems much ado about nothing if you ask me." He leaned in on the table. "Frankly I don't understand this bullying nonsense; the involvement of Cardinal Arinze, et cetera. Dispensation should be a very simple matter. All you have to do is whatever they want you to do, easy as that."

As he spoke it became clear that although he had made himself familiar with my father's case, he did not quite see where Dad was coming from, or what he hoped to accomplish. He walked us through the procedure of resigning from the canonical priesthood. But Dad knew the process; he had been refusing to submit to it for thirty-five years. What he wanted, he explained, was to have his marriage recognized without having his priesthood denied. He did not want to choose between sacraments. Baptism, he felt, entitled every Christian to all of them.

"I'm not going to do it, John," Dad said. "I've seen too many people throw themselves down in the mud over this, subjugate themselves to this. I'm not going to do it. Marriage is a fundamental human right." His index finger tapped on the tabletop: Fundamental. Human. Right. "I didn't ask the hierarchy permission to marry because I have permission from God, I had a *vocation* to do so."

McIntyre sat patiently. He looked at my father like a seasoned dog trainer sizing up an overexcited pup. Raising his shoulders and then his hands into the air, he made a shrug of dismissal.

"Nothing is going to change," he said. "What you need to understand is there are two fundamentally different issues of canon law at work here. You are approaching this as if it were a matter of *juste*—justice, more or less—when in fact it is a matter of *gratia,* charity. You are asking for rights but they don't do rights. They do charity: anything you get from them will never be because you have it coming but because they deign to give it. And in this case, they won't."

He smiled sadly, then added, "Why put yourself through this? Just drop the whole business."

"What would happen if I did?" Dad asked.

"Well, if they were feeling mean they'd follow through, haul you before the tribunal. More likely, and with all that's going on, much more likely, it would—" He raised his hands into the air, and spread his fingers like a puff of smoke. "Just. Go. Away." He used the last word like landing gear, lowering his hands to the table. He smiled kindly at my father's disappointment. "But look. I'll do some checking. Ask some questions. See what I can find. Meantime, don't worry. We'll figure it out."

With that, it was time for lunch. A scholar and a gentleman of the old school, he insisted we join him in the faculty dining room. Dad seemed impatient to continue the discussion of his case, but in the dining hall there were larger matters at hand. Everyone seemed obsessed with Bishop O'Malley's appointment. Boston College is run by Jesuits, who, as a self-governing religious order, usually remain aloof where matters such as selecting new men to watch over parishes are concerned. The school, however, happens to be directly across the street from the Archbishop's Residence, which crowns sixty acres of prime real estate the ever-expanding undergraduate campus had been coveting for years.

From the few tables within earshot, I eavesdropped on an excited hubbub concerning what the future would bring for O'Malley and the church in Boston. The prevailing opinion seemed to be that the new bishop would sell the residence to get the archdiocese out of the debt so many abuse lawsuits had incurred. O'Malley's appointment meant that victims would be paid; BC would expand; life would go on.

Father McIntyre had his own opinion. Eighty years old, fifty years a Jesuit, he had seen the Catholic Church move toward reform and away again, toward and away, like some great breathing beast.

"People keep saying they think this guy will bring change," he said. "That's bullshit. He's not interested in change. If he was, he sure as hell wouldn't have the job." He winked; he was retired now, and could speak however he pleased.

"And would you get a load of that guy!" he said. "That robe! That hemp belt! I just got a new belt myself, two weeks ago when I was in Germany. It's a very nice belt: Hugo Boss, fifty-five euros. But I don't go showing it off to everybody."

"You've got to admit it makes a good picture," I said.

He smirked. "Sure, sure, but you know something?" He leaned in close, like he was letting me in on a secret, then he whispered, "We're not always on camera."

As for the possibility of O'Malley making a lasting difference in the Archdiocese of Boston or the wider church, he said, "He wouldn't know how to make a lasting difference if he wanted to. Know why?

No sense of history. The man doesn't have degrees in theology or ec-clesiology or canon law. How is he going to change the church with-out really knowing how it works?

"His degrees are in Spanish and Portuguese literature, for God's sake. All that means is he's probably read *Don Quixote* in the original."

The canon lawyer looked across at my father and me and tilted his head, smiling slightly at the connection he was too kind to make. Then he clucked his tongue and let loose the hint of a laugh, perhaps at the thought of his church not as a breathing beast, but as a wind-mill, turning its arms when the wind was strong enough, then always settling back to stasis; never really moving an inch.

"Come to think of it," Father McIntyre said, "maybe O'Malley is the right man for the job after all."

While it remained to be seen what impact this latest change in the church would have on my father, there was another, earlier reforma-tion whose effect on his life was both less ambiguous and more imme-diately felt, even though it took place much farther from home.

When Pope John XXIII convened the Second Vatican Council in the fall of 1962, he railed against "prophets of doom," those who believed there had never been a worse time to be alive, people behaving as if "the end of the world was at hand." He offered the Council as an al-ternative to such pessimism. What was needed in these times, he de-clared, was not fear of the future but an embracing of it, an engagement that would position the church as a body not enduring dark last days, but existing fully within history, with much to look for-ward to even as it learned from its past. "Divine Providence," Pope John said at the start of the Council, "is leading us to a new order of human relations."

Despite such rhetoric, though, it soon seemed the prophets of doom might have been right. Seen from the vantage of the American church especially, the world looked worse in many ways at the end of Vatican II than it had before it began. The Council was convened in the month of the Cuban Missile Crisis, and before it came to a close in late 1965 the nation's first Catholic president would be killed, Pope

John himself would die, and the country would begin its long slog through the parallel spiritual crises of Vietnam and the most violent era of the civil rights movement (the duration of the Council saw such events as the murder of Medgar Evers, the church bombing in Birmingham, and "Bloody Sunday" in Selma, to name a few).

The '60s came late to American Catholicism, but when the changes of those troubled years finally arrived, they were as turbulent inside the church as out. During the three years of the Council, nearly every element of the faith Catholics had known all their lives was reconsidered. The Latin of the Mass was replaced by the vernacular. Marriage was affirmed as an equal sacrament to holy orders (separate but equal, of course). The laity was encouraged as never before to become more involved in worship, liturgy, and the work of the church. For the first time, non-Catholics were not considered damned (not officially, anyway). Many of the assumed divisions upon which the faith had so long stood—remember the catechism: God and man, church and world, etc.—seemed a little less divided than they had before.

There was an element to the Council that was only surface reform—perhaps not much different than, decades later, the appointment of a photogenic friar to give the appearance of change in the Archdiocese of Boston. In fact, that was precisely what many high-level Vatican officials believed the purpose of the Council would be: a big show that would quiet dissent but ultimately not disrupt anything.

Yet the true setting of the revolution of Vatican II was not St. Peter's Basilica but the living rooms and kitchens of Catholic households around the world. For those who saw scenes from the Council on television or read reports of it in the press (most famously in the *New Yorker*, whose "Letters from Vatican City" series was a surprisingly riveting read), the very fact that the fathers of the church would even discuss change was enough to trigger countless personal, individual revolutions. The long-term effects of the Council's practical reforms are still debated, but even in the shadow of reactionary factions who ultimately would undo Pope John's optimism, it would be impossible to overstate the change the Council made in the faithful's relationship to the faith.

The same was true, perhaps even more so, for the clergy. Some nervously, some hopefully, priests followed the Council in every way they could, making both official accounts of the sessions and gossip concerning the main players coffee-talk in American rectories and seminaries for years. Around Boston, news spread of how Cardinal Cushing, almost totally lacking in the Latin of the proceedings, had offered to pay for a simultaneous translation system. When his offer was rebuffed by the conservative Italian cardinals who were running the show, Cushing went home to Brighton, figuring he could do more good in a place where he spoke the language. Anyone sympathetic to the linguistically challenged archbishop of Boston would have enjoyed the poetic comeuppance later suffered by those same Italians, who, though they thought they would control the conversation of the Council with their superior command of Latin, were said to sound "like quacking ducks" compared to the articulate orations of a group of Dutch reformers. Those library-basement theologians were finally having their day in the sun.

And so too was a new way of thinking about being a priest. Suddenly the church a generation of clerics had been trained to serve had changed to such a degree that many of them began to see themselves as activists and social workers as well as men of God. The prevailing theme of Vatican II was *aggiornamento,* a "bringing up to date" that would help a tradition nineteen centuries old become more current without the loss of principles it held to be timeless. "The church is not an archeological museum," Pope John said, "but the ancient fountain which slakes the thirst of the generation of today as she did that of the generations of the past." The Council, it seemed, was an attempt to balance eternal hopes and immediate needs. Some wanted to take this idea a step further: like their fully human, fully divine model, these priests hoped to be both fully religious and fully secular. Inspired by their pope, they planned to rebuild the church from the ground up, to help it serve the modern world by living and acting like modern men.

Fresh from seminary, Father Bill Manseau was one of them. Zealous, idealistic, naïve—he was ordained when he was younger than I am now. In a newspaper snapshot I have of his first Mass he stands swimming in his vestments like a boy playing dress-up. In the picture, his back is to the congregation, as the priest's back always was in those days; he lifts the host into the air as if it were a baby bird being returned to its nest. As the concentration on his face makes clear, at the moment he was the one being lifted, being changed. Transubstantiation: once this contact was made, it would be impossible to go home again, to ever not be what he had become.

And what was that, exactly? Everything and nothing. He had never lived on his own; never been more intimate with another person than he'd been on those guilty dates during his minor seminary summers; never earned a salary or paid bills or owned a car. He'd never even done his own laundry. Nevertheless, as far as he was concerned, he was ready to save the world. He decided that the only way to get past the contradictions he'd encountered at St. John's was to embrace them. He decided, in short, to be Christlike.

"I must love everyone," he wrote one day not long after his ordination: "If I do not, we all are lost." Jotting down this thought in one of the tattered reporter's flipbooks he carried inside the crisp black suit that was now his proudly worn uniform, he underlined *everyone* and the second *I*, making the connection he saw between the two impossible to miss. He then named a few of the people he *must* love: "George and wife . . . Frank and wife"—a clear statement, it seems to me, of whom in fact he did not.

It's easy to imagine the scene: he was twenty-five, black suit hanging off his thin frame, the new priest on the block in his first church, and Mrs. George comes to the rectory to chew his ear over the success of the bake sale, or to give him grief for allowing a folk duo to sing during Mass. Tedium taxes charity: whether it's the drone of her voice or the smell of cigarettes mixed with perfume, it's something, something about her that makes him think for just a moment: *Oh won't this woman just leave?* He thinks it so loudly, so harshly that he can't imagine she hasn't heard. When finally she turns and moves toward the door, he reaches for his notebook, overcome by the distance between what a priest's life should be and what his is at this moment. He sets the notebook on his knee and presses the pen so hard to the page it feels as though he is writing on his own skin, *I must love everyone.*

So far it had been a challenge. When he left St. John's it was with a head full of radical ideas that he thought the world was waiting to hear. ("The Bible is an *action,*" he wrote. "It is the framing of an *explosion* . . . It is the *marriage bed* of God and his People . . . It is a coiled spring which rockets us into a new dimension of living!") As a parish priest, he quickly realized it would take some work to get his new parishioners to share his excitement. He had seen the changes of Vatican II coming before they started, and so had been given a chance to assimilate them into his idea of what it meant to be a Catholic. Not so in a suburban church. Even at a well-heeled and well-educated parish like St. Elizabeth's in Milton, his first assignment, it was going to take quite a while for change to trickle down. ("Be more open to their stiffness," he wrote; "it's not their fault.")

At times it seemed it was going to take even longer to win the respect he had expected like a birthright upon ordination. His hair always neatly parted and slicked across his head, his thin lips often pursed as if he was keeping a secret, he was too fresh-faced, too young-looking for the work he hoped to undertake. When he walked through St. Elizabeth's in his alb, the white gown worn beneath vestments, the parishioners often took him for an altar boy.

Even when he did manage to connect with his parishioners as fellow Catholics, that connection was often marred by his difficulty simply relating to them as people. "Each man must be met on his own ground," he told himself. "I must read the Sports Page." And it was worse with women. Eight years spent exclusively in the company of men had not made it easier talking or working with the opposite sex. How could it? Just to be in a woman's presence made him feel he was the opposite *of* sex. Since his first year of seminary, even to drop by his parents' house was to be reminded of his separation from the world of long hair and any dress frillier than his cassock. As a boy he'd shoveled driveways to buy stockings for his mother; now, when he visited home, the same nylons drying in the bathroom were enough to send him rushing back to the rectory. Such was the uneasiness with bodies that was his training's other indelible mark.

But, as he also wrote that year, "the things we find hardest to do must become the first things we do." So one weekend he resolved to hold a women's retreat in the basement of St. Elizabeth's. Such activities were coming into vogue in many American parishes by then. Among the liturgical experiments that spread through the church in the wake of Vatican II was lay involvement in a three-day session of intensive prayer and worship called a Cursillo. Imported from Spain, the Cursillo ("short course") was an early flash in what would later be known as the charismatic movement, which delighted in blurring the lines between what was considered safely Catholic—sacred ritual, dignified liturgy—and that which was sniffed at as strictly Protestant, that is, all displays of faith deemed overly familiar or emotional. Starting in the early '60s, charismatic Catholics crossed the boundary between these with a Pentecostal fervor. Bill himself had been to his first Cursillo earlier that year; now he wanted to share the fire.

In his notebook, he made notes for a sermon:

"Salvation History is the world's greatest love story!" he planned to say.

Grace is God-the-lover reaching to embrace us and guiding us to embrace others in the Trinity's divine person of love: The Holy Spirit.

Christians are love-people—loving and being loved in Christ, in the risen Christ with his wounds. To be in Christ is to share in his wounds and move love around!

When we come face to face with God thru Jesus, He sets us free and we really begin to live! Christ opens up a new way of living, which we must take if we are to give new life to an old world. He charted a new course—He was loyal to His Father alone—and because He did so, He showed us the way out. These are our marching orders.

At the retreat's end, Father Bill thought it had gone very well. And apparently others did too. One woman was so moved that, during the punch and cake reception that followed the final prayer, she kept trying to wrap herself around him in a giant bear hug. She was a large woman, full of life and almost splitting the seams of her dress. All Father Bill could see every time she came at him with bare arms open wide were two enormous breasts about to burst from their covering and fall down upon him in an avalanche of polyester and flesh.

"Oh thank you, Father!" Mrs. Avalanche said as she swooped down upon him. "I had such a wonderful experience!"

"Glad to hear it!" Father Bill nodded, stepping behind one of the basement ceiling's metal supports.

"So moving!" she cooed as she followed him to swoop a second time.

"Great!" he said, ducking to the other side.

"And life-affirming!"

A turn, a head fake, a quick pivot, once more around.

"I can just feel my faith growing and growing . . ."

"Terrific!" Bill cheered, terrified he would grow and grow as well if he should fall into the abyss of her bosom. He forced a grin as he cha-cha'd around the pole, dancing forward and back to keep four inches of metal between himself and embarrassment. Why was it he could speak so passionately of God's embrace, but recoiled in fear when his divine ideal became a fleshy possibility?

From his notebook, January 12, 1963: "The cup the Lord offers me is the cup of humiliation—to be His brother I must accept it. It is the only way that I can grow. I accept it gladly and joyfully without further hesitation! I ask only that the Lord protect His own interests."

Despite such minor indignities, he loved being a priest. He worked six days a week at the parish and used his only day off to teach an Introduction to Sacred Scripture class at Boston College. A few of his fellow priests looked down their noses at his fervor; even his pastor let him know such Protestant-seeming goings-on were not appreciated. It was a hard rebuke to ignore, especially since merely being in the pastor's unsettling presence often made Father Bill shake with fear. ("I should remind myself the man is insane," he wrote, "and try to treat him with compassion.") Yet the occasional mediocrity and shortsightedness of his fellow churchmen only spurred him on. "I must do the works which Jesus shows me to do," he told himself, "not just conform to the static religious patterns of past years. Jesus did not conform to the dead letter but reached into the spirit of his religion and thus startled his contemporaries with the power of God. I will not be saved by merely upholding the system."

Of course, as the '60s rolled on, there was a lot of that sentiment in the air. Just as Bill had found a new way to think about being a Christian in texts hidden in the basement of the seminary library, he soon found a new way to act on it in books—two books, specifically.

The first was by Hans Küng, a young Swiss priest who emerged as the brightest star in the constellation of those reforming European theologians. Küng's book *The Council, Reform, and Reunion* explained the spirit of Vatican II in a way that made the implications of the faraway proceedings in Rome come to life. The ultimate end of the Council, Küng proclaimed, was unity, a bringing together of all the separated branches of the Christian faith.

To Bill this was nothing short of revolutionary. The American Catholic worldview remained parochial enough at the start of his priesthood that when President Kennedy was assassinated that year, Bill could not understand why on earth non-Catholics were as upset as he was. JFK was *our* president, after all. What did *they* have to feel bad about? Küng made him doubt the assumption behind that question. And once the elemental divide that had separated Catholics and Protestants was breached, it was only a matter of time before the other divisions that seemed to govern the world—white and black, rich and poor, clergy and laity—would be challenged too.

No less revolutionary was that Küng's challenge to the church was not just in how it related to the world beyond it, but in how it related to itself, the role of its members in the body they made. "When it comes to abuses in the Church," he wrote, "the sum total of being a

Catholic does not consist in swallowing them." It was only in being honest with its members about itself that the church's goal of unity could be attained. Not only can we suffer, he said, "we can criticize." More importantly: "We can act."

That Küng's effect was immediate on the young priest my father was then can be seen in the influence of another book he discovered early in the '60s. Written by a Protestant, just a few years before it would have been as off-limits to Bill as if it appeared on the Vatican's infamous Index of Forbidden Books. Priests and seminarians in those days required special permission to study non-Catholic theology. This book, however, would've been hard to ignore.

First published in 1962 and then reprinted throughout the decade, *The Cross and the Switchblade* caused a sensation. It told the story of the Reverend David Wilkerson—"the thrilling true story of a country preacher's fight against teen-age crime in big-city slums." Wilkerson had left behind his family church in rural Pennsylvania for a street ministry in New York City. For a radical in the making like Father Bill Manseau, Wilkerson's book was like a grown-up Boy Scouts' manual, complete with lessons on how to identify native species—as in the case with Wilkerson's encounter with the Mau Mau street gang of Brooklyn: "Some of the boys wore brilliant red jackets with black armbands and the two letters MM sewn boldly on the back. Others wore tight tapered trousers, bright shirts and continental shoes with thin soles and pointed toes . . ." There were also helpful notes on communicating with the locals, as when Wilkerson first meets the president of the gang: " 'Slip me some skin, Preacher,' he said. I was still innocent of the slang of New York, and when he held out his hand I tried to grasp it. 'Just slip it, Preach,' he said, and he slid his open palm against mine."

Forty years later Wilkerson's book reads like an epistle to the cast of *West Side Story.* The most menacing description he can offer of the gangs he ministers to is that "nearly all of them wore sunglasses." It depicts a sanitized slum, suitable for churchgoers, where gang insignias are "sewn boldly" but nothing ever seems terribly dangerous. Yet to Bill, *The Cross and the Switchblade* was the real thing. Though it

told the story of a Protestant preacher, he saw in it a man much closer
to the priestly ideal he had formed in his youth than many of the
priests he'd met since his ordination. He even went down to Brooklyn
to meet Reverend Wilkerson in person. He spent an afternoon ob-
serving Wilkerson's "Teen Challenge" ministry house, where recovering addicts and former gang members always found an open door.
Started just ten years before, Teen Challenge was already a national
movement; it gave Bill an idea of what could be accomplished when a
man devoted himself to what he believed God wanted him to do. Not
much more than that came of the meeting, but nonetheless Bill had
gotten out of it what he'd hoped: to see the Holy Spirit at work. As he
had only lately come to see it, the Spirit was just as likely to be found
with a Protestant preacher in the streets of New York City as it was in
the great meeting of Catholic bishops going on half a world away. And
if that was so, Bill wondered, wouldn't the Spirit also be found even
closer than that?

Returning north, he sought out the Boston Teen Challenge House
and saw that the same problems and the same solutions could be
found in his own city. It was there, in a converted brick house, that Father Bill first heard the wild sounds of Pentecostal prayer: a dozen
voices shouting at once in a language he had never heard before. It
was such a far cry from the tepid paternosters of his daily devotion or
the choreographed drama of the Mass, he thought it sounded like the
ranting of the devil himself. Budding ecumenicist though he was, the
Catholic in him couldn't help but run from the room. Only when he
had composed himself did he go back in and join the prayer. Before
long he could shout and holler his praise with the best of them.

"We cannot be hot-house saints," he wrote. "I must learn as much
about the world and ways of the world as I can so that I will be able to
communicate with it and really transform it. Separateness is fatal to
the command of Christ: Go teach the world."

Jesus gave him marching orders, Hans Küng gave him justification,
The Cross and the Switchblade gave him a model. "I must seek the
meaning of my life in a ministry among the very oppressed," he

wrote, and from then on he watched for signs that might show him where to begin.

"Praise to Jesus Christ for making me a radical," he wrote. "I am like an arrow hurtling to its target!"

He hoped it would be the worst place he could find.

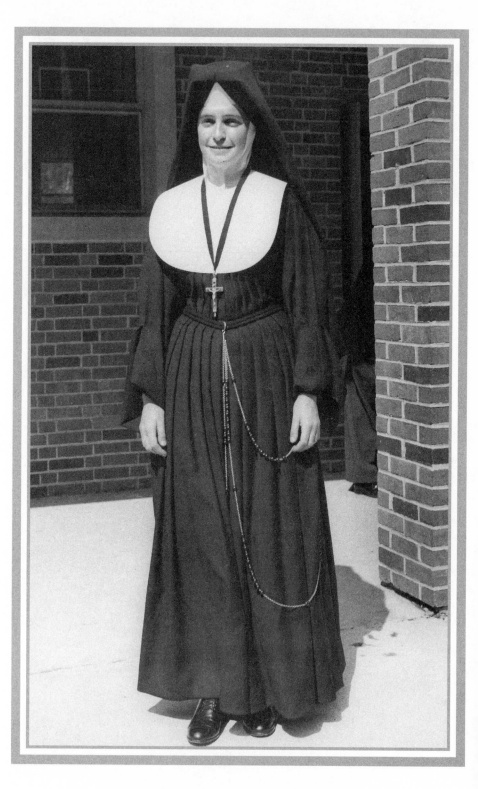

FROM MANY WOUNDS

When a new batch of Sisters of St. Joseph arrived at St. Francis de Sales parish in the fall of 1966, Father George Spagnolia let them know that working there would not be like what they had experienced in their previous positions as teaching Sisters. Ordained just three years, Spag had already become the kind of activist priest who tried to be where the action was, so it might have been as much of a boast as a warning when he spelled out the way of life in the neighborhood. "You don't live in Roxbury," he liked to say, "you survive it."

Sister Thomas Patrick, the nun formerly known as Mary Doherty, had taken her vows at Bethany five years before. Since then she had taught in parishes on the outskirts of the city, in classrooms full of kids much like those she had grown up with: white, Catholic, almost-middle-class. Her third-graders at St. Joseph's in Medford or St. Clement's in Somerville may not have had the backyards and swing sets of their suburban peers, but they hadn't come to school hungry either. With the obvious exception of the days spent huddled among the other Sisters and their students watching the funeral of the president, teaching in parish schools had been just what she'd expected. In fact, her hours in the classroom were not all that different from what they had been during her own school years, back in Dorchester at St. Margaret's Elementary. For all the changes the world had seen by then, it had been comforting to learn that even as seen from the other side of the habit, Catholic education remained much the same. So long as the students kept their hands folded on their desks and memorized the same four R's she had—reading, writing, 'rithmetic, religion—they, and she, had had little else to worry about.

St. Francis de Sales, though, was a crumbling parish in the poorest part of Boston. Literally on the wrong side of the tracks (the steel stripes of the Huntington Avenue trolley marked the border with affluent Brookline), it occupied a section of the city that had followed a demographic trajectory similar to that of many of the nation's troubled urban areas: white flight in successive waves. The Brahmins moved out when the Irish moved in, the Irish moved out when the Jews moved in, then the Jews moved out too. By the middle of the century, to most of the white residents of this famously segregated city, the name given to the neighborhoods in Boston's southwestern corner had joined what they considered a list of synonyms: black, desperate, dangerous, best-to-be-avoided . . . Roxbury. In those days when Catholics in Boston spoke of the ghetto, they weren't talking about the self-imposed exile of religious provincialism anymore; they meant only the curve of Tremont Street that brought you where no one from Dorchester, Southie, or Brighton went if they had any choice.

The reputation was not just local. Two years before Sister Thomas Patrick arrived at St. Francis de Sales, President Johnson had named Roxbury one of the ten worst slums in the country, the Northern front of his "War on Poverty." Though in the rest of the city there was much talk of the "New Boston" being built downtown with its high-rise Prudential Tower and the concrete expanse of Government Center, in Roxbury garbage piled up for weeks at a time even along its main drag, Blue Hill Avenue. Johnson's program, part of his plan for creating the so-called Great Society, was designed to target the causes of poverty—bad schools, inadequate health care, unemployment—but everyone in Roxbury knew that the uneven treatment their section of the city received came down to the color of their skin.

For an Irish girl from Dorchester, it was quite an education. Growing up, all she had known about the people she first learned to call colored and now were called Negroes was that they fitted neatly into the catechism's divided universe. Maybe not by doctrine, but certainly by practice, white and black had always been as distinct as man and woman, spirit and flesh, church and world. Now she lived in an area whose white population had dropped 30 percent in ten years. The parish school was 98 percent black, with relatively few Catholics among them, though the Sisters of St. Joseph (98 percent white) taught every class. The actual teaching was much the same as anywhere—the Sisters were barely aware that many of their catechism students were actually Baptists, attending St. Francis de Sales only for an education marginally better than they would receive in one of the city's public schools. Yet the neediness of the neighborhood raised the stakes, called out for more commitment.

On one of her first days on the job, a boy no more than ten ran up to her in the recess yard, a small square of asphalt kept separated from the surrounding streets by a chain-link fence. In September 1966, Sister Thomas Patrick still wore the old-fashioned habit she had received at Bethany, from the medieval underwear to holsterlike pockets to the heavy cloak thrown over it all. The boy ran at her so fast he nearly tangled himself in its folds.

"Sis-nah, sis-nah!" he cried.

Most of these Baptist kids had no idea what a nun was, or why they should say "Sister" to a complete stranger, a white lady no less, so you couldn't expect them to get the terminology right all the time. *Sis-nah, Shishtah, Stah*—these days Thomas Patrick answered to anything remotely sibilant followed by Boston's vowelish *r*.

"Sis-*nah!*" the boy howled. "He called me *black!*"

When he stepped away, she saw he was in tears, his finger pointing across the faded grid of decades-old hopscotch and box-ball squares. Thomas Patrick looked and saw another student of hers glaring back. Then she glanced again to the boy by her side. To her eyes, they were the same exact shade of brown, both neatly dressed in the blue pants and short-sleeved white button-down that was the school uniform.

"He called me *blaaaaack!*" the boy wailed again, shrieking as though it was the worst insult he'd ever heard.

Covered head to toe in inky serge, she and her fellow Sisters were certainly the darkest figures on the playground, like shadows cast by their far more colorful students. Among kids who ranged from the high yellow of Roxbury's West Indian community to the deep blue-black of one African immigrant family, if anyone was just plain *black*, it was the nuns. Yet here was one child jabbing another with the word like a knife.

She knew then she didn't understand this question of race at all. Yet the first boy's tears combined with the second boy's spiteful glare let her know it had something to do with the rage of helplessness and self-hate, which she did know something about. She was reminded of those feelings every morning when she woke and looked in the mirror at a face she judged much too old for a woman of twenty-six. She was reminded every time she brushed her teeth. Almost ten years after they had been inflicted, the wounds covered by the pink and white mask of her dentures still stung with the feeling of being separate, worthless. Is that what the boy felt when his classmate called him black? Is that how it felt to have what you are turned against you?

Before Roxbury, she might as well have lived on another planet for all that her time as a nun had prepared her for the realities of the inner city. The closest she had come to witnessing actual human suffering in her previous assignments might have been at St. Joseph's in Medford, when one of the superiors, Sister Paulita, would assemble the junior Sisters in the chapel to deliver show-and-tell sermons on the Passion.

As soon as the younger women had settled into their pews, Sister Paulita would point up to the crucifix that hung above the altar, and then down at one of them—often right at Thomas Patrick, with a finger stabbing the air.

"You see that?" Sister Paulita would ask.

"Yes, Sister," Thomas Patrick would answer.

"Are you sure you see it?"

"Yes, Sister. Yes."

"Good. You know who did that?"

Trick question. "Um . . . Pontius Pilate, Sister?"

"Wrong!" Paulita boomed. "You did that! You!"

The other Sisters inched away in the pews, but they weren't getting off any easier. The old nun's finger shot in the direction of one Sister, then another. "And you! And you!" Paulita hissed. "You and you and you and you! You all did that to my lovely Savior!"

She always said it with such conviction the younger Sisters could only bury their faces in their sleeves. Jesus, they thought, maybe we did.

Or perhaps she'd seen real suffering at St. Clement's in Somerville. There was that stooped old widow who sat in the back of the church every day for morning Mass. When time came for Communion she'd approach the altar weeping, on her knees, mumbling her prayers in what could have been Portuguese behind the lace of her church hat's veil.

The morning priest at St. Clement's favored the Mass of the Dead because it was the shortest of the liturgies. No incense at the Introit, no blessing following Communion, he could wrap it up and get back to his newspaper in about fifteen minutes. There was always so much to do before the start of school that the nuns often didn't mind the hastily said Mass. But apparently the widow liked it for a different reason. With all her moaning, she seemed to appreciate the added asceticism of the stripped-down service, especially the fact the Mass for the Dead required the celebrant to wear black vestments over his alb.

Whenever Thomas Patrick watched that poor woman creep to the Communion rail, she guessed that surely some great tragedy must have occurred to make the woman's mood as black as the priest's cloak behind the altar, as black as the Sisters' habits in their pews, as black as the widow's own mourning dress, the hem of which swept St. Clement's side aisle six days a week.

One day the usual celebrant was ill, held up in bed, and some young man fresh from seminary took his place at morning Mass. Apparently caught up in the liturgical changes of the Council in Rome, he decided to forgo the somber Mass for the Dead. When he appeared at the altar in springtime green rather the expected black, the widow leapt up off her knees and shook her fist in the air.

"You Protestants!" she shouted. "You goddamn Protestants!"

The Sisters bit their lips to keep from laughing at the thought that maybe there had been no tragedy at all; she just really liked black.

As ridiculous as Sister Paulita or Mrs. Blackmass seemed when Mary looked back, they did raise a more serious question: Was that the kind of suffering that was supposed to be at the center of the faith? The suffering of self-righteous old ladies nostalgic for a death-obsessed church?

Many of the Sisters of St. Joseph didn't know much more about it than that. Cloistered away as they were, and with children their only contact, news of the racial violence in the South and of the body count in Vietnam bypassed them entirely. They didn't even watch television—not that they didn't try. On one occasion Sister Thomas Patrick snuck away with Sister Marie Therese to try to watch Yul Brynner in *The Brothers Karamazov* on the new television in the parish school. Such was the hold the life had on them—so internalized had its restrictions become by that point—that they lost their nerve before the screen flickered to life. They rushed back to their rooms instead, fearing a stern talking-to above all else.

For Thomas Patrick, that was about as bad as it got until Roxbury. To be a Sister was to strive for the perfection of devotion, and such a pursuit could not be sullied with the messiness of life. Even when Michael Doherty fell off a ladder and died, in the spring of 1963, the details of it had been kept from her. She would always wonder if her father had been drinking, or if his heart had just given out, but she never knew. She wasn't allowed to attend his burial. No matter the state of the world or one's family, the Sisters lived as if the only death that mattered was Christ's.

And so, though her time in the habit had not been exciting, it had been not particularly stressful either. It had often been sad, but overall it was exactly as she had hoped it would be, safe. Ten years since she entered the novitiate, she chafed occasionally at the more arbitrary strictures of convent life, but all in all there was a certain security to the routine, the reliability of the habit and the rules that came with it.

Now the rules seemed to be changing, however. The Sisters of St. Joseph had not followed the Council in Rome as closely as had some of the priests of the diocese, but they had begun to feel the binds of their life loosen. At St. Francis it was as though the chaos of Roxbury had seeped through the convent walls.

Like all the local parishes, St. Francis attracted an endless parade of hard-luck cases. Alcoholics and addicts made a circuit of the churches in Roxbury, and when they didn't make it to St. Francis, Father Spag and several of the Sisters of St. Joseph would go to them. In St. Philip's parish, one of Spag's seminary colleagues, Father Jack White, was engaged in a similar kind of inner-city ministry. When urban renewal closed down the St. Philip's sanctuary, Father Jack had turned a residential building into an unorthodox worship center called Warwick House, where the more adventurous priests and nuns in the area ministered to locals who wouldn't set foot in a building that looked like a church. Freed from ecclesial architecture, not particularly concerned with following archdiocese rules, Warwick House became a meeting place for the city's misfits and radicals. Thomas Patrick and several of the other nuns from St. Francis would head down as often as they could. Their new Sister Superior was far more lenient than most superiors of the order; she didn't object to the Sisters being involved in the world around them.

One of the regulars at Warwick House was a homeless street poet. He seemed to take a liking to Sister Thomas Patrick right away. To let her know he thought she was okay, not like some stuffy old nuns he had met in the past, he gave her an original composition, typed up on a sheet of tissue-thin paper. The poem summed up his philosophy of a black man's life in America. He called it "Ain't That a Bitch."

> *The blood escapes from many wounds*
> *And whip marks scar my back*
> *Yet no one comes to give me aid*
> *Know why? Because I'm black.*

> *Freedom's but a word I hear*
> *A thing I cannot see*
> *It's measured out in minute specks*

Because I'm ebony

I find it everywhere I go
Some show it, some hold back
But all in all it's still the same
Can't do much . . . I'm black.

There was that word again. Whether on the playground at St. Francis or in the kitchen of Warwick House, it seemed she couldn't go anywhere without running into it. Understanding its meaning was an unlikely enterprise for girls raised in the Irish enclaves of Boston, where, at least around St. Margaret's in Dorchester, the closest they'd come to it growing up was the olive-skinned man whom the neighborhood kids called Nigger Murphy like it was the most natural thing in the world. Yet lately it had occured to a few of the Sisters of St. Joseph that trying to fathom what it might mean to be black was essential if they hoped to do any good in the place they now lived.

In Roxbury, they soon discovered, black was two things at once. In the schoolyard it could be a cudgel. Thomas Patrick's students knew a jingle about skin tone and its implications as well as they knew any of the songs they sang while skipping rope; the complicated history of race in America distilled to a few rhyming lines: "If you're white, you're right / if you're yellow, keep it mellow / if you're brown, stick around / if you're black, get back."

Even while the younger kids played, though, a new slogan was blowing through the chain-link that surrounded the school: "Black is Beautiful" were the words on every teenager's lips as all across the ghetto older kids began to find new ways to wear the label that had made them cry as children. The Black Panther Party sponsored youth fairs in Franklin Park. Over on Intervale Street, the Black Muslims had established a temple among a line of buildings that had been churches, then were synagogues, and now were up for grabs. Such was the atmosphere in Roxbury at the time, the feeling that change could come suddenly and irrevocably, that the leader of that temple, the Nation of Islam's Mosque No. 11, was a man who first achieved local renown as a calypso singer called Gene Louis "The Charmer" Walcott, but now preferred to be known as Minister Louis X. And such was the confusion of the times that when Louis X's temple opened its doors on Intervale's row of former synagogues, the Boston phone directory had at first mistakenly listed him as another rabbi in the once predominantly Jewish neighborhood: Rabbi Eugene L. Walcott. Later he would be known as one of black America's most controversial figures, Louis Farrakhan.

There were no less dramatic changes going on within St. Francis de Sales' small community of nuns. Every week something else occurred to upset the comfort of their routine. One week Sister Geraldine Marie's brother came home from Vietnam, and then Sister Joan's brother was reported MIA. Another week, Martin Luther King came to town and twenty-two thousand people joined him, marching from Roxbury to Boston Common, from the forgotten black edge of the city to its proud green heart. The nuns who marched were changed forever by the experience; the nuns who didn't wished they had. Of all the upheavals though, few approached one caused by ten inches of fabric. The change they felt when it was announced that the Sisters of St. Joseph would shorten their habit to just below the knee was seismic. For the first time in a decade Sister Thomas Patrick felt the sun on her legs, and she wanted more of it.

Later that year, it was announced that the head of the Sisters of St. Joseph, Mother Catalina, was on her way to St. Francis de Sales for an inspection. The Sisters couldn't have been more excited. With all the good work they'd been doing in the community they expected a rave review.

They got the opposite. The outreach they had been engaged in was not proper for Sisters of St. Joseph, they were told. To hear the superiors of the order tell it, you'd think they should be back in the novitiate reciting the Maxims of Perfection. Whatever was going on in the streets around them, they should just stay put in the convent, teach their classes, and not call attention to themselves.

Mother Catalina's response prompted several of the Sisters to announce it was time they stopped living in the convent. Regardless of what their superiors felt, they would go get an apartment in the city and live as nuns in the world. They called themselves the Bread Community, and believed their presence beyond the church walls would be like yeast in the flour, tiny grains of action causing the whole loaf to rise.

They asked Thomas Patrick to join them, but she wasn't ready to go that far. She lived in the world by joining the card games the winos set up while they were drying out at Warwick House. Soon they all knew her as the nun you didn't have to watch your mouth around, and every interaction with them was a minor disturbance in its own right, if only because it was there she began to see more of the life of the city in which she lived, and seeing it, she was able to imagine herself living as more fully a part of it.

I have a picture of her at the time, dressed in a modern black habit, being removed from a forum on Black Revolution in Roxbury. Stokely Carmichael, chairman of the Black Panther Party, was the featured speaker; Muhammad Ali, newly minted as a minister of the Nation of Islam, was scheduled to be in attendance. Carmichael was the man who coined the phrase "Black Power" and set white America shaking; his presence did no less in Boston.

It's another scene easy to imagine: eighteen hundred souls crowded into the auditorium of the Boston Technical High School. Stokely takes the stage: "Every Negro is a potential black man," he said that night. "We must begin to have undying love for our people or face genocide from the whites." Elsewhere in that same year he explained what undying love might entail: "We are preparing groups of urban guerrillas for our defense in the cities . . . It is going to be a fight to the death." He was just hitting his stride in Roxbury when a couple of Irish-eyed nuns showed up in the back of the hall. They were there because they taught in the city, because they knew the boys who would grow up and maybe die in these streets, because they cared in such a way that they could not imagine they would not be welcome. Had they made it that far, they would have walked in with their newly shortened habits brushing the knees of the revolutionaries, sweeping into a room of bow-tied Muslims and Black Nationalists like nine hundred years of Catholic Europe. Their hearts were in the right place, but they were not, and the nuns were quickly pointed toward the exit.

In the photograph my mother stands framed by stone stairs and a metal doorway, a couple of serious-looking Panthers behind her. The one in the doorway must be even younger than she is, a boyish face staring out from a black beret and black leather overcoat. Sister Thomas Patrick glances up and smiles as she comes down the stairs. A few steps back, the Panther shakes his head, having just explained for the last time why she's got to go. The other Panther is smirking. *Who does this nun think she is?*

As the years had passed in the convents of parishes around the city, she had become less and less sure, but now she was beginning to make sense of it. She had been a nun all her adult life—she didn't know how not to be one. But what that meant had changed gradually. It had meant one thing when she was a postulant at Bethany, and then quite another at her first assignment, teaching third-graders day in and day out in Medford. It had meant one thing on visiting day in the novitiate when families would bring them treats and toys and remind them they were special, and it meant something new and unexpected when her father died and her superiors wouldn't let her attend his burial. The meaning of her life had always seemed to swing back and forth between those two old feelings: chosenness and a complete lack of control.

Now though, like the definition "black," her life seemed to be changing. She'd gone into the convent to give her life to God, to lose herself in the anonymity of the habit, the mask of the veil. But wasn't it by wearing the habit that she had found herself? Every year that passed as a Sister of St. Joseph she chafed more and more at the rules, at the demands of her superiors, but living the life of a nun had also put her more in the world than she ever would have been had she stayed, all those years before, in the shadow of St. Margaret's in Dorchester. Her family lived not five miles away—ten minutes on the MBTA—and yet she never saw them. Not only had she been kept from her father's interment, but her brothers' weddings, her sister's graduation from Monsignor Ryan Memorial High School. Once she had only known who she was in relation to those people and places, but now her life was different, her own. How else but as a nun could she be who she had become?

Every so often Spag would have the Sisters over to the rectory, sometimes to talk about parish concerns and programs, other times just to have a little social hour, a break from all the trouble they dealt with in the neighborhood. The rectory was a much more comfortable place than the convent, and Spag pretty much had the run of it. St. Francis's pastor was chaplain to the Massachusetts House of Representatives—basically a lobbyist in a Roman collar, Cardinal Cushing's man on the inside—which meant that at his home church he was more or less an absentee landlord, his name on the sign out front but himself rarely seen in the rectory or behind the altar. So the place was Spag's and as such became an unlikely refuge for the younger nuns of the parish. The older ones wouldn't dream of snooping around in there.

One evening when the Sisters dropped by, Spag broke out a bottle of something, passed glasses around, and they all had a fine time. Spag poured one nun's glass, then another, then another.

"Mary, would you like a bit of this?" he asked.

"Oh no, Spag," Sister Thomas Patrick answered. "I don't really drink."

"Maybe you just haven't found one you like yet."

"Maybe," she said.

Late that spring, after a CSJ gathering on Cape Cod, she was able to spend the night with her brother and his wife. She came back with exciting news.

"I think I found a drink I like!" she told Spag. "A Tom Collins. My sister-in-law made one for me. It wasn't so bad."

"You don't say," he said.

A week later, at the end of the school year, Spag invited a few of the younger Sisters over for a celebration dinner. They trooped up to the rectory from the convent and had just taken their seats around the table when Spag appeared with a pitcher of cloudy white liquid. He had looked up a new recipe for the occasion: a little vodka, a little lemon, some club soda, lots of sugar. "Tom Collins!" he announced, and poured Sister Thomas Patrick a tall glass.

Aside from Communion wine, it was the second drink of her life, but it went down like Kool-Aid. Sister Joan didn't much care for hers.

"Well," Sister Thomas Patrick said, "if you're only drinking half you don't mind if I finish that do you?"

Spag made them each another; Sister Thomas Patrick had both.

Soon enough it was the nuns' curfew; time to head back to the convent. But one of them wasn't going anywhere; at least not without help. She sat slouched in her chair with her veil falling across her face.

Father Spag hoisted her to her feet; Sister Eileen slid under one arm; Sister Joan under the other. Out of the rectory, down the walk, the three Sisters crept through the dark toward the convent steps, approaching the statue of St. Joseph, their patron, husband of the Blessed Virgin, staring dumbly down as the nuns stumbled by. He seemed to frown at the sight. Watching with those unmoving eyes.

Oh keep your judgments, you sterile saint. Hadn't she spent most of her life as accepting as you were, as docile as plaster? And what good had come from following your lead?

But on the other hand: what a risk he took, when you think of it. All expectations dashed by divine whim, and still he stuck around. What a leap of faith it takes to get on with it after God has done His worst.

Up, up, up the stairs, and then the Sisters squeaked down the tile hallway to their rooms. Somehow they got Thomas Patrick to her bed, under her covers. The room spun so fast it was a wonder the blankets didn't fly away.

CITY ON A HILL

Roxbury: To most priests in the Archdiocese of Boston, news of an assignment there would have been received as a rebuke. To Bill, it sounded perfect. After four years working in relatively peaceful parishes on the edge of the suburbs, he sought permission from Cardinal Cushing to begin an experimental ministry in the heart of the most troubled part of the city. As odd a request as it would have seemed, Cushing was getting used to it by then—not too long before, he had granted a similar petition, sending Bill's old seminary buddy, George Spagnolia, to oversee the school at St. Francis de Sales. Cushing agreed to Bill's proposal with one condition: Father Manseau would officially be stationed at another parish in Roxbury, both to keep a roof over the young radical's head, and to ensure that his superiors could keep an eye on him.

Bill's new church, All Saints, was on Roxbury's Fort Hill, a rise of crooked city streets topped with a stone watchtower commemorating the Revolutionary War fort that had been erected on that spot in 1775. It was now home to another revolution: with its abandoned buildings and home costs lowered by the highest crime rate in the city, Fort Hill was becoming Boston's gathering place for hippies, Black Panthers, and other '60s fringe groups. Most conspicuously, the street leading to the tower, Fort Avenue Terrace, had been claimed by a loose association of dropouts and musicians from the Cambridge folk scene. In Roxbury they called themselves the Fort Hill Community, which before long was a commune of fifty or so—a dozen couples, a score of towheaded hippie kids—who lived on next to nothing but managed to renovate four falling-down Victorians within a couple of years. The Hill People, as they also called themselves, had started as a utopian experiment but soon turned into something of a cult, led by a rail-thin folkie turned nihilist guru-god named Mel Lyman. In their alternative paper, *Avatar,* the Hill People mostly published Lyman's messianic musings and screeds:

> *I am going to burn down the world*
> *I am going to tear down everything that cannot stand*
>   *alone*
> *I am going to shove hope up your ass*
> *I am going to turn ideals to shit*
> *I am going to reduce everything that stands to rubble*
> *and then I am going to burn the rubble*
> *and then I am going to scatter the ashes*
> *and then maybe someone will be able to see something*
>   *as it really is . . .*

So much for peace and love. Such rants made the Hill People few friends in the black community that surrounded them. Lyman's followers patrolled Fort Avenue Terrace through the night, every night, and elsewhere on the Hill teams of Black Panthers could often be seen doing the same. Many of the commune's neighbors already lived in rubble and ashes, thank you very much, and they didn't need some Harvard Square banjo player taking over their streets and shoving their hope aside.

Nor did the presence of the Hill People do much for the reputation of the neighborhood's few other white residents, living not far from the watchtower in another monument to Roxbury's long-ago Yankee past. On this hill covered with the broken shells of empty apartment buildings, the All Saints rectory occupied a grand residence that had formerly served as home to the governor of Massachusetts. A mansion large enough for the family and staff of the state's chief executive, it was now home to barely a handful of priests.

The clerics at All Saints generally kept their distance from Lyman and his gang. On Bill's single foray into the commune, for the parish census, he wandered into one of the buildings and found a dozen or so hippies crowded into a dark room, staring out at him as if he were a ghost. They already had a stand-in for God in their leader Mel (thus spoke the *Avatar:* "Mel Lyman is the Truth and the Life and if we express the truth it is because of Mel Lyman and it is Mel Lyman"). A decade later, Mel would be dead at age forty, but at the time the Hill People believed he was immortal, so they didn't have much use for priests.

The feeling was mutual, but that was a fact easily overlooked by the rest of Fort Hill's inhabitants, who couldn't help but notice that white men claiming godliness—priests or hippies, what did it matter?—had the nicest homes around.

When Father Bill arrived at All Saints there were just two other priests in residence. His new pastor was "Circus" Ed Sullivan, so called because he was the chaplain for the Barnum & Bailey Circus. Whenever the show came to town, Circus Ed would be there to confer his blessing on the performers and animals, splashing them with holy water as they brought a parade of acrobats and the stink of manure to city streets. The other priest in the rectory was Father Rafferty, whom everyone called "Rackets" because he used his stature and position as a priest to pull off, in broad daylight, some rather questionable salvage operations. He kept a truck in the rectory driveway and every so often he would round up a gang of hoodlums from the neighborhood, pull up to one of the many condemned buildings nearby, and with his crew he'd strip the place of its copper pipes, load them in his truck, and sell the metal for scrap. Bill never knew what happened to the money, but he was sure it never found its way to the collection plate.

Every morning on his way out of the rectory, Father Bill would pass the miniature big top Circus Ed displayed like a year-round crèche in the sitting room. Every afternoon, out in the driveway, he would see Rackets Rafferty's salvage truck. This was the church Bill had given his life to serve? This was the promise of the Council? The nicknames said it all: sometimes the church seemed filled with clowns and crooks. In his last years at seminary, he had earned a nickname himself: "Ivory Tower" Bill, they called him. He often scolded himself for feeling superior, but there was no denying that among priests like these he did not belong.

It was hard to know just where he did belong in those days. While he had been well liked by many of his suburban parishioners, others had considered him something of a zealot, too often conveying the sense that there was an unbridgeable distance between his lofty goals and their everyday concerns. Even his family seemed to react to him that way. They had all been thrilled to have another priest in the family, but the reality of it—of his black-suited presence at holidays or on an otherwise casual Sunday afternoon—made the air heavy whenever he returned home. One photograph he kept of the family said it all: it showed his parents and their children gathered before a picture window in the living room of their house in Lowell. Jeannette and Leo Manseau squeeze in close together with their daughter and three younger sons; their oldest, a boyish twenty-seven in his Roman collar, stands apart. Light from the window streams between Bill and the smiling huddle of his family. The young priest looks away from the camera, as if impatient to be on his way.

Though All Saints was his official assignment, as Bill saw it his true work began as soon as he reached the bottom of Fort Hill, heading down from the grandeur of the former governor's mansion to parts of Roxbury into which not even the hippies would venture. He started talking to people on sidewalks, then going door to door, making house calls to learn about the problems of the neighborhood. ("Rats and hatred and rotten buildings and stinking hallways," he wrote.) Sometimes he'd leave his collar behind and get an earful of what people really thought about the church.

He drew his inspiration then from another reform movement growing in popularity in the wake of Vatican II—the "Secular Institute," which like the Cursillo encouraged Catholics to find new ways of thinking about the faith. Through the involvement of both priests and the laity, members of the Secular Institute of Pius X, as the group he joined was called, sought to help those most in need by going beyond the boundaries of parishes and religious orders, by establishing groups for outreach and ministry—*in saeculum*—in the world. "Priests in neckties" is how the institute's founder, Father Henry Roy, referred to its members. And though Bill still wore his Roman collar most of the time, nonetheless that notion, that image, was powerful to him. Hans Küng himself had worn one when he toured the country proclaiming the good news of the Council. To Bill the sight of it proclaimed something else as well: a priest that could look like any man could fight for any man. As he saw it, the Secular Institute was like an undercover army serving God, focused on the neediest because they were the ones who bore the brunt of society's hostility and negativity, which, rather than any individual or political body, he regarded as the real enemy. On his walking tours of Roxbury he had seen this enemy first hand.

"Now is the time for a counter-attack," he wrote. "We are to renew the world for our generation. Our groups are cells of the new life. It is a new life in an old world, so we must be ready for loving struggle. We are not struggling against people but the ideas which propel them and trigger their action. We are on the move!"

Bill found a home for his "cell" when he came upon an abandoned storefront on Shawmut Avenue, in the shadow of the Lenox Street Housing Project. It wasn't much to look at: a funeral parlor gone out of business, its three small rooms still had the smell of flowers and must to them. Yet when he hung a sign out front that said *Catholic Messengers of the Bible,* Bill felt he was becoming the priest God wanted him to be.

A chemist's son, after all, he couldn't have found a better laboratory for the kind of religious experiment he had in mind. The storefront's street-facing wall was an enormous plate-glass window. Inside the window there was a closet-sized office, complete with one lone shelf just wide enough for a telephone. Whenever he got a call, Father Bill would stand in the window for the world to see, this pale white presence in an all-black neighborhood, a priest behind glass like a stuffed bear in a Roman collar. He wanted people to be curious, to wander over just to see what it was all about. Soon enough they were coming over in the evenings for Bible study and hymn singing in the center's main room, a meeting space big enough for a packed house of thirty people and a makeshift altar. A few always returned the next day for soup cooked up on the hot plate he kept in the back.

Sometimes they wanted more than soup. People would wander into the storefront, find out this was some kind of religious place, and wait around to see what more it had to offer. Unlike the All Saints rectory, where Rackets Rafferty was known to set his Alaskan husky on unwanted visitors and had even drawn a revolver on a couple of panhandlers, the Catholic Messenger Center gained a reputation as worth the effort of a visit. If any of the drunks in the neighborhood wanted to dry out, Father Bill or one of his volunteers would give them a lift to Bridgewater State Hospital—and not only there, but back again. Unlike the Fort Hill hippies, the Catholic Messengers didn't want to drive the locals out; they wanted to become fully a part of the place, making Roxbury's problems their own.

Soon a regular gang from parishes outside the city began dropping by to help out. College kids from Michigan spent the summer living in an apartment Bill rented above the store. Suburban church ladies drove in from colonial homes in Lexington and Wellesley. One came down on the weekends and painted bright murals of Gospel scenes over the funeral-gray walls. A Capuchin priest who was also a practicing lawyer was enlisted to give free legal advice to anyone in need. With all that was going on at the Catholic Messenger Center, word quickly spread that the young priest who had started it could be counted on to give more than his blessing.

He did have his limits, though. One regular was a homeless poet who was always asking to stay the night on the center's floor. Father Bill wasn't having any of it. You can take the boy out of seminary, but you can't take the seminary out of the boy: a righteous life was first of all an ordered life. The Catholic Messenger Center was a place to pray, sing, and organize, maybe to occasionally get some hot food in your belly, but a flophouse it was not.

"Sorry, we've got rules here," Father Bill said.

"C'mon, just tonight, Father. You know how cold it is out there?"

Bill wouldn't listen. "Head on down to the shelter," he told the poet. "If I let you stay once, this place will fill up every night."

No one gave much thought to the poet's absence for a few days after that. Then news reached the center that when Father Bill turned him out he had set up camp in an empty building, one of the crumbling concrete shells that blighted the neighborhood. With no windows to break the wind and not much by way of blankets to cover himself, by morning he was dead, frozen in the Boston winter.

"Death by exposure" is how the newspapers would have put it, but if anyone felt exposed, it was Father Bill; exposed as a man who claimed to be helping the poor but often came up short. A classic and unforgivable sin of omission. Could he really claim the Gospel as his guide if he could so easily forget that most basic command: "Him who comes to me I will not cast out . . ."? Couldn't he be counted on to keep a man alive by simply opening the door?

"My Jesus mercy on him and me!" Bill wrote. "How else has the Lord come? Perhaps he came in the alcoholic I was flip with on the phone, causing him to hang up. Yes. He was the Lord. He came and I turned him out."

Bill wasn't sure what to do with the regret. The condolences of his suburban volunteers weren't much help. It took two locals—two guys from the neighborhood who could always be seen walking and talking, drinking and philosophizing up and down Shawmut Avenue—to show him. Bill had met them over at Warwick House: Billy Mays and Bob McCreary, both about Bill's age, though the lives they'd lived couldn't have been more different. Billy was from the neighborhood, a great big guy and a real bullshitter, talking nonstop about this or that scheme. Bob was the more laid-back one, a bearded hipster fresh to Roxbury from San Francisco. He had family in town, and besides, he said, "You can only stay high so long."

The first time he came by the Catholic Messenger Center, Bob told Father Bill he wanted to talk business. Swaying back and forth as he spoke, he was as drunk as the center's regulars tended to be. What was unusual was the business he had in mind.

"Hey Father," he said. "I want you to take me down to see Cardinal Cushing."

"You have business with the Cardinal?" Father Bill asked.

"No, you do. You're gonna ask him to give me a loan."

"A loan?"

"Yeah, man. Fifty thousand dollars. That's all I need to start up my nightclub. Soon as I do that, I'm all set. Pay him back in no time."

The neighborhood was so full of grifters and con artists that Bill almost told him to get lost, but the death of the street poet had taught him a hard lesson. "Jesus said, 'I am the light of the world . . . '" he wrote. "I must let Him be the light that shows me other people; the light that shows me, as I follow Him, how he becomes one with them.

"Are they depressed? So is he.

"Are they hungry? So is he.

"Are they jobless? So is he.

"Are they drunks? So is he.

"Are they thugs? So is he.

"Are they liars? So is he.

"Jesus said, 'so if the son makes you free you will be free indeed.' What freedom! Freedom not to judge men as bums, as thieves . . . but as Jesus in need of respect, care, affection, healing."

"Tell you what, Bob," Father Bill said. "You come see me on Sunday. Sober. And then we'll talk about it."

Sure enough that Sunday he came back to hear what the priest had to say. The two of them sat on the rectory steps. Bob seemed to have forgotten his nightclub plan, but he had another idea for a new neighborhood nightspot. A halfway house, where the drunks could go when they needed to dry out, clean up, find work; a place where they could get a night's sleep without wondering if they were going to get stabbed or robbed before morning. Bill had seen a few of the places the neighborhood's alcoholics and junkies usually found to crash; he remembered the railroad spike one of them clutched even as he slept, just as Bill had held his rosary when he was teenager. A crucifix in the palm was the best way to keep from touching yourself, Father Tom had said. In the face of the real world's problems, the moral dangers of his youth now seemed absurd.

But what more could he do? The Catholic Messengers were spread thin already.

"Isn't there a place over in South Boston?" he asked. "We could shuttle guys to it, same as we do down to Bridgewater."

Bob had to laugh at the thought. A black man in an Irish neighborhood wouldn't have to worry about keeping safe in the shelter; the cops would get him before the other drunks had a chance. And the people who ran the shelters weren't much better. Anyone's welcome, they'd say: didn't we have a black guy in here a couple of years back?

Bob and Father Bill talked the whole day, sitting on the stoop of the former governor's mansion, in the shadow of the Revolutionary War watchtower. Before the conversation was done they had decided to find a way to create a safe place for homeless and alcoholics right there in Roxbury.

Later they told Bob's friend Billy about the halfway house plan, but he wasn't so sure he wanted to be involved. Bob had wanted his nightclub; Billy wanted to find someone with a big boat so he could sail around the world.

"I'll make a deal with you," Father Bill said. "Give this a try. If it doesn't work out, I'll find you a sailboat myself."

Before long they had hatched a plan to acquire abandoned buildings and turn them into safe havens in the middle of the most dangerous place in Boston. They decided to call their new venture Open Ear Associates. Bill had learned the hard way from the street poet's death: if they didn't listen to each other they would never accomplish anything.

Not that it was going to be easy. First things first, they needed cash to get under way. Bill had already done some fund-raising for the Messenger Center, so he sent Billy and Bob down to a few of the old-money Yankee charities that made their homes in the quiet streets around the Common.

"You're crazy," Bob told him. There was about as much chance of a Beacon Hill Brahmin writing a check for drunks in Roxbury as there was of Big Billy Mays marrying George Wallace's daughter.

But Bill, as ever, was a true believer. "The Holy Spirit is on our side," he would say. "You'll see."

They saw, all right, and so did the charities—those bluebloods saw the Open Ear's emissaries coming and had made up their minds before Bob and Billy made it through the door.

"You've got to come down there and show them some white," they would tell him, and Bill would know just what they were talking about: White collar. White face. In Boston these assets went a long way.

The three of them trooped back down to Beacon Hill for a few more rounds. Each time, before, they went, Bill said a prayer. "Jesus I am so grateful for what you have done for me and are still doing . . . To be here in Roxbury is beautiful. Use me as you want, only hold on and watch me carefully as I get my footsteps secure—it is your work and I don't want to botch it up."

The other men weren't Christians, and he didn't ask them to be, but still he'd add, "Let's pass the Spirit around now . . ." and then they'd get to work.

As soon as they got inside the first office and sat across from yet another uptight Bostonian, it was clear the spirit wouldn't be going too far today. Behind his Protestant desk, buttoned up in his Protestant suit, sitting stalk-straight and humorless in his padded-leather Protestant chair, he was a fellow who made it immediately clear that he believed the only thing worse than a black man asking for money was a Catholic.

Never mind. They'd come all this way and Bill wasn't about to hump back to Roxbury without at least making his pitch. He stood up in that posh Beacon Hill office and explained to Mr. Oldmoney why it was exactly that Boston's black community needed a halfway house of its own. One of the reasons Bob liked Father Bill so much was the fact that he understood what a lot of New England do-gooders didn't: that white institutions didn't even know how racist they were; that white charities had no idea the extent to which the ways they thought were helping were actually doing the opposite. When Bill made their case, he let the charity man have it with the fullness of his Roxbury-radical, parish-priest turned storefront-preacher Gospel fervor.

It was a wonder nobody called the cops.

On their way back to the Catholic Messenger Center, his two colleagues shook their heads at the spectacle they'd just seen. But they were not unimpressed. Though they didn't get any money that day, it came soon enough. Not by grace but by sheer stubborn will, they soon acquired one abandoned building, then another, and renovated them with a skeleton crew. The plan hatched on the steps of the All Saints rectory eventually led to the first halfway houses for alcoholics in Roxbury. Whatever Rackets Rafferty or Guru Mel Lyman could take apart, Ivory Tower Bill would try to put back together.

"I swear, Bill," Bob said. "You've got some big brass balls hidden in that black suit of yours."

As much good as the Catholic Messengers tried to do, in the summer of 1967 the situation in Roxbury went from bad to worse.

In early June, not far from the Shawmut Avenue storefront, a sit-in at the Grove Hall Welfare Office had gone awry when the Boston Police Department stormed in to break up the demonstration. A group called Mothers for Adequate Welfare had occupied the building in a style found more often on college campuses in those days—linked arms, chains around the doors. We shall not be moved.

It was late in the afternoon when the police broke a glass door and went in to bring the MAWs out so the office could close for the day. Outside, a group of men had gathered more as spectators than anything else. Police cruisers weren't exactly a unique sight on Blue Hill Avenue, so at first they watched only half-attentively. A bunch of crazy ladies getting themselves in trouble, that's all the protest seemed.

After a while, though, some on the sidewalk began to wonder why the police were taking so long to clear out a few mothers and their kids. Through the windows movement could be seen, but it wasn't clear what was going on inside the building. Maybe it was just the orderly exit of demonstrators who had decided they had made their point. Maybe one stubborn MAW was in there gripping an office chair to her chest, giving the cops a piece of her mind. Then one woman put her head out an open window and, loud enough to find every ear in Roxbury, shouted, "They're beating your black sisters in here!"

All hell broke loose. The men who had been milling outside

charged in to give defense. The police who had been breaking up the sit-in charged out to keep them from entering. Reinforcements were called in on both sides: white cops speeding in from Dorchester and Southie in response to radio calls; black Roxbury residents running down Blue Hill to see what was happening and inevitably getting caught in the fray.

The clash at the welfare office was immediately all over the news, interrupting radio broadcasts, stopping the presses of the dailies' evening editions, and then it was all over the streets. Earlier that year, after the riots in the Watts section of Los Angeles, Martin Luther King had named ten cities in the U.S. that were likely to erupt in more riots in that hot summer. Roxbury was the first to prove him right, with Newark, Detroit, and Harlem to follow.

By the time night fell on that first day of violence, over a thousand cops had been mobilized in Roxbury, most patrolling the streets in full riot gear, quick to club anyone in reach. Hundreds of others set up in Franklin Park, ready to sweep in—like the cavalry or a death squad, depending on which side you were on. For three days, the poorest section of the city burned.

A writer from the *Boston Globe* gave a personal account: "Driving through Grove Hall, in the Negro district, flashing press credentials on every block, you knew you were in a sick country. The fires, the looting, the armed camp. Stores that had been in the community for 50 years suddenly had seen their death . . . glass and brick everywhere . . . people running from one doorway to another . . . meaningless shrieks in the night . . . the area could never be the same."

"Hundreds of residents peeked precariously from behind lowered shades, and the cigarettes in some of their hands sparkled in the blackness . . . And you thought surely that some very decent people were inside those walls, children with hope and adults with a sense of responsibility."

At the corner of Intervale Street and Blue Hill Avenue, he continued, "police attempting to establish order were hit from the rooftops. Bricks and bullets fell among the ranks of the police. They rushed some dangerous yardage down darkened Intervale, armed

with carbines and riot guns and fired round after round at their ele-
vated tormentors . . . And you wondered why the dead weren't everywhere."

The *Globe* would not go so far as to blame the police, but the local
press in Roxbury saw it differently. While the *Globe* headlines proclaimed Roxbury "riot-torn"—as if it was hit by a storm, neutral, dis-
passionate, with no one to answer to—headlines in the *Bay State
Banner,* the paper people actually read in the neighborhoods now in
flames, declared: "Roxbury residents brutalized." It devoted three
columns to injuries suffered at the hands of the Boston police. "You'd
think these cops were from Mississippi," one witness said.

Even the Hill People reported the incident: "Too many people attempt to reduce this and similar situations to police brutality," the
Avatar wrote. "Sure they're brutal, brutal in a way that few of those
who stay out of their clutches can imagine; yet, as Hannah Arendt said
of Eichmann, they're also banal. There is no archfiend among them,
no Satan brooding upon the abyss of Roxbury . . . To ascribe such epi-
cally malignant proportions to the cops is madness. There's just not
enough to them. They only act with their instincts, instincts ultimately programmed by the mood of society. Throw them into a tense
situation and whammo—click, whir, bang—off they go like so many
beasts swarming over an intruder."

Driving down Blue Hill Avenue that night, that's just what it looked
like to Father Bill. A swarm. He could see the smoke rising outside his
windshield. Cops everywhere; people running. All the clergy in the
area had been called in to try to calm the situation, to get anyone they
recognized inside. He scanned the streets for a familiar face. Then suddenly noise of riot outside the car was inside, as the window beside
him shattered. A hail of glass filled the car's interior. He looked down
on his seat and saw a ball-peen hammer among the shards of glass. It
had a black handle, silver head, a blue and white price sticker affixed to
the neck. I know exactly what it looked liked because I used to play
with it as a boy, pounding nickels flat as a knife-edge in the garage of
my parents' house. When it came flying into my father's possession,
the hammer had likely just been looted from the hardware store on

Blue Hill Avenue, whose windows had been smashed along with those of two hundred businesses. Bill looked through his own shattered window and saw the person who had broken it. She was just a girl, maybe fifteen years old.

As the fighting continued, Father Bill abandoned his car and took to the streets. He recorded injuries in his notebook:

1. *26 yr old, 43 Hallworthy Street. Hit with a baseball bat*

2. *White man struck by an unknown Negro*

3. *Lt Jos. Donovan, firefighter, shot by rifle in finger (arm)*

4. *Charles Caine, resisting arrest, struck by service baton. "Walking from bus 10 police surrounded me and began to beat me. I had my hands in the air. They had to pull one of them off of me."*

5. *Ronald Kelly. Intervale St. Struck by bricks at 2 am . . .*

The list goes on, followed by a note to himself: "We must be shrewd enough to realize that our values are either radically with God or not."

Even when he returned to the Messenger Center and discovered that his own window had been smashed, that a trash can had scattered glass shards in a halo on his floor, he had no trouble distinguishing which side he was on. In the aftermath of the riot—dozens wounded, a half-million dollars in damage, a miracle no one was dead—Father Bill marched so long with the MAWs and their supporters that his black shirt turned gray in the summer sun.

Some of Bill's fellow priests looked down their noses at all this activism, wondering what helping alcoholics, street people, and black welfare mothers had to do with the reforms that were taking place in the church. ("Don't you come preach on my sidewalk!" one monsignor told him.) Saying Mass in English was one thing: what Father Bill seemed to be up to was something else altogether.

To Bill, though, it was all done in an answer to the call begun by Pope John and now taken up by his successor, Pope Paul VI. If there was to be true unity in the faith, Bill felt, there must be unity in the world, and unity in his city first of all.

Though they were definitely a minority of the Catholic clergy, there were others who saw it as he did. They were a new breed: self-styled "street priests" working in the worst neighborhoods of Boston. Across town at St. Francis de Sales there was Spag, a regular at sit-ins and protests, with a big billy-club lump on his head to prove it. Downtown there was another St. John's graduate, Father Paul Shanley. Decades later he would be the lone Boston priest convicted in the sex abuse scandal, but back then he was making news with his ministry to street kids and drug addicts. Throughout the city there were others, joined together in the Association of Urban Priests, and all over the country could be found more of the same: men in Roman collars were showing up in news photos of civil rights marchers in the South; priests linked arm in arm with Martin Luther King, or running righteously from the law, like the leaders of the Catholic wing of the protest against the war in Vietnam, the brother priests Daniel and Philip Berrigan. Even in conservative, Catholic Boston, priests were becoming a common sight at draft-avoidance marches. Perhaps because they themselves were exempt from the draft, they were occasionally the objects of particular scorn. According to legend, a cop once stopped four older priests on their way into a diner around the corner from a protest in Post Office Square. The clergymen tried to explain they were out-of-towners, had no idea there was a march nearby, but the cop wasn't buying it. Apparently wanting to keep all the radicals penned in where the authorities could keep an eye on them, the cop shouted, "Get back to the parade you motherfuckers!"—as if suddenly every priest was a peacenik.

That Catholic involvement in the struggle for civil rights and against the war began in the wake of Vatican II was no coincidence. What these priests had learned from the Council was not only that the church could change, but that the world could too. More importantly, they learned that they, as Christians, as Catholics, as priests, were called upon to change it, to heal the rifts that seemed to be the cause of each problem. Gone were the catechism's endless divisions: white and black, rich and poor, Catholic and Protestant. The new gospel was reunion in all things.

"'Unless the grain of the wheat fall into the ground and die . . . '" Father Bill wrote, "'it remains just a single grain; but if it dies, it bears much fruit . . . '" It was a line of Scripture quoted often enough by churchmen who believed simply being a priest was sacrifice enough. Now more than ever, though, the passage spoke not just of sacrifice but of actual death. The possibility of it, anyway: what seemed to him the necessary danger of a life lived by faith.

> I must proceed wide open, with arms held wide, to reconcile my white and black brothers through meeting their needs . . . We are windows in the house of the world through which men may look to see God and through which His light and warmth reaches them. I beg God to clean me or if necessary to smash me and remake me so that men—*all men*—will see His light and feel His warmth.
>
> As I grow older, the passing values of much of society are seen for what they are and the basics become more obvious. Unity continues to grow in my estimation as an imperative—human unity on all levels—sacred unity. Religious denominations, races, etc., more often than not they are idols; obstacles to reality. I do not fully know who Jesus is but I am obeying him and I am discovering life in a new way. The enigma of his person remains while my loyalty to him increases.

With all his talk of unity, it now seems inevitable that one day Father Bill would realize the greatest rift to be healed was the one that remained within himself. It began in fits and starts, occasionally bubbling up in the pages of his notebook like a wound that wouldn't heal: "Way, deep within something is happening to me and I'm not even sure what it is," he wrote. "It seems to be strength and calm, but also there is a radical openness to total life which I don't understand in terms of my commitment as a priest. Jesus, I am your disciple—make me what you want me to be."

Apparently what Jesus wanted him to be was in constant motion. With these feelings brewing at home, it's no surprise that it was just at this time that his desire to see the Spirit at work wherever it might be had begun to take him out of the city. First to Billy Graham's World Congress on Evangelism in Germany; then to a meeting of charismatic Christians in Bogotá, Colombia, then at small gatherings of like-minded Catholic activists at universities around the country.

Many of the stories from my father's life as a priest I have learned anecdotally, through years of asking and listening. Some of his exploits, though, I've been able to read about. A book called *Catholic Pentecostals,* for instance, recounts the earliest stirrings of a new movement as it occurred at Catholic colleges like Notre Dame:

"The opening meeting was characterized by prayers of praise, as we shared the good news of what the Spirit had been doing in the different communities represented. Through the gifts of prophecy and wisdom, the group found directions from the Lord toward greater awareness and involvement in the grave and pressing concerns of war, race relations, and poverty. Again and again we were pointed toward the realization that our responsibility is as great as the power of the Spirit who moves us. As a concrete tangible sign of our willingness to begin at least to follow these promptings of the Spirit, Jim Byrne, a Notre Dame senior, was inspired to suggest that the money which had been collected at Saturday's dinner should be turned over instead to Father William Manseau of Boston for his work with the poor in the inner city. It was, and prayer and songs of praise continued through the night."

Later, the authors continue, "Father Manseau gave the homily, and it reinforced our direction toward involvement in the concerns of society. We must share with all God's children the gifts, the power and love which we have received."

As Bill measured it (and of course his measure was far from much of the world's), he was becoming a success. Making a difference. But still there seemed to be something missing in his life.

Late in May 1968, Father Bill was flying from Boston to Dayton, Ohio, to yet another conference of charismatic Catholics. With a few hours to himself on the plane, he felt the weight of it, and thought he knew what would lessen the burden. "God, I want to be human," he wrote. "I want to love a woman and be loved by her."

He could not have written the words without feeling the treason of it. After almost fifteen years of being preoccupied with the priest-hood—with preparing for and then embodying the *celibate* priest-hood—the idea of loving a woman was in some ways a denial of all he had wanted to be. And yet how could this longing for unity—what was it but that?—how could that be sin?

"O, God, have mercy on me," Father Bill continued as the plane rose into the sky. "The more I give myself to your spirit the more I long—in honesty—to know the experience of making love, freely, fully with my whole being . . . I am speaking to you in all honesty, simplicity, and sincerity, Father. Lead me. I trust you."

As the plane climbed his thoughts drifted. Wasn't this the life he had dreamed of when he was in seminary? "The Father always speaks His word through the Spirit," he had written, and now here he was a minister of that Word, an advocate and an emissary of that Spirit. It had taken him to Germany, where he saw the Spirit at work to heal a war-ravaged nation, and to Colombia, where he'd seen the streets swarm with hungry children—hungry for food, he thought, but also hungry for love. Hungry for God.

"The sky is magnificent deep and light and blue," he wrote, "very white fleecy clouds below us. How I thank you for the privilege of flight, Father. What beauty is revealed."

He stared out the window, the world so far below. He was thankful, yes. But not content. He tried to let all the morning's concerns go. But he could not. He had one wish he had not yet uttered because to do so was to give voice to the fear that life as a priest, as the kind of priest he had been, was not, would never be, complete.

"Oh, God," he prayed, "I want to be a man."

•   •   •

Back in Boston, back to work. One day early in the summer of 1968, Father Bill left All Saints rectory and went down to the storefront to set up for his evening prayer meeting. He still celebrated Mass regularly in the church, but he had discovered that his informal Bible studies were the best way to make contact with the people he wanted to reach. However much he thanked God for flight and the excitement of his traveling ministry, there was still much to do on the ground.

He had a few college students helping out for the summer, but there were still plenty of chores that fell to the pastor of a shoestring ministry: sweeping up, or arranging two dozen folding chairs for worship around a makeshift altar of sawhorses and an old wooden door.

How was the trip? one of the college kids asked.

Fine, fine, he said but still he was preoccupied with those airplane thoughts that had come unbidden, unsettling him during an otherwise peaceful flight. So wrapped up was he in the thought of it, it's a wonder he didn't miss it when the boy kept talking, when he asked what would turn out to be one of the more important questions of Bill's life.

"Hey Father Bill," he said. "Have you seen this nun who plays cards with the winos?"

My father became a priest, he once told me, because he wanted to help people and he knew only two ways to do so: become a priest, or a nurse like his mother. But men didn't become nurses then, so between these two options there wasn't much of a choice. Yet something of the nurse remained with him in seminary, even after ordination: a clinical approach to the soul. It was not a distance he strived for, or made a point to maintain, it was simply who and what he was: a man more comfortable with a handshake than a hug, and more comfortable still with a priestly blessing, his hand held a foot or more away from the face of any member of his flock. He lived to reach out to people, but he would not, could not, reach so far as to risk muddling holy intention with human contact. In Roxbury, though, he had come to wonder: Was he really trying to love everyone if he was not truly with them? Was he ever actually reaching them if he remained so removed? How could you really love bums and junkies and winos if you didn't sit down with them on their terms? Now perhaps he'd find an answer.

The day before, the volunteer explained, a few Sisters of St. Joseph had stopped by the storefront to have a look at the new ministry in town. Though they were disappointed not to meet the charismatic young priest they'd heard would be there, soon one of the nuns could be heard laughing, the bums joining in. The game was gin rummy. Hand after hand, she kept winning. Yet even while they grieved their losses, the storefront regulars loved playing cards with this young nun. They loved that she stayed with them, shouting and laughing like it was the most natural thing in the world.

This was a story, Father Bill thought, of someone living among the people no one cared about—of truly loving them in the way he hoped he could. This was someone from whom he might learn a thing or two about living, and maybe something about loving as well.

Bill kicked open the last folding chair and set it on the floor. Later he would question God in his notebook—*Father, do you lead a man in stages? Do you sometimes lead him into an entirely new life?*—just now, though, he had more earthly concerns.

"Who is she?" he asked.

HEART-SHAPED
STONE

Christianity is a faith of inversions. The undying dies so the dying can live. A virgin bears an infant who will carry the weight of the world. The worst sinners become the greatest saints. All this is so, the thinking goes, because the Kingdom of Heaven is so far removed from the life we know that every established order must be overturned before it can be attained.

So when Father Bill started asking around about the card-playing nun, he was really only doing his part. *Ad majorem Dei gloriam,* he might've said in his seminary days, for the greater glory of God.

Even before he met her, he had begun thinking about marriage. The idea of it, anyway: the theoretical joining of hypothetical souls. He'd been wondering how such a joining would be affected if one of those souls happened to belong to a priest, and he'd been considering what the implications of the act would be, not just for the man and the woman involved but also, more importantly, for the church.

"I had come to a junction in my life," he'd tell a newspaper reporter later, "when I really felt that in order to be faithful to the Gospel, I should enter into the deepest relationship possible for a Christian, marriage."

Marriage for Dad began as an intellectual exercise, an experiment in engagement with the world. "I was convinced that if the Christian Church were to have an effective impact in a society rampant with racism, militarism, nationalism, materialism, and alienation, the people of the church must learn their treasure, their identity as free sons and daughters of God, from one of their own kind, not from a member of an elite, separate caste of priests living an encapsulated kind of existence." A hopeless romantic Dad was not.

He had been thinking about marriage, in other words, for the same reason he became a priest, for the same reason he asked to be sent to Roxbury: because he wanted to save the world. Armed with his faith of inversions, he thought the only way to do so was to turn it inside out, layer by layer, beginning with his church.

Yet with that question, *who is she,* even his intentions were inverted. Soon after he'd asked it, marriage stopped being a curious unlikelihood and became a life-changing possibility.

16 July 1968

O Father, deep within my being I feel a call to follow you in a new way—trusting beyond knowledge that it is right—it is so insistent—Lord Jesus, accomplish your will in me. Whatever it may be. I am bewildered as to which course to follow.

The course became a bit more clear one Wednesday evening at the Catholic Messengers' regular meeting. After welcoming the dozen or so Roxbury locals, a handful of visitors from the suburbs, and the small group of priests and nuns from nearby parishes, Father Bill led a Bible study and gave a short sermon. He had been struck in those days by the notion of people of faith as pilgrims—not in the *Canterbury Tales* sense of a parade of characters making its way to a holy place, but in the sense of the founding American myth. As he saw it, people of faith were those who set out to live in an unknown land; they were those called to board ships and cross the ocean, whatever the dangers might be.

He might've turned to the story of Jonah for an illustration of the kind of faith he was talking about, but a better choice was a story of Paul. In the Acts of the Apostles, the tale is told of how St. Paul, arrested for teaching about Jesus, is transported by ship from Caesarea to Rome. When a storm rushes in and waters rise around the vessel, the prisoner Paul announces that he has heard from an angel what must be done. As the ship begins to sink, the sailors throw all of its cargo overboard. Then they throw its tackle, and then its supply of food. Only when they have discarded all that has been weighing them down is the ship free to follow the wind where it would lead, letting them find the ground God intended for them. Only by throwing over all that once seemed necessary were they able to survive.

Bill noticed four or five Sisters of St. Joseph sitting in the crowd as he preached, each in their order's recently redesigned uniform. Compared to the yards of drapery they had previously worn, the nuns' shin-length skirts could not have seemed more revealing; when they sat in their metal folding chairs, it was difficult not to steal a glance at their ankles, their calves, their knees. Nuns' knees! The novelty alone was enough to draw the eye.

Even more distracting was the fact that their head coverings had also changed. Before this sartorial reformation, the veils themselves had drawn all the attention. With white starched wimples surrounded by deep black wings, the faces buried within might as well have belonged to mannequins. The anonymity of the uniform was the point, after all. Now, though, the lighter, shorter veils seemed like curtains opened to reveal the features they framed. As Bill preached, their young cheeks and bright eyes were a jarring surprise. They were not just nuns, he realized, but women.

And one of these women, Bill noted, he had not seen there before. She was quite pretty, he thought, and seemed to listen attentively to what he had to say.

It was too soon to tell more than that about her, though. Fresh faces were always turning up at the Messenger Center on Wednesday nights. Precious few would prove themselves serious enough to become regular volunteers. Most were just curious; they'd politely introduce themselves at the end of the meeting, wish him well, and never return. He couldn't immediately discern who had come to join the cause, and who was there merely for the spectacle of a priest preaching like a Protestant, so while he spoke he tried not to give the new nun too much thought. He had to wrap up his sermon, after all. He hadn't yet reached the end of the story of Paul's transport to Rome: the shipwreck that showed the apostle's captors they were dealing with a man of God.

Once Bill had finished, he joined his small congregation to mill about and talk over coffee. One of the men from Shawmut Avenue cracked a joke and a raucous laugh rang out above the chuckling of the others. It came from the nun whom he had not seen there before, and it was a laugh so big and full of joy Bill thought he had never heard anything like it. He knew then that she was the one he had heard about, and he walked toward her as if blown by a strong wind.

From then on Bill tried to turn up wherever she might be. He passed by St. Francis de Sales when he could, craning his neck around every corner in hopes of catching a glimpse of the nun he'd learned was called Thomas Patrick. If they were going to meet accidentally, he wanted to be prepared.

On Fridays he made sure to drop by for the evening liturgy at War- wick House. According to the Sisters who frequented the Catholic Messenger Center, that was the place to be. Some of the senior nuns of the congregation didn't care for all the experimental devotions that went on there—they didn't have much patience for worship tinged with guitars and tambourines, and had even less for services that found priests and nuns, whites and blacks, everyone holding hands and sway- ing as they made the Our Father into a song—but there was no keeping the younger Sisters away. Now there was no keeping Bill away either.

It was just around this time Bill's youngest brother had gone off to college and given Bill his old car, a fire-engine-red Volkswagen Bug. Bill used it mostly for the work of the Catholic Messengers and the halfway house—making trips to the hardware store, transporting the most serious dependency cases to Bridgewater State Hospital—but he saw no reason not to put it to more personal use now and then.

One afternoon he got behind the wheel and just drove around the neighborhood, down from Fort Hill, into Lower Roxbury, scanning the sidewalks as he rolled by. Sister Thomas Patrick had mentioned she liked to take a daily walk away from the convent. Permission to move freely about town had never been granted to her at her previous assignments and she wanted to take advantage of it while she could. There was no telling when Mother Catalina might send word that she was to be transferred back to the outskirts of the city, where the relatively peaceful atmosphere left the senior Sisters with time on their hands to keep a tighter rein.

Bill drove up Shawmut to Ruggles Street, near the area which only now, a year later, was beginning to heal from the three days of burning and violence that the riots brought, and then he saw her. Walking alone quite happily, she seemed to be recognized here and there by her former students and their families, greeted the way all nuns were, with a combination of respect and concern, as if she seemed both familiar and fragile to every soul who caught her eye.

Bill pulled up alongside her. "Excuse me, Sister. Would you like a lift back to St. Francis?"

"That would be fine," she answered.

In the car she told him she'd grown up not too far from there, just down Mass. Ave. into Dorchester, so she was glad to be back in the city after her assignments in the suburbs. She admitted that, no offense to the other parishes, St. Francis de Sales was by far her favorite. Why was that? Bill asked. It was a different sort of place, she explained. Being in Roxbury almost felt like being free.

"Well, Sister Thomas Patrick," Bill said, "I think I know what you mean."

"I'm glad," she told him. "And please call me Mary."

In the summer of that year, Father Bill officiated at the wedding of one of his brothers. He had seen several of his four siblings married by then; he watched them begin families of their own while he remained, to his mother's pride and his increasing consternation, celibate and alone.

As the priest in the family, he was never without a role to play—he had even introduced his sister Barbara to her husband through Young

Christian Students, a Catholic action group at Lowell State Teachers College. Celebrant of weddings and baptisms, he was always taking part in the creation and sanctification of new life—but always from a distance, a distance that more and more felt to him like nothing so much as death. While his brothers, his sister, and the friends he had before seminary got on with their lives, became new fathers, new mothers—entirely new and renewed people—it seemed to him his current course would only lead to stagnation. Another wedding, another funeral, what did it matter. He would always be only the man in the collar, the man in black. "Can I ever truly live?" he wrote in his journal. "Must I always be dying?"

This time, however, when he drove back from performing his expected family role, he would have company. As it happened, his brother Skip's wedding was to be held not far from Regis College, where, Bill knew, Sister Thomas Patrick was taking classes during her summer off from teaching third grade at St. Francis de Sales. Usually it took a combination of trains and buses to get back to Roxbury from Regis, so when the handsome young priest offered to pick her up on his way home from the wedding, she gladly accepted.

He had already learned a few things about her. From the other Sisters who visited the Catholic Messenger Center, he'd heard that, like so many of the nuns in the city, she was an Irish girl, and a Red Sox fan, usually the one shouting loudest from the bleachers on Nuns' Day at Fenway Park. And he had heard she was a card player, of course. On the ride home from Regis to Roxbury that day, Father Bill hoped to learn more.

"Feel like taking a walk?" he asked, as if they were just a man and a woman out for a drive in the country. He'd taken off his collar after the wedding but was still dressed head to toe in priestly black. She was just as conspicuous—a habit is still a habit, even when it's hemmed at the knee.

They stopped at a wooded path around a pond, and walked just long enough to stretch their legs, talking little, keeping a comfortable distance. Father Bill, ever the Boy Scout, kept one eye constantly on the ground, the way he'd learned to watch for arrowheads when he was young. At one point he stooped, picked a stone from the trail, and dropped it in his pocket without a word of explanation. Not that Mary needed one—he learned later that she used to do the same with bottle caps on Roseclair Street. She'd tack them to her shoes and dance a clacking jig.

Back in the car, moving east toward Boston, she gave him some news.

"I've been thinking about leaving," she said.

Leaving. Period. No need to explain what the word meant. So many had been abandoning the convent lately that in their circle "leaving" could mean only one thing. Those who stayed in the convent were said to be Still In. Those who left, no matter what they went on to do with their lives, were simply Out.

"Leaving?" Bill asked. "Why's that?"

Silence, and then a long exhale from the passenger seat.

"We've had some trouble with the motherhouse about ministry in the city," she said. "The superior doesn't want us active outside of the schools—at your storefront, or at Warwick House. But that's where people need help most, isn't it?"

"It is," Bill said.

"So I'm afraid I'll be transferred from Roxbury this summer, and I can't go back to the way it was at the other convents."

"What will you do?"

"I've been thinking I might want to work. And maybe to get married. Someday."

Look ahead, Bill. Keep driving. He focused on the sounds of the road rolling beneath them. The sounds of moving forward, and of leaving behind.

Bill rolled down the driver's side window; Mary's veil flapped against her cheek. As much as he wanted to, he did not give voice to his intention, his hope: to marry and yet not to resign his ordination; to find a way to be a married priest, though such a thing hadn't existed in the church for nearly a thousand years.

He was not alone. For several years now there had been news and rumors of priests who had found ways to be married. There was the well-known Jesuit Bernard Cooke, who filled lecture halls in the mid-'60s with his talks on the changing church, something of an American Hans Küng. In his book *The Challenge of Vatican II* he had found seeds of a married priesthood planted in no less a garden than the Council: "The notion of a priesthood common to all baptized Christians is prominent in the documents of Vatican II," he wrote. If such could be said of the privileged sacrament of holy orders, it was not such a large leap to suppose that the sacrament of marriage could be common to all as well, including priests. Cooke leapt there and beyond: "To the extent that people are not genuinely free, you do not have Christianity," he wrote, and later he exercised that freedom by leaving the priesthood and marrying. Across the ocean there was another prominent writer and priest, the English theologian Charles Davis, who decided it was time he "accepted the risk of a wider and receding horizon." He did so also by marrying, and by leaving the Roman Catholic Church entirely.

Bill, however, was not willing to leave the priesthood or the church. They were both too much a part of him—more than a part, in fact: "priest" and "Catholic" were not two twigs of the bundle of sticks that was his identity; "Catholic" was the tree he was cut from, "priest" was the string that tied it all together. How could he cut that string? How could he stop being what he was to the roots? Why should he? John XXIII had said himself that it was not impossible: "Ecclesiastical celibacy is not a dogma," he admitted. "I need only take a pen and sign an act, and tomorrow the priests who want to do so will be able to marry." Even Cardinal Cushing said it: "One day the Catholic Church will admit married men to the priesthood." That this was the trajectory of the Council's reforms seemed obvious and exciting. It was only a matter of time, Bill believed, before the Vatican did something further with the changes it had begun.

As it happened, he was right, but the further action the Vatican eventually took was not what he'd expected. Pope Paul VI had replaced John XXIII in 1963, and though he convened the final sessions of Vatican II, later he backed down on many of the changes his predecessor had set in motion. In the encyclical *Humanae Vitae* he would reaffirm the church's stance on birth control. In *Sacerdotalis Caelibatus* he would do the same concerning mandatory celibacy. But there was no way of knowing that then. Riding in the car that day from Regis to Roxbury, Father Bill saw no reason not to be hopeful.

Which perhaps is why, before returning Sister Thomas Patrick to the convent that day, Father Bill dug into the pocket of his black slacks and produced a small stone. Muddy and gray, with rounded angles and a cleft down its middle, when held just so and tilted back, its form was unmistakable. A heart-shaped stone, lifted from the dirt not long before, and now lifted again. Earlier that day, with the same hand he had held a Communion wafer before his brother and the newest member of his family. Held it as an invitation, a coming together. Now, he made another offering. The body remembers and mimics itself; his hand just so, he held the stone lightly between two conse--crated fingers. At the sight of it, Sister Thomas Patrick instinctively lifted and cupped her hands. And why not? This too was a Communion, a coming together, a transformation. A stone becomes a heart, as bread becomes body, if it is given in love. When she received it in her palm she did not yet realize she would keep this stone the rest of her life, that she would put it in her jewelry box and one day her son, their son, would ask to hear its story. And though she too saw that this moment was a kind of sacrament, when she closed her fingers around the stone and accepted it as a gift, she did not say *Amen*. Instead, she said simply, "Thank you."

My mother left the Sisters of St. Joseph three months later, and by then it seemed she was part of a parade. Many of her Sisters had "friends" by then, priests with whom they would take day trips, priests who would drive them home to visit with their families. They all believed the church was changing—weren't they proof of that themselves? They were the church, after all, and the fact that they had been altered by the times was as obvious as their naked knees.

Sister Thomas Patrick knew what she wanted to do but kept putting it off. She had been a nun for ten years—did she know how not to be one? It was a risk to be sure, but she had learned by then that even though a risk meant danger, it also meant freedom. She sat down at a table and composed a letter, surprising herself at the leap she had made from uncertainty to total resolve:

Dear Mother Catalina,

    Greetings of peace and love! Hope you are well and able to get some rest and enjoyment out of this beautiful summer.

    I'm here at Regis now and quite caught up in studying for final exams. I was going to wait until retreat to write to you because I'd have some extra time. And, to be more honest, the new assignments might have been out by then and I wanted to know if I was getting changed from Roxbury. This really isn't important now, and I felt I was being selfish, knowing that every day is important to you.

    A letter, another letter, like mine will bring more pain and for this I am sorry. After much prayer, thought, and talking it over, I have decided to leave the community and return home. I regret that a choice could not have been made earlier to convenience you but this was something that could not be rushed . . .

As soon as her wishes were known, she made plans to move out of the St. Francis de Sales convent, back home to Dorchester. With most of her siblings married and on their own, there was room enough for her in the Doherty house, where only her brother Frank and her sister Rita still lived. Before she returned to the world, though, she had some shopping to do. With Rita at her side, she wore her habit for the last time in public, browsing in the uniform she'd worn since she was a teenager to find a dress to wear when she walked out the convent door.

Bill hadn't left All Saints yet, but that didn't stop him from coming around. The first time he visited, Mary's mother Margaret had no idea he'd come as a suitor. Maybe she just chose not to see it; she was so pleased and proud to have a priest drop by the house. He was about the same age as her oldest son, but she wouldn't hear of calling him anything other than *Father.*

As for Bill's parents, Leo and Jeannette Manseau knew something was happening to their son before he said a word. He had been losing weight, was visibly anxious much of the time. One of the housekeepers at the rectory had noticed it too. "Father Manseau," she said, "if I didn't know better, I would guess you were in love."

When finally Bill confessed to his family that this was the case—and that he hoped to marry a woman named Mary Doherty, if she would have him—Jeannette wrote a letter to her oldest son. "The Devil sits perched atop rectories," she warned, "waiting for clergy to lure away with just this kind of temptation." One of her other sons had already given her grandchildren; what was there to be gained if her firstborn stopped being a priest?

Bill tried to explain that he had no intention of leaving the priesthood, but that only increased the grief Jeannette felt. To give a son to the church was a great honor; for that same son to fall away was an even greater shame. As painful as his mother's letter was, Bill tucked it away in his bureau drawer for safekeeping; he knew her disapproval was an awkward kind of devotion, a wish for him to have the perfect life for which he'd been chosen.

But then that was all that he wanted too, and he was sure he would not find it if he stayed another day in the rectory on Fort Hill. It had come to seem to him as strange and unhealthy a place as the hippie commune down the block. He requested and was granted a leave of absence from Cardinal Cushing, and then, with Mary's help, he found a small apartment. Whether or not it was intentional on some level he later would not be able to say, but when the last box was packed and moved from his rectory bedroom, he had forgotten to include his eucharistic chalice, the one left to him by his mentor fifteen years before. It had been to him a symbol of the kind of priesthood to which he had once aspired; was it possible he had simply overlooked it? Or was this too something to be thrown overboard if he was to get where God wanted him to go?

Once Bill was out of the rectory, things began to happen quickly. During the week he kept himself busy with a new job as a counselor for a drug rehabilitation clinic, and on the weekends he would pick up Mary in Dorchester and the two would go out together as if they had

no reason not to. On Friday nights they went downtown for dinner
and movies—*The Odd Couple* was the first, as far as they recall. On Saturday afternoons they went walking on Castle Island, a strip of beach
surrounding a 19th-century fort that once kept the city safe from
ocean attack. With tall granite walls and green grass growing on top,
it was a like a medieval ruin transported to the New England shore,
the castle that gave the island its name.

It was on one such walk when Bill asked Mary to be his wife. He
explained all his hopes and plans for the married priesthood, made the
case that their marriage would help bring change to the church, proclaimed how exciting it was and how happy they would be.

She politely declined. She was only just out of the convent, she explained. She was working and making her own money and finishing
her teaching degree. Finally she had the kind of freedom she had
dreamed of for a decade in the habit. Why on earth would she turn
around and get married now?

Bill let the matter drop, admitting that maybe he was getting ahead
of himself. They kept walking that day, and came back every week for
a stroll on the beach. On one fall day, Mary tried to tell Bill something
she hadn't mentioned to anyone since she had confessed it as sin when
she was seventeen years old.

"A priest tried to kiss me once," she said.

Bill just listened; she didn't have to say it was a memory that pained
her. The effect of it, if not the details, was there in her face. He took
her hand and they walked in silence around the Castle Island fort, its
great granite walls blocking the ocean breeze. The stopped and read a
plaque explaining the fort's design: with the grass on top it was all but
invisible from a distance. Only by walking around it could you see
what was hidden below.

Through the winter they continued to spend days and evenings together as often as their new lives would allow. On New Year's Eve 1968
they celebrated at a party at the Ritz, and it seemed about as far removed from the storefront in which they'd met as the moon. On
Valentine's Day 1969, Bill gave Mary a watch and her brothers were

beside themselves. It wasn't the fact that a priest was making advances toward their sister that bothered them; they just knew they'd never hear an end of it from their wives.

On Sundays they went to Mass at the Paulist Center downtown, focal point of Catholic peace activities in Boston. Later in the week, they'd make the trip to an ecumenical gathering place called the Packard Manse, where all manner of radical Christians and church reformers appeared and spoke. One night a dance was held after a lecture by the poet-priest Daniel Berrigan, vocal opponent of the war in Vietnam. A few years later he would go into hiding, wanted for draft-card burning by the FBI. When Mary saw Father Berrigan on the dance floor, his graying hair and gaunt cheeks purple in the psychedelic lights, she walked right up to him and told him how much she admired him.

"And would you mind giving me an autograph?" she asked.

"Not at all," he said.

It had been fifteen years or more since young Mary Doherty had haunted the back gate at Fenway waiting for Ted Williams and his teammates to appear. By the time she'd left for the novitiate, she had amassed an entire book full of the scribbled reminders of such encounters. Now, in the replaying of that act, the same innocent question, the same cordial reply, she knew how much she had changed. Mary still knew a hero when she saw one, but now her heroes were not mere ballplayers. They were priests and rabble-rousers who risked all to do what they thought was right.

She thought of the question Bill had asked her on the beach, of all that he hoped to accomplish, and more importantly, of how he had listened when she tried to explain a hurt so old it seemed it would never go away.

If he asked again, Mary decided, she would say yes.

She had a feeling she would not have to wait too long. He had shown himself to be a persistent man.

(Herald Traveler Staff Photo by George Dixon)
FR. MANSEAU AND BRIDE

JUNE 14, 1969

The following summer they were married, in a ceremony performed by three priests, but without a church. Though Father Spag had suggested St. Francis de Sales would be available for the occasion, and another friend had offered St. Leo's on Esmond Street, they didn't want anyone to suffer for their actions. Both bride and groom considered their wedding as Catholic as they come, but they knew Cardinal Cushing would see it differently. Any priest who let such a notorious couple marry on archdiocese property or with its official sanction would have had hell to pay. "Oh, I'd have been deep-sixed for sure," Spag said. "But what are friends for?"

They opted instead for a ceremony in Margaret Doherty's house in Dorchester, in the shadow of St. Margaret's but well beyond its red-brick walls. When Bill arrived at the wedding site, he found a crowd of reporters and photographers waiting for him.

"You the priest?" they asked him. "The one getting married?"

"I am," he said. "And what are you all doing here?"

One of the reporters explained that a source in the city records office, where Bill and Mary had registered for their marriage license, had passed along a tip that one of Boston's so-called street priests was about to marry a former nun. They were there, the reporter informed him, for the story.

Bill pushed his way through to the stairs. "We'd be happy to talk with you after the ceremony," he said, "if you would all be kind enough to wait outside."

"When and where, Father?" one of them shouted.

"About two hours," he called down to them as he closed the door behind him. "At the entrance to Florian Hall. Just before the reception."

Inside his future mother-in-law's home, Bill saw that the place was already packed to the walls. Forty folding chairs crowded the homemade altar at the front of the tiny living room. The friends and family who had arrived early smiled and waved in his direction. A portrait of Jesus, pointing to his exposed heart, looked down from the floral wallpaper in a gold-painted frame. Mary's brothers stood glaring out the window at the newsmen loitering on the sidewalk; they'd seen one of them shout something as Bill came in but hadn't heard if it was a remark that deserved a stronger reply.

"Just say the word and I'll go out and pop him one," Mary's brother Danny said, and the other Doherty men nodded in eager agreement. They hadn't expected their older sister's wedding to be such a spectacle, but they knew what to do if things got out of hand.

"Where's Mary?" Bill asked.

"Upstairs," her brothers said.

When Spag and the other priests arrived, they rushed through the gauntlet of reporters, declining to comment or to be named. Not that they were ashamed to attend or to celebrate such an occasion. Had any of them stopped to answer questions they might have admitted what they believed in their hearts, that this wasn't just a wedding, it was the start of something. It was a sign of the times, as Scripture put it; a sign not only of how things were then, at the end of a tumultuous decade, but a sign of what their faith could become.

Instead they said nothing. Public participation in this event was an offense inviting excommunication; it was a crime against Roman Catholic law. For the bride and groom there was no choice. And unlike the friends who had insisted on performing the liturgy for them, if they were barred from practicing their religion, they at least would have the solace of each other, and of the family they would make.

Upstairs, Mary's sister Rita helped her smooth the crocheted shoulders of her silk wedding dress. That it was borrowed mattered little; to wear such a simple white gown after so long confined to layers of coarse, dark fabric felt as extravagant as if she had wrapped herself in pearls. When the wedding photographer arrived, the two Doherty girls showed off their Irish smiles and then posed as Mary slid a garter up her thigh. Only after Rita had led the photographer from the room, to give the bride a moment's peace, did Mary notice the thick leather prayer book resting on the dresser. With the exception of the last few months, she had used it every day for the previous ten years, all through her time in the convent. Its binding had been bent so often it was now worn to the gray-blue of a coming storm. Flipping it open, Mary saw its pages too had aged; there was a jaundiced yellow beneath the words of prayers she had long since memorized. Only the book's cover held its original shade. It was the lone square of nunnish black in this room filled with clothing and flowers the colors of porcelain, milk, and bone. Could that really be all that was left of what she had been?

Rita called from outside the door, "It's time!"

From the rooms below, Mary heard music and voices—*People of God sing out with joy, Jesus invites us all*—and when she opened the bedroom door she saw that the procession of celebrants had begun. With no wedding aisle to speak of in her mother's small home, they had decided to parade down the stairs. Three Catholic priests in full draping vestments moved through the narrow hallway like curtain dealers displaying their wares. Their old friend Father Spag led the way, singing with gusto and eyes glued to his hymnal.

Then it was her turn. She moved slowly down the stairwell and into the foyer. Through the front door's window, she could see reporters and photographers still lurking on the sidewalk.

Never mind. It wasn't the time to worry about what strangers would make of her life. Turning the corner, she came upon friendlier faces. On one side of the room sat her brothers, her mother, her aunts, and cousins. On the other, her new family, who had been heartbroken by the thought that they had lost their priest to her, but who now only seemed to watch her with joy in their eyes. Scattered throughout both sides, she saw faces from Roxbury, Milton, Wellesley, Framingham,

Dorchester, Somerville, and Medford, from all the places she or Bill
had worked in their decade of service to the church. She saw her sister
nuns in their recently shortened veils. A few of them sat beside Bill's
fellow priests. Maybe their weddings would be next.

Finally, she saw him. Glasses shining with the pop of flashbulbs, his
thin lips opened in a broad grin at the sight of her. She walked down
the aisle and stood at his side.

Standing at the front of the room before the homemade altar, beneath the Sacred Heart of Jesus, they heard their friend Spag ask a
question they never thought would be theirs to answer.

"I do," they both said, and they were joined in a sacrament they
knew their church would call a sin.

As the liturgy ended, they sang a closing hymn with their families
and friends:

> *His word is searing deep in my soul.*
> *It lights. It fires. It pains.*
> *He calls for all that's closed up within.*
> *And in our love we shout out to all,*
> *"Our God is Love. Our God is Love . . ."*

And they then went out together to face the world.

At the spontaneous press conference that followed the ceremony,
Mary greeted the reporters, smiling for the cameras and gripping her
husband's arm. He did most of the talking.

"Through careful consideration for over a year, and after much
prayer and talks with theologians, I made my decision," he said. "One
has to marry a person, not an idea . . . We believe in the goals of the
church and love the church very deeply," he continued. "We have
committed our lives to the church, and believe we are doing this for
the good of the church."

As if in search for some sign of disapproval, the press sought out the
mothers of the bride and groom. Good Catholic ladies that they were,
surely they would be devastated by the scandal of it all. Margaret Do-

herty, however, took it in stride. In a crowded room containing her seven grown children she said, "I feel like any mother would, like I felt at all the other weddings." For her part, Jeannette Manseau put on a brave face. Had they asked six months before, when Bill first told her the news, she might have given a very different answer. Today, however, she simply smiled and said, "It was the most beautiful and impressive ceremony I've ever seen."

Mary, meanwhile, handled the press the same way she had handled the card-playing winos. She spoke plainly, made them laugh, and won them over.

"Our plans," she told reporters, "are simply to live happily ever after."

Part Four

PROCREATION

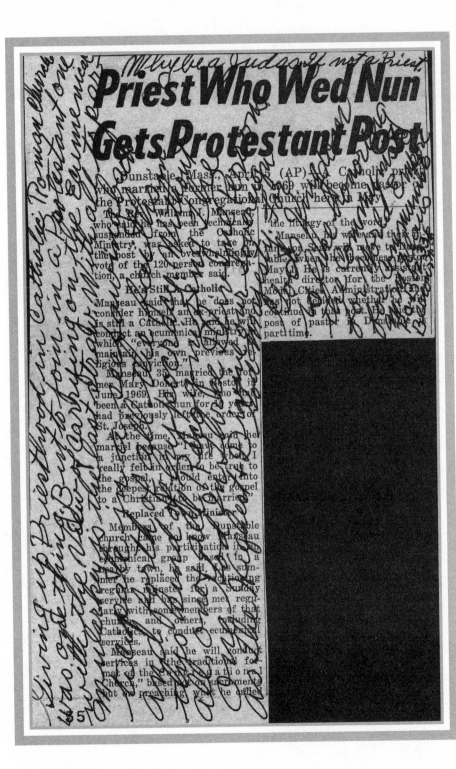

Priest Who Wed Nun Gets Protestant Post

Dunstable, Mass., April 5 (AP) — A Catholic priest who married a former nun in 1969 will become pastor of the Protestant Congregational Church here in May.

The Rev. William J. Manseau, who said he has been technically suspended from the Catholic Ministry, was asked to take on the post by an overwhelming vote of the 120-person congregation, a church member said.

He's Still a Catholic

Manseau said that he "does not consider himself an ex-priest" and is still a Catholic. He said he will conduct an ecumenical ministry in which "everyone is allowed to maintain his own previous religious conviction."

Manseau, 35, married the former Mary Doherty in Boston in June, 1969. His wife, who had been a Catholic nun for 10 years, had previously left the order of St. Joseph.

At the time, Manseau said he married because "I have come to a junction in my life where I really felt in order to be true to the gospel, I should enter into the deepest relation of the gospel to a Christian, to be married."

Replaced Former Minister

Members of the Dunstable church came to know Manseau through his participation in an ecumenical group based in a nearby town, he said. Last summer he replaced the vacationing regular minister for a Sunday service and has since met regularly with some members of that church, and others, including Catholics, to conduct ecumenical services.

Manseau said he will conduct services in the "traditional format of the Congregational Church," based not on sacraments but on preaching, what he called

the liturgy of the word.

Manseau, his wife and their three children, Shaw, will move to Dunstable when he becomes pastor May 1. He is currently assistant health director for the Boston Model Cities Administration and has not decided whether he will continue in that post. He will do the post of pastor in Dunstable part time.

5

PREACHING, WAITING

My father stood before a crowd of men like him, fifty married priests, and read aloud a letter to his bishop. "My dear brother, Bishop Richard," he said. "Easter season greetings to you . . ."

Thank you for the visit we had on April 11, 2003 at your residence to discuss the petition which I had made originally to His Holiness, Pope John Paul II, to grant me a dispensation from the obligations connected to the priesthood in the Latin Rite of the Roman Catholic Church and the response which you have received from Cardinal Francis Arinze, Prefect of the Congregation for Divine Worship and the Discipline of the Sacraments. I was glad that you and my son, Peter, had an opportunity to meet. I regret that you felt that it was not appropriate for him to be present during our visit as it would have been instructive for him . . .

The married priest group—CORPUS, the Corps of Reserve Priests United for Service—is part social network, part professional association, part support group. They had gathered, as they do at least once every year, to discuss their various initiatives: optional celibacy, the ordination of women, pensions for former priests. This time they met in Dallas, where just a few months before the U.S. Conference of Catholic Bishops had convened to formulate the church's official response to the crisis caused by the sexual sickness of some its clergy.

That the fifty men meeting here now—most of them fathers and husbands for thirty years or more, all of them ordained—might present
one part of a remedy never occurred to the bishops; to them, priests
who want to marry are part of the same problem as priests who mo-
lest children.

That is not as much of an exaggeration as it might seem. Before
leaving Massachusetts for Dallas, Dad heard what his Jesuit canon
lawyer had learned when he started asking around about the issues
we had discussed with him at Boston College. Father McIntyre told
him there were two cases like his currently making their way from the
Archbishop's Residence in Brighton to the Vatican; two priests of the
Archdiocese of Boston who had been informed they would be
brought before a church tribunal if they did not resign their ordinations. According to Father McIntyre, one of these priests was Paul
Shanley, accused of, among other things, raping a Catholic-school boy
in a confessional; the other was my father, guilty of marriage in the
first degree.

The fact that canon law regarded a priest who married and a child
rapist as having committed the same offense—"carnal sacrilege," a
defamation of the sanctity of the priesthood, a sin against the church
itself—had only strengthened my father's resolve to defy the Vatican's
demands. It had also made him eager to share his predicament with
his fellow canonical outlaws, this gathering of married priests. And so
he continued to read:

> *The requirements of Cardinal Arinze, which you communicated to me,*
> *that I cease all ministry and dissociate from all affiliations that support*
> *my ministry are requirements that I cannot accept in good conscience . . .*

The crowd nodded its approval. Many of these men had been
through similar conflicts with the Catholic hierarchy. Inspired by Vatican II's call for unity, as my father had been, they had all sought ways
both to be married and to be priests. Some of them had done so quietly, taking leaves of absence from their parishes or religious orders,
marrying in secret, and keeping their heads down ever since. Others

had gone through the process of laicization, which in essence required them to declare they had been mistaken about their vocations all along; required them, in other words, to say that whatever good they had done during their time as priests, however fully they embodied the priestly ideal, they had never truly been up to the challenge. As it does in the annulment of a marriage, canon law views celibate priestly service through the lens of its end. If an ordained man does not die with his collar on, if God forbid he dies instead wearing a wedding band, the church regards him as if he had never been a priest at all.

The men in this room knew better, though. They were the American wing of what had become an international movement, with organizations in twenty-seven countries. Over one hundred thousand priests have left the church in the last forty years; many of them now are members of such groups as Leaven in Ireland, Vocatio in Italy, and Rumos in Brazil, groups of men who could not so easily forget what they had been told at their ordinations: *Tu es sacerdos in aeternum.* You are a priest forever.

> *As my letter of October 18, 2001, made abundantly clear to His Holiness, I have continued to exercise the ministry which was entrusted to me on the day of my ordination, February 2, 1961. The modalities of that ministry changed on June 14, 1969, when Mary Doherty and I celebrated the sacrament of marriage . . .*
>
> *Mary and I took this step in conscience based upon our belief in our inalienable right to marry and found a family, which had been most recently reiterated by now Blessed John XXIII in his Encyclical Letter,* Pacem in Terris. *Because this right is "universal, inviolable and inalienable" it cannot be surrendered nor taken away. It may be refrained from use for a while or even forever, but it may not ever be surrendered. It perdures. It is a divine law.*

At this point in the letter, in case the bishop had need of a reminder, my father quoted Scripture, with chapter and verse. Genesis 1:27–28: "So God created man in his own image, in the image of God created he him; male and female created he them. And God blessed them and

God said unto them, Be fruitful, and multiply, and replenish the earth." Genesis 2:18: "And the Lord God said, It is not good that man should be alone . . ." Genesis 2:24: "Therefore shall a man leave his father and his mother, and shall cleave to his wife: and they shall be of one flesh."

"Amen," a voice among the married priests said.

Dad read on:

I have taken very seriously my calling as a Catholic priest in a church which is in the process of reform and renewal in head and members. It has not been an easy task. I have obtained two doctorates in ministry to increase my skills as a Catholic minister of the Gospel and have devoted my life to the cause of the Christian ministry and the reform of our apostolic Church.

To accept the requirement from Cardinal Arinze and yourself that I leave this vocation I have received from God is unthinkable. To agree would be to abandon the gifts I have been given and to turn my back on the People of God. As Peter and the apostles answered the high priest and all the senate of Israel, "We must obey God . . ."

Another line from Scripture, but only half quoted. The remainder of the quote, left to the eloquence of the ellipsis, was in fact the point of the whole letter. "We must obey God," Acts 5:29 says, "rather than men." Rather than you, dear brother bishop. Rather than you, Cardinal Arinze. We must obey God, Dad let those three dots say, rather than His Holiness Himself.

"This is a dynamic moment in history," my father had written and now said in closing. "I pray regularly for your ministry."

When he reached the end of his letter, he scanned the text again. As a page of words resting flat and static on the kitchen table at home, his statement had seemed so humble, appropriate for a priest addressing his bishop. Now, speaking it aloud, all but nailing it to the wall, the audacity of it hung in the air. Had he really preached divine law to the apostolic administrator of the Archdiocese of Boston? He had. Had he actually quoted a papal encyclical as defense against the wishes of a cardinal? He had. Did he truly believe his renegade ministry was as valid as any in the Catholic Church? Yes, he did, and so did the men around him. These married priests were precisely the group Bishop Lennon, Cardinal Arinze, and the rest of the ecclesial hierarchy demanded he disassociate from. One by one they were bad seeds, individuals who couldn't get with the program. Together, though, they were a thorn in the Vatican's side, an image of what my father prayed the church would one day be.

When Dad looked up from the podium he saw fifty married priests on their feet, joining his prayer with applause.

I was not there that day in Dallas, but I know the people who were. Many of those priests and priests' wives (not a few ex-nuns among them) were the same men and women who came to our house for the dining room liturgies that are my earliest memory.

Through all the years of my childhood, families like ours were always around: mothers who had left the convent without looking back, fathers restless for the sacred in their newly ordinary lives. Like my parents, they were part of the mass exodus that emptied rectories, seminaries, convents, and religious orders in the late '60s and early '70s; men and women who broke the rules that had made them because they knew even then that if their church did not change its attitudes toward sex, toward family, toward God, it would tear itself apart.

They were, in other words, a movement. The particulars of my parents' story are all their own, but the broad strokes—the faith of inversions; the priest and the nun who loved their church so much they had to make it change—are more common than you might think. Just consider the ubiquity of Catholic clergy in the culture a generation or two ago—they were everywhere, cultural icons as well as men and women on the street. Compare that to the mild shock one feels today simply seeing a nun in the airport. Where did all the Father Mulcaheys and Sister Mary Catherines go? The old ones died; the young ones left—many of them to be with each other.

Eventually such unions became a nonstory. My parents, though, were among the first, and so in their marriage's earliest days, the summer of 1969, the story of the "priest-nun wedding" was everywhere. For the relatives of the bride and groom, the dream of having clergy in the family suddenly turned into the nightmare of, as the saying of the time had it, "bringing scandal to the church."

In Lowell that season, my father's parents were denounced publicly from the pulpit of the church they had attended since their oldest son was born (they never went back), and my mother's mother heard similar disapproval at St. Margaret's in Dorchester (she still goes there today). My Aunt Rita's own Catholic wedding was disrupted when the celebrant refused Communion to my mother, the matron of honor, upon learning why her name was so familiar. These incidents, to mention only a few, made it abundantly clear that despite my parents' Catholic bona fides, they were now persona non grata in many parishes of the diocese.

The grumbling didn't stop at the church door. Thanks to the press that had shown up at the reception, Bill and Mary found themselves at the center of the Catholic sex scandal of the day. After running the story on Page 1 the morning following the ceremony (LOWELL PRIEST MARRIES BOSTON NUN, one headline read), newspapers around the state were overrun with letters protesting both the wedding and its coverage.

From a letter signed "Disgruntled Reader": "The news media won't stop playing up these distasteful incidents until the Church is split, the country and the world . . . If some of these 'kooks' didn't get so much publicity, their foolish ideas would soon die out, but you make heroes of them."

Another note, from a priest in my father's hometown, blames their marriage on "a complete hopeless and idiotic type of seminary and convent permissiveness, where they measure priest and nun candidates with a tape measure around the head and not as God does by measuring the Heart. This has made religious life today as confused as a Chinese fire drill or a blind dog in a meat market."

Other letters complained that by running such a story, the press "put the Catholic Church up for ridicule by non-Catholics . . ." and displayed "a brazen lack of respect for the dignity of the priesthood," and that the story of the "wedding" (as often as not referred to in quotation marks) was "in very poor taste and offensive to the sensibilities of a large number of readers . . ."

All through the fabled Summer of Love, my parents learned that news of their marriage had spread around the world. My mother's childhood neighbor Jimmy Connolly wrote to his parents to tell them that he'd read about the wedding in Saigon, and asked that they please pass on his best wishes. Other letters from the far corners of the world were less pleasant. "Dear Priest," a letter from Korea begins:

> *How utterly sad to read of your defection, of your betrayal of Our Blessed Lord! No doubt you were shocked when you read during your seminary days about Luther's defection and his illicit union with an equally traitorous nun, and rightly so. You had some decency in you then, you loved God like any real genuine Catholic should . . . You talk about entering into "the deepest relationship possible with a Christian." Strange that Our Blessed Lord did not know this. Neither did his wonderful Mother. When did "shackin up" become such a meritorious experience? I suggest you see a doctor, friend, and may God forgive you.*

Only my father's mother thought to respond to all of this. In a letter to her hometown paper, the *Lowell Sun*, Jeannette Manseau wrote:

> *My Dear Editor,*
>
> *We are still glowing from our deep spiritual and joyful experience of last Saturday evening at a wedding reception in Dorchester (held in a spirit of humility to honor two wonderful people) where the rich and the poor, black and white, Religious and laity, sat at the table of the Lord and rejoiced together. This was love and unity in action in the deepest sense of the words . . .*
>
> *We are sickened and very sad about some of the reactions and thinking of a few individuals who seem to regard marriage as an institution of shame while it is the complete opposite. Marriage represents love, discipline, sacrifice and respect. That's why Almighty God instituted it in the very beginning of the world.*

As moving as the substance of my grandmother's letter is, more telling is the fact that it seems she never sent it. When she died a dozen years later, my father's sister Barbara found this note bundled together with a stack of rewrites and false starts. In all of them, she protested that the families involved felt no shame nor should they, but tucked away as her handwritten pages were, it is easy to suppose that, for the priest's mother at least, writing it did not make it so.

Bill and Mary, for their part, were surprised by all the attention, but unfazed. They had the business of being married to attend to. Though Bill had wanted to stay in Roxbury to continue his ministry, the thought of raising a family there—among the crime and the poverty, every day passing windows still boarded over in case of another riot—was enough to set the new Mrs. Manseau to tears. So they bought a house not far from the neighborhood where Mary grew up, both working to make up the difference in housing costs from next to nothing on broken and dangerous Blue Hill Avenue to a little more than that over the border near Codman Square in Dorchester. Mary continued her position as a clerk at the State House until she completed her degree and secured a teaching post in Boston. Bill likewise found a secularized version of the job he had been doing for years: he worked now in the Boston office of the Model Cities program, a Great Society initiative through which, Bill hoped, he could continue to help the poor while he took on new challenges: paying bills, starting a family . . . all the humdrum rituals of adulthood from which the collar had so long preserved him.

Negative publicity aside, they had received such an outpouring of moral support as a result of their decision to marry that it was difficult not to feel a divine hand at work in their lives—a hand stirring things up, yes, but also leading them through the cloud.

As the dust settled, though, new problems arose—within the marriage as well as around it. He was a man of thirty-three who had been coddled by his mother and then by his church, never fully leaving the sway of either. She was a woman of twenty-eight who within a year went from the convent dormitory to her wedding bed. He was the button-down revolutionary; quiet in manner but hell-bent on shaking up the ecclesiastical status quo—and willing to use his marriage to do so. She was the loud one, the talker, the shouter in the bleachers at Red Sox games, but sometimes she was content to let the church be what it was. She loved her church, even though she'd just left the convent to marry a priest who refused to resign his ordination. Not that the church always pleased her. During their first years of marriage, awful rumors spread through some circles. When an unrelated woman named Mary Doherty was checked into a hospital psychiatric ward in the city, word got around that it was the priest's wife. The story that reached the newlyweds was that Father Bill beat Sister Mary and caused her to have a nervous breakdown. The part of it that pained Mary was not merely that there were lies being told about them (there would always be lies, after all), but that some people— some *Catholics*—seemed to wish these lies were true.

Bill and Mary had believed that the church would mature with them—that in a year, maybe two, priests who married would be welcomed back to active ministry, not as prodigals in need of forgiveness, but as pioneers, explorers who'd cleared a trail for others to follow. Yet the changes brought by Vatican II were not as far-reaching as they'd hoped. There would be no married clergy any time soon. And other hopes went unrealized as well. Optional celibacy? Out of the question. Woman priests? No way. The many advances that Pope John XXIII had made toward creating a church retooled to serve the modern world were undone by each subsequent pontiff: Paul VI, pope for a month John Paul I, and especially John Paul II. In 1979, in fact, as if to drive nails into the coffin of the Catholic reform movement, the great Hans Küng, voice of a generation, was formally silenced by the Vatican, forbidden to teach theology at any Catholic institution, or even to be referred to as a Catholic theologian. As far as Rome was concerned, dissent simply did not exist.

Without the support of his diocese or the church, my father became something of an itinerant preacher. Missing the life of a full-time minister, he left his stint at Model Cities and became a clergyman in exile, affiliated with the only churches that would have him— Protestant churches, in other words. Places he had been taught to avoid like any other occasion of sin were now his only refuge.

When he took a position at a two-hundred-year-old Congregational church in Dunstable, a bucolic country town an hour's drive from Boston, it was hardly a threat to the church on the level of the Reformation, but again he found himself in the news.

"Ex-priest Holds Protestant Rites," one paper's headline read in 1971. Because of the worldwide attention the wedding had received, it was not just local news. "Priest who wed Ex-Nun is Pastor," wrote the *Pittsburgh Post-Gazette.* In Toronto: "Married nun, priest hired by U.S. church." The *New York Times:* "Censured Priest Takes New Pulpit."

> DUNSTABLE, Mass., April 10—A censured Roman Catholic priest who will assume the pulpit of this town's Congregational Church May 1 expects to be able someday to resume his ministry in the Catholic Church despite the fact that he is married.
>
> "The Catholic Church cannot publicly approve what I am doing," said the Rev. William J. Manseau, "but canon law is being rewritten in Rome right now and the whole matter of priestly celibacy is being discussed."
>
> . . . The 36-year-old clergyman said his Catholic faith was "as pristine as the Pope's."

As far as he was concerned, Dad was the Catholic Church's advance team. Any day now the hierarchy from Brighton to Rome would catch up to him, follow on the trail he had blazed. Until then, he would hold on for the inevitable. A caption from one newspaper photograph in those days sums up what had become his true vocation: "William Manseau . . ." it said, "preaching, waiting."

In the meantime, little changed. As word spread that the priest who had married a nun was now the leader of a Protestant church, a segment of the Catholic population once again responded with anger out of proportion with the issue at hand. The more addled among the faithful mailed in letters of outrage from around the country, often including defaced newspaper clippings to underline their disdain. My parents received multiple newspaper photos of my father with horns drawn on his head; beside the headline on one of them, A CHANGE OF

VESTMENTS, someone had written, "Oh the devil is glad." Others were more direct: "You are an <u>ex</u>-priest, Big Boy, whether you like the description or not, and your wife is an <u>ex</u>-nun," a man from New York wrote.

In all the talk about a married clergy no one seems to question about the congregation. I certainly would not go to any services by a married priest—especially anyone married to an ex-nun.

Start your own style of Church, why don't you, like Luther. Eventually, I guess, you'll be sorry.

The locals were no more sympathetic:

Read in Boston papers where you left the priesthood. Good riddance to an old bum like you. How can you be a Catholic and a minister of a Protestant church at the same time? You can't be. You must be crazy. You are French. The French people are a bunch of dopes, so are you. The Catholic Church is better off without you. You could not have been a decent priest.

A particularly ambitious hate-mail writer from Chicago made the new minister's name into an acrostic poem:

To Rev William J Manseau

WILL *of God gave you a priesthood,*
In domain of parents' creed,
And they thought of it as a blessing,
    An oak tree from Catholic seed.

Made a sacrifice to lead you,
Join the group of chosen men
Master blessed as His disciples
    Strive to ban the present sin.

Aim was theirs to see priest true,

> *Ne'er lose fealty to Pope*
> *Serve him well—accept his dicta,*
> > *And become his future hope,*
>
> *End not then, the faith mom taught you,*
> *Admit error you have made,*
> *Urge Mary to be a nun 'gain*
> > *Have your present actions fade.*

The start of another letter hints at the real reason behind all this anger:

> *Reading your statement in the paper made me sick. You were never a real priest or was your religious wife a real sister. Just make believers. You both know that real priests and nuns don't change like you did. You want to make excuses for your cowardly act. You know very well that Our Lord said take up your cross & follow me, leave behind mother & father & every one close to you, go out and walk the highways of all nations & preach & whose sins you forgive are forgiven & whose sins you retain are retained. Our Lord didn't want weaklings; you wouldn't be a weakling if you had a real Love of God.*

The signature on the note is barely legible, but the "Mrs." that precedes the name is plain enough. A married woman, a Catholic, probably a mother, and yet the thought that the men and women who served her church should want some of the same things from life as she did was unimaginable. "Real priests and real nuns don't *change* like you did . . ." She is not just responding to scandal but to the whole catechism-ordered universe being turned on its head. After the turmoil of the 1960s, it seems many reacted to my parents' wedding and then to their seeming defection as if all the changes the church had recently endured had been shaped into bricks and tossed through their windows. How else to explain such bile spilling from the pens of the devout:

> *Don't you think that you have done enough harm to the church and your-*

self without you putting your pictures in the paper and now becoming a
minister? You took vows when you became a priest, so did your wife the
nun. No Catholic will ever have any faith in a priest that don't live his re-
ligion. . . .

Life is short & you will have to live with yourself & face God. You will
not be a good minister! Why try?

Just as he had done at his wedding, when Bill took his new pulpit,
he tried to keep scandal-hungry reporters out of the church, but some
seem to have snuck in with the crowd. According to one report of his
first day on the job:

"Rev. Manseau, dressed in a dark business suit, and wearing a white
shirt with dark green tie, appeared nervous when he began his sermon . . . 'Well the photographers are all outside, and we're all inside,'
he said."

But never mind that, he told his new congregation. He'd come to
deliver a different story than the one the press wanted to tell.

"You see the world differently when you fall in love," he preached.
"Wow, it's beautiful." Then he went on to make a scriptural connection between miracles of the Old Testament and the New, God's creation, and Jesus giving sight to a blind man. He had seen for himself
the ways in which these were stories about the same process. To par-
ticipate in creation, he had discovered, was to open himself up to see
in a new way.

Earlier that year Mary had given birth to a son, my brother Sean. My
sister Kathleen followed three years later, and then me. This, all of it—
marriage, fatherhood, the whole universe of postcelibate possibility—
was the eye opening he referred to, the actualization of all his theories
of how best to serve God, how best to move the faith forward.

"You must all open your eyes," he preached, "to see the world
through love!"

As a writer for the *Boston Globe* reported, "Rev. Manseau spoke for
more than twenty minutes and didn't have a note in front of him.
Asked later for a copy of his sermon notes, he held out a Bible."

Had it been possible, he might have simply held out his life.

HOLY FAMILY

Happy families are all alike; Catholic families are all unhappy in their own way. As I was growing up, though I knew that without it my family would not exist, the church often seemed the greatest threat to peace within our home. Life had been so pleasant for my parents during their time with the Congregationalists in Dunstable that my mother, ever the Irish optimist, could only believe something bad was about to happen. Sure enough, after they left that bucolic old New England town, family tensions mounted, all of them caused by questions of faith.

In the beginning, these were not questions of what we believed, but how. For all the various churches we attended through those early years, we remained an unshakably Catholic family. One somewhat paradoxical reason for this was that, though he eventually held affiliations with a handful of denominations, Dad never thought of himself as anything other than a Catholic priest. He would admit to anyone who asked that he was technically "not in good standing" (as one euphemism for "excommunicated" had it), but really that was a matter for the paper pushers of the Vatican bureaucracy to work out. "It's ecclesial politics," he'd shrug. "They're so out of touch in Rome it will take a while for change to trickle up."

Never mind that he was challenging gravity. As far as Dad was concerned, the hierarchy's entrenched opposition to a married priesthood was foolishness that would meet an end of its own making. In the meantime, he had it on higher authority that what he was doing was not just right but necessary.

There was a short time at the start of their marriage when Mom was as excited about the Catholic reform movement as Dad was. She wrote a holiday letter every December in which news of the growth of the family was entwined with details of their initiatives on behalf of bringing change to the church. They *were* change, after all: every day in a household headed by a priest and a former nun was like a do-it-yourself extension of Vatican II. It was a grand project, in its humble way, and they were in it together:

Dear Friends,

Happy Christmas and God's choicest blessings on the coming New Year. All the Manseaus and the Dohertys are very well, thank God. It's Christmas again and time to share the goings on of our life with you. We recently attended the third annual convention of the Society of Priests for a Free Ministry in New York. Bill was elected Vice-President for the New England area, and so we continue as we have for the past three years to promote the work of SPFM. Along with many other priests in the country we hope that the Church will eventually see and accept the fact that the ministry of married priests is a valid one . . .

Yet as annual meetings came and went and none of the changes they hoped for seemed any more likely, my mother's enthusiasm for the struggle waned. In the first five years of their marriage, they had moved from Boston to Dunstable, Dunstable to Chicago, Chicago to Maryland, and then back to Massachusetts, all for my father's work. What's more, as three young children grew, it became more and more clear that fixing what was wrong with the church was not going to feed us, clothe us, or get us off to school on time.

All of which made my mother a far less enthusiastic pioneer. Of the two, though Dad clung stubbornly to his vocation and Mom seemed to regard her time in the convent as a long, strange dream from which she was glad to have awoken, it was she who remained the more traditional Catholic.

By the time they returned to the Boston area in the mid-1970s, settling in the northern suburb of Tewksbury, the scandal of their wedding had been largely forgotten. We became involved with our local parish, St. William's, and did our best to seem like any other devout family in town. Mom served as a frequent reader and lay minister at Mass. My brother, Sean, trained to be an altar boy, like his father before him. My sister, Kathleen, joined the children's choir. Two Decembers in a row I was conscripted as a Christmas pageant Joseph. During the performances, I would stand between the altar and the pews with a six-year-old Virgin Mary dressed in a baby-blue bedsheet. My role was to lead Mary around the front of the church as we mimed scenes from the story of the first Noel: the long road to Bethlehem, the fruitless search for shelter, the unlikely birth that changed everything.

At that age, I couldn't help but associate the Nativity story with my parents. Hadn't they also wandered and waited, hoping that by following God's lead they'd find a new beginning? I'm sure I did not understand then that though Mary and Joseph traveled together, they might have had very different ideas about what that beginning might mean. Had I known more about my parents, I might have guessed that even if Joseph seemed to be leading the way, it was really Mary who was calling the shots.

Likewise, I realize now that it was my mother who was the driving force behind our involvement in the local parish—our reengagement, as a family, with the institutional church. After my parents' unorthodox union, Mom wanted nothing so much as a return to Catholic normalcy. The facts of their lives made this next to impossible, but she did her best to maintain the illusion of it. Even as my father served as pastor of one Protestant congregation or another, she wouldn't hear of the family failing to receive Communion at a "real" church at least once a week.

Nor was she satisfied when other married priests, their wives, and their children gathered to celebrate Mass in our dining room. At the time, I had no idea of the significance of these homey affairs, when two dozen or so would convene at our house for weekend get-togethers.

Now, however, I see these liturgical cookouts as what they were: the backyard barbecue as suburban heretics' convention. Imagine Martin Luther at the grill in plaid shorts and loafers, Joan of Arc in the kitchen making macaroni salad—it's overstating the case to equate the great saints and schismatics of history with the unassuming men and women who met at our house for Eucharist and hamburgers, but the prompting issue for each of them was the same. No less than Luther, they hoped to bring new life to the faith through individual access to the divine.

I can remember one summer Saturday when we were expecting the usual crowd—the Married Priest People, my siblings and I called them. Two hours before our guests were due to arrive, Dad had decided to take care of some yard work.

Out by the back porch, a forsythia bush that had grown clumpy and wild the previous spring that day looked brittle and dead, a mess of spindly wood blocking the screen door and the stairs. Dad lugged a metal stepladder from the garage, and I watched as he climbed up to trim the bush from above. He was dressed in work clothes: white cotton gardening gloves, faded Boston College T-shirt, an unmarked blue baseball cap, and a pair of stiff dungarees that never seemed as comfortable to him as his black clerical slacks, the ones he still wore from time to time with his black suit coat, black shirt, and white plastic collar.

That Dad was a priest was one of the first things I knew of the world. Earlier that year in my CCD class we'd been assigned to draw a picture of our baptisms. I drew my father: an orange-crayoned priest with a round head and carefully parted hair, standing next to a gold bowl rendered in Crayola yellow. Floating above the scene I'd drawn a cartoon word balloon the size of a half-dollar, too small for all the words I'd meant to write, room enough only for sacramental abbreviation—*i bapt u peter*—in my scrawled grade-school hand.

I couldn't remember the day of my baptism, of course, but I knew my father had performed it. I'd seen the photographs: Dad in glasses and vestments, myself a bundled infant in my godmother's arms. Perhaps that's why it never seemed strange to see him in priestly attire, in the uniform of a man made for Sundays.

Far more unusual were these Saturday work clothes: the novelty of

Dad high up in the air, snipping the branches' spidery ends with garden shears, then stretching to cut close to the trunk with a handsaw. I was too small to be any real help, but still I loitered at the foot of the ladder, catching the tiny dried leaves as they shook off their branches.

My mother called out from the porch, "Really, William, can't you leave well enough alone? They'll be here soon!"

I'd seen photographs of her as well: at twenty-two, wrapped in yards of dark fabric and the square-topped wimple of the Sisters of St. Joseph; at twenty-seven, in the order's newly shortened veil. Unlike Dad's priest suit, these were garments I'd never seen beyond the pictures, so to me they seemed somehow less real, as if in the photographs my mother was dressed for Halloween.

"The tree looks fine!" Mom called. "All it needs is a little rain!"

Dad kept sawing; can't leave a job half done.

"Well don't let him play so close then!"

"He's fine, Mary," Dad said, but then added, "Stand back, Pete." So I started circling the ladder, darting back in to gather the clippings, then out again to drop them on an old wool blanket we used at the beach. When we had a good pile of branches cut, I folded the corners of the blanket into the center and then followed as my father carried the bundle across the road to the swampy edges of Long Pond.

"Why are we cutting the tree down, Dad?"

"We're not cutting it down, we're cutting off the dead branches."

"Why are we cutting off the dead branches, Dad?"

"To make room for the living ones."

We put the blanket down by the side of the road and shook the pile of clippings into the black mud of the pond's edge. Bits of color scattered down with gray branches into the muck.

Dad stooped at the knees and leaned in for a closer look.

"Well would you look at that."

He pulled off one of his gloves, then reached into the pile, gathered a few of the branches he had just cut, and held them out for me to see. Tiny green and yellow buds were breaking through the bark, like oak roots bumping up a sidewalk. Not dead at all. Dad shook his head. Whether it was wonder or regret, I couldn't tell.

"It just goes to show you," he said. There was no separation between the Gospel and the world for my father; standing on the edge of a swamp, he couldn't resist a homily: "Even when a thing seems dead," he told me, "there's always a little life left, trying to break through."

Dad dropped the branches back onto the brush pile, but I picked them up and brought them home. My mother put them into a tall glass vase and then put the vase on top of the altar cloth she'd spread across the dining room table. Now the real preparations began: Dad removed his vestments from their dry-cleaning bags in the front hall closet. My sister, Kathleen, stood on a chair to rinse out the blue ceramic chalice for the dining room Eucharist that would start the party. Mom cajoled my brother, Sean, from his basement bedroom hideout. I was the youngest, too small to do anything but take it all in.

Soon the guests began to arrive. I could never remember all the names, but I knew they were families like ours: the fathers still priests, the mothers once nuns, the children never quite sure what their roles should be. We all filed into the dining room, where the table had been set with improvised liturgical elements: the ceramic chalice filled with pink Zinfandel; a dinner plate piled with torn bits of Near East pita bread. And the forsythia branches, their yellow buds beginning to open with their cut ends now in water.

That's how I think of these gatherings now: flowers growing on branches cut from their roots. It was a common theme of the sermons we heard, and not without scriptural precedent: there was the stem of Jesse—the prophet Isaiah's promise of Messiah coming against all odds—and the staff of Joseph, the tale of the divine selection of the Virgin Mary's husband, the old carpenter whose walking stick bloomed to make clear to all who it was that should care for the Son of God. Whatever the biblical reference, the stories told at these household liturgies tended to have the same moral: that life could spring forth anywhere—spontaneously, stubbornly.

When all the guests had crowded into our tiny dining room, Dad or one of the several priest/fathers in attendance would stand at the head of the table in his vestments. If it was too hot for all that finery, the celebrant would make do with just a stole over his short-sleeved Oxford shirt, like chaplains in some tropical war zone. The other adults packed in around the table were usually dressed for the season and the summer activities that would follow the liturgy, badminton and swimming, the prospect of which made it difficult for the kids to sit still.

One of the mothers would always see you if you went for the door, so the escape tactic that worked for me was to slump lower and lower in the big dining room chair until I was entirely under the table. Hidden by the curtain of the tablecloth, I'd be free to dig into my pockets for pieces of the miniature magic kit that at the time was my favorite toy. The best trick involved an orange plastic box into which a nickel would be placed. I would snap the lid on top, shake the box so I could hear the coin rattle inside, then take the lid off and—abracadabra, hocus pocus—the money was gone.

Hocus pocus—a bit of fake Latin, I would later learn, a medieval parody of *Hoc est corpus meum,* the ritual words of transubstantiation, the spell for which my parents' friends now waited. Magic above the table, magic below.

"This is my body," I would hear Dad say. "This is my blood."

The familiar formula let me know it was time to climb back into my chair, back into the world of priests, their wives, and their children, the extended family of our peculiar Catholic exile.

The Married Priest People were a ragtag community, full of men and women who had been through the ecclesiastical wringer. Some priests who left their service in the church found other work right away. Using the diverse skill set they'd acquired in their parishes, they became teachers and professors, social workers and businessmen, or, as my father eventually did, psychologists, lending their priestly ears to the clinical confessions of therapy and analysis. The men who made such transitions without difficulty were the minority, though. After a decade or more spent sheltered in the church, most, my father included, had a hard time readjusting to the world. Their families, like ours, seemed kept afloat by strong-willed women, who often found themselves supporting their households while their husbands struggled to find their secular sea legs. It was, it seems to me now, a community that included an inordinate number of damaged people; damaged by the church, damaged by leaving it, damaged by loving it still.

Mary Lou from Pennsylvania was sometimes there; a former rectory maid who'd had a clandestine marriage with a priest. She had cared for him through an illness years before but as they both got older and she could no longer take care of him, he returned to his religious order's motherhouse to live out his days. Though her husband was still living, Mary Lou was three hundred pounds of widowed grief in a massive floral-print muumuu, with a watch she wore not to know the time with, but as a place to keep his picture. She kept it taped to the watch face and showed it off every chance she got. As it happened, she died before her husband and left instructions for her ashes to be delivered to him.

Another occasional visitor was a married bishop who claimed to have been approached by secret Vatican envoys who had selected him to be the founder of an American Catholic Church made up entirely of married priests. This kind of talk was not at all uncommon. The Married Priest People were great starters of organizations. Though radical in their approach to faith, they had been so thoroughly institutionalized by their seminary educations that the number of reform groups at times seemed to increase like spores in a Petri dish. The Society of Priests for a Free Ministry gave rise to the Fellowship of Christian Ministries, which prompted the creation of a rival group, the Corps of Reserve Priests United for Service. As in the church itself, in each of these organizations there were committees and subcommittees, conferences and conventions. There were presidents and chairmen and regional officers, all of whom through the years championed so many competing agendas that as a movement they mirrored perfectly the institution they were trying to reform. With factions always breaking off, restructuring, starting anew, calls would come in on a regular basis for Dad to serve on a planning board, raise money, or write something for the latest married-priest newsletter. When the bishop phoned the house to speak to my father, my mother would grab the receiver and cover it with her hand. "Don't you agree to *any-*

thing," she'd warn my father as she handed him the phone. "The man thinks the pope is calling him twice a week—"

"Well, you never know," Dad would muse. "Stranger things have happened."

"Just don't. He's *crazy.*"

The others gathered at our table were less extreme but no less sincere; their devotion to the Catholic Church, and to the changing of it, informed every part of their lives. My father and his fellow married priests had come to think of themselves as "tent-makers," free-roaming ministers modeled after St. Paul, who financed his travels by crafting and mending the temporary dwellings of the desert. They practiced their livelihoods in support of their ministry and brought their ministry into their homes because, they believed, families could not live by bread or the institutional church alone. The result was the strangeness of Catholic ritual transposed onto the ordinariness of our suburban household; symbolic actions that felt like theater in an auditorium-sized church around our dining room table had an intimacy and immediacy that moved me before I was old enough to wonder why.

All well and good as far as my mother was concerned, but no matter how moving or genuinely supportive such at-home liturgies were to these men who wore exile as their cross, Mass in the dining room was not, could never be, church as she understood the word.

This is the hold of the Catholic worldview that my mother developed in the parishes and convents of Irish Boston: even as she married a priest, even as she accepted and agreed with him that he should remain a priest despite the protestations of his superiors, it seems my mother could not help but view priests who married as damaged goods where performance of the liturgy was concerned. She'd left the Sisters of St. Joseph with none of the looking back that plagued my father, but still there was something of the nun in her. She needed music and vestments, candles and incense, stained-glass windows and the tinkling of bells in order to feel that she had worshipped properly. Nevertheless, for all her ambivalence, my mother would still join the others in the torn bits of pita bread that passed for the Eucharist those weekend evenings. Why shouldn't she? Chances are she had already attended an actual Mass earlier that day, so her ritual bases were covered.

My father meanwhile insisted that "church" was not a place but an occasion, a holy occurrence—something that happened, as the Gospel says, "whenever two or more gather" in Jesus' name. As for communion, it was just what it sounded like, a coming together with God. It was the church's insistence that centralized authority was necessary for sacramental experience that led to the great abuses of its power. Et cetera, et cetera, et cetera. Don't get Dad started. Imagine this discussion casually asserting itself at 7:30 on a Sunday morning. My mother looks down at her mug of tea, lifts the teabag and lets it drip back into the cup. "Yes, dear," she'd say, "I'm sure it's still a *real* sacrament when you do it." And then she would bundle us up and out the door to church.

In those days my mother had a crayon box full of liturgical expressions to choose from in the towns around Boston, and different reasons for choosing each one. There was our local parish, St. William's, a Wal-Mart of a church just down the road, which offered a thirty-two-minute Mass for a quick, bland ritual fix, followed by powdered donuts. Other times she also attended St. Agnes' in Reading or St. Mary's in Chelmsford; occasionally she'd head back down to Dorchester for a vigil at St. Margaret's. Each church boasted this or that priest or choir, whose liturgical or musical styles were appropriate to various moods.

For a number of years we also trooped down to St. Francis de Sales, the Roxbury parish where my parents had met. All their old friends were gone by then and the old church building had been torn down, but the community was thriving. It had taken over a Baptist church a few years before—not just the building but a fair number of its members, who each Sunday set the place rocking with two hundred hands clapping and the only full-Gospel Catholic choir I'd ever heard. The parishioners weren't just attentive, but involved, with shouts of "Preach it, Father!" ringing from the pews. When as a child I learned that this parish had played a role in my parents' meeting, it was the first time I had ever considered the world that existed before I was born. I could not help but connect the sounds I heard there—the shouting, the singing, the Roxbury rhythms so foreign to my suburban ears—with the beginning of the possibility of my life.

This church or that—it made little difference to me. I *loved* church, any church, loved going to Mass the way other children love their first storybook, content to hear it read aloud until its binding breaks. My parents would shake their heads at the lack of spirit in our local parish, but I even loved that one. God was in the details: I loved the chill of the holy water in the font perched like an ashtray at the door. I loved to slide across the wooden pew in my Sunday slacks. I loved the creak of the kneeler dropping into place and I loved the silence of two hundred people praying before the ceremony began, when the first nasal strains of the children's choir wailed from the loft above the back rows. Gone were the ancient Latin introits of my parents' Catholic childhoods, replaced by '70s-style liturgical ballads I can still hear ringing in my ears:

> *And he will raise you up,*
> *on eagle's wings*
> *Bear you on*
> *the breath of dawn.*

When the children sang it was high and thin and quavering; when the adult soloist took over, the notes were as fat and made-up as she was. Whoever was singing it was awful by any formal standard, but there was a searching quality to the voices that seemed appropriate to their purpose, something in them that made me believe it—all of it.

> *He'll make you to shine*
> *like the sun*
> *And hold you in the palm*
> *of His hand*

And I didn't just believe it—I tried to become it. I had memorized the Mass in its entirety by the time I was seven or eight. I could recite not only the parts that the congregation spoke or sang together but also those meant for the priest alone. A boy whose father is a carpenter might pretend to build a house out of the sofa cushions; sitting in the pew with my family, my fingers fluttering above a cup only I could see, I pretended to turn wine into blood. I had seen my father perform the priest's magic trick a thousand times at home. Though I knew when to say the words of the statement of humility that preceded Communion—"Lord, I am not worthy to receive you . . ."—I don't think I ever believed them. Not worthy? How could I be not worthy? Wasn't this my birthright? Wasn't this the family business?

Soon enough I became aware that the answer was yes and no. The tensions surrounding religious observance in my family gradually shaped my own conflicted attitude toward the church. As Dad's pursuit of ecclesial reform continued, he less often attended Mass with the rest of us. Though he was elected president of the Society of Priests for a Free Ministry, Mom stopped attending the married-priest meetings. On at least one occasion she followed Dad up to a gathering in New Hampshire and, as it would later be recounted in family lore, "blasted him to Cork and back," calling him out of a room full of his fellow radicals and demanding he forget his reformation dreams for a day at least and come home to deal with his family.

"One needs to marry a person, not an idea," Dad had said just after his wedding, but given his continued devotion to the cause, his wife would have been justified in wondering if he had wed her or simply the idea of being a married priest. And if that was the case, where did that leave their children?

In a word: stuck. Between our father's unabated radical inclinations and our mother's gradual return to a more traditional Catholicism, we were caught in the middle of two religious ideals: loyalty to community and the courage to go it alone. My parents wanted desperately to raise good Catholic children, and they remade us in that image every chance they got. My brother the altar boy. My sister singing solos in the St. William's children's choir. Me in a bathrobe with a towel on my head as a Christmas-pageant Joseph. Yet our ambiguous place within the faith eventually caused an inevitable rift. In any parish we attended, we didn't know where we fit—and the feeling was mutual.

Nowhere was this more apparent than in St. William's religious education program. One evening a week every child in the parish would be dropped off at the church school building for lessons that were only slightly improved from the catechism that had taught my parents about the essential divisions of the Catholic universe forty years before. My family didn't fit into such easy categorization, and so my teachers' explanations of the way the world supposedly worked only increased my confusion.

I remember one day the lesson for the class was the sacraments. We third-graders had received our First Communion the year before, and we all had seen pictures of our baptisms, so we moved through those quickly and headed for murkier waters: holy orders.

Mrs. Crocker, my CCD teacher, was sitting in front of the classroom at a desk like ours, slightly lower than an adult's thigh, the sliding tote tray removed to make room for her knees. A teacher's edition of the third-grade textbook lay open in front of her, but she riffed on the sacraments extemporaneously. She didn't need any book to tell her about being Catholic.

"Why don't priests get married?" Mrs. Crocker was saying, with no sign that she expected a response. "Because they love God sooo much." She smiled and hugged her arms to her pink sweatshirt as if God were an invisible teddy bear. I think by then I had already understood that God could sometimes make people act in ridiculous ways, but still I paid close attention. My ears always perked up at the mention of priests; the word itself offered a chance to learn something about my father.

"Priests don't get married," Mrs. Crocker continued, "because they only want to serve the church and don't have time for a wife or children."

Wait a minute. The answers seemed fine: Dad did love God that much; he did only want to serve the church; and, sure enough, he did not have time for a wife or children. But the question she'd asked seemed wrong.

I raised my hand halfway into the air.

"Do you have a question, Peter?" Mrs. Crocker asked.

"Sometimes priests get married," I said.

Mrs. Crocker's head flopped back in amusement. "Oh-no-no," she laughed, clucking her tongue. I had clearly not been paying attention. "Oh no, they don't."

"Yes," I said. "They do."

She stopped laughing, tilting her head.

"No," she repeated slowly, "they don't." She patted the teacher's edition of the third-grade CCD textbook; I might not listen to reason, but who could challenge so high an authority? "They don't get married, ever."

She stood up, turned around, located a nub of chalk, and began to write on the blackboard: tall, thin letters, scritching and scraping as she dragged the chalk up and down as if she were zipping and unzipping a winter coat. Only when she'd moved away could I read what she had written:

V O W S

"Priests don't get married," she said, "because they take *vows.*" She said the word slowly, rounding her lips and opening wide to let the *o* float out of her mouth like a bubble. The rest of the third-graders instinctively repeated it, and the room echoed with the sound.

"But so do married people," I said.

"Those vows are different."

"Not always."

All eyes were on her. My classmates' heads, I realized, had been moving left to right between us. I'd just scored a point, but it was her serve now, and she was just staring at me. CCD teachers were volunteers, church mothers who barely had time to read through the lesson before class each week; they had no reason to know or care what "not always" might entail where canon law was concerned. She tried to change the subject, to move through to the next point on her outline, but I was eight years old, convinced I was right, and would not be satisfied until she accepted it.

"And nuns get married, too," I said.

That did it. She stood with a huff and marched toward the door, her cheeks burning red over her pink sweatshirt. "Let's just send you off to the deacon and we'll see what he has to say about this."

The deacon, William Emerson, the parish's director of religious education, knew my family well. He smiled when I explained what had happened in the classroom and sent me back with a message for my teacher.

"So," Mrs. Crocker smirked, "did the deacon set you straight?"

"No," I answered. "He says I'm a Special Case."

She blinked at me for a long moment, and then turned away.

"Well, then," she said.

I don't know for certain if that's when she decided not to call on me anymore, but she never did again.

The class moved on to another sacrament—anointing of the sick, which we third-graders found to be simultaneously the most boring and disturbing of the sacraments, and also a little gross. Our textbook depicted it as the one sacrament performed exclusively in hospital rooms; judging from the photographs, it seemed to require both a bedpan and a crucifix.

It didn't bother me that day. My mind was filled with priests, nuns, and the vows they take. I wrote in my notebook the deacon's phrase, a Special Case, and considered the matter settled, for now.

EX DAMNATO COITU

Inevitably, as I reached the age of teenage dissent, I decided I'd had enough church to last a lifetime. There were the usual reasons: boredom, laziness, the predictable testing of religious limits known in some Protestant circles as PKS: Preacher's Kid Syndrome—far less common among Catholics, but in my case it applied. More than all these reasons, though, I was driven away from my Catholic upbringing by a sense that as a family we were in the faith but not of it; a nagging feeling that the church we were raised to place at the center of our lives did not in fact want us.

"According to them," my father once told me, "you're a bastard." Dad was speaking of the ecclesial hierarchy, and he used the word "bastard" in its technical sense: Despite the fact that more priests had been present at their wedding than perhaps at any other in the history of the Archdiocese of Boston, the church refused to recognize my parents' marriage, and so considered all of their offspring illegitimate by definition. More precisely, among the many classes of *bastardi* referred to in canon law (the children of prostitutes, the children of incestuous relations, etc.), I was *"ex damnato coitu."* Born "from a damned union."

I didn't need to be told. It must have been around my twelfth or thirteenth birthday that my early fascination with the spectacle of ritual began to be stifled by the questions of an adolescent mind: Why on earth would I want anything to do with a church that felt as it did about the circumstances of my birth? How could my parents expect me to respect an institution that had nothing but disdain for their marriage? For that matter, how could I respect them for continuing to love such an institution? In passing down the Catholic tradition to their children, it seemed they wanted us to enter into the worst kind of dysfunctional relationship. Devotion to the church looked to me like nothing so much as the enablement of an abusive spouse: no matter the psychological or emotional beating my parents endured, they would keep coming back. If that was what faith meant to them, this bastard wanted none of it.

My siblings shared my gut rejection. Each of us put up with CCD classes until the age of fourteen or so, and then, like most of our friends, as soon as we had made our confirmation, receiving the anointing that initiated us as adults into the church, we thought of the sacrament as nothing but a license to leave it behind. After all, hadn't our father's own life suggested that the best way to be true to our religious impulses was to recognize that the church could be wrong?

As a result, my brother, sister, and I began to struggle against our parents' beliefs in ways they found incomprehensible. It is only as an adult that I can imagine the rebuke that must have seemed. Dad had given his life to an ideal—to be married and to be priest; to be both father and Father—only to have reality make him feel as effective as a plumber who couldn't fix his own damn toilet. When he went back to school in the late 1980s to earn the degree that would allow him to begin his counseling practice, even that felt as though it had increased the distance between what he wanted for his family and what we wanted for ourselves. The degree was a doctorate in ministry, more of which seemed to me to be the last thing we needed.

My brother, the oldest, eventually bore the brunt of Dad's frustration. Sean put our father through what must have been the worst humiliation a priest with children could imagine: seeing a son thrown out of a series of Catholic schools for arguing with the rigid clerics who taught theology. Sean by then had grown from an altar boy to a Dungeons & Dragons–playing, heavy-metal guitarist; his hair hung to his shoulders, earrings studded the lobes of both ears. "Scholarship recipients," one letter of expulsion proclaimed, "should better reflect the Catholic values of the school."

Back in his Roxbury days, Dad had never cared whether the people he helped as a priest were believers or not, but as a father it was something else. His firstborn had been an affirmation of all he hoped to achieve with his combined priesthood and marriage. To see Sean scorn the faith was to have all that he had worked for thrown into doubt.

At least, that is how I must understand it now for the rage we sometimes saw to make any sense. My most vivid memories of our father are of that priest overseeing his dining room liturgies as if they were high Mass. He was a man older than any of my friends' fathers, with a carefulness to his words and actions that kept him forever at an emotional distance. My brother's dominant memories of him, however, are of a younger man, a man closer to the street preacher he had been, a man of passion and charged encounters, capable of ferocious indignation. The father my brother remembers might as well be another person altogether, and yet I know they are the same, conflicted memories of a conflicted man, torn between the vows he had broken and the family that at times seemed broken by them.

When Sean was young, he tells me, he was bored at Mass one Sunday and spent the bulk of the hour fidgeting in his seat. He made his hands into the shape of the building we were in, small fists clenched together with both index fingers pointed up—*This is the church, this is the steeple*—then he folded out his palms and fluttered his interlocked fingers—*open it up, and see all the people.* Time passed more quickly, he had discovered, if he could pretend he was floating over it all, looking down from above. But imagined escape lasts only so long: the whole way home Dad stammered with anger, enraged that Sean had not seemed to be listening to the sermon. He was all of eight, exactly one year younger than the time elapsed since our father had last been acknowledged as a priest by his church. "You didn't hear a single word of the homily!" Dad shouted. For my brother, it is a memory that fairly well sums up their relationship for the next ten years.

There was a great deal of silence in our house during that time, jarred only by the moments when Sean tried to make clear that he didn't want to fight, didn't want to attack their faith. He simply no longer wanted anything to do with it.

Usually these confrontations happened in the evening, and were to me only disembodied murmurings rising from the heating vent in my bedroom. With the kitchen directly below me, I could hear the voices as if the metal grate where the wall met the floor was a radio built into the molding. My father's sighs of frustration, my mother's pleas for peace, the pendulum swing of bravado to whine in my brother's complaint: when I was just reaching an age when I was able to lie awake at night and drift off to sleep thinking about my family and God and what the two had to do with each other, these were the sounds that informed my dreams.

On one occasion I was there to actually see one of these quarrels unfold. I remember I was watching television with my sister, turning down the volume so we could better hear the rising tones down the hall. When finally I opened the door and peeked toward the kitchen, I saw my mother sitting at the kitchen table with her eyes closed as my father and brother stood on opposite sides of the room, the oven and five feet of linoleum between them. Mom put her hands down on the tabletop as if in need of balance. Her lips bent and by the way her shoulders shook I could tell she was crying—crying, I thought then, because my brother would not go to church.

Of course, I know now that church is rarely just church. For a family like ours, church stood for tradition and continuity and hope and death, not merely for all that was right but for all that was inevitable. For my parents, whether their children attended, believed in, and identified with their church was not simply a matter of obedience, it was about the possibility of the worst kind of failure.

At times this meaning was made more apparent than others, and the argument I witnessed was one of them. Not long before, my parents had been out at an Irish dance with a few of my aunts and uncles. Mom still loved the jigs and reels she had learned as a girl in Dorchester. She danced with one of her brothers when a song called for a partner; Dad preferred to watch from the side. Midway through the night, she collapsed on the dance floor. A heart problem first identified in the medical exam prior to her entry to the convent thirty years before had finally shown itself again. Rushed to the hospital that night, she learned that if she did not have open-heart surgery she would likely not survive the year.

The thought of it filled her with dread. It was not so much the prospect of dying as the implication that we, her children, would be all but orphaned in the process. For years, Mom had been the primary financial support for the family while Dad worked for what she then considered a lost cause. She was convinced she would die and we would be left in the care of this priest who couldn't even persuade their eldest son to attend Mass.

Sitting at the kitchen table the night I peeked down the hall to see them fight, Mom may have been crying about church, but by then the very word carried with it a divine rebuke: after leaving the convent, after marrying a priest, still burdened by the long-ago hurt she kept as hidden as the holes in the top of her mouth, maybe she felt she had it coming.

Dad's face burned red beneath the enormous metal-framed glasses he wore back then. "Mary, please," he said when he saw my mother's tears. "Don't throw pearls before swine."

I didn't know then that these were words from Scripture, but from the way Sean fell silent, from the way he turned and left the kitchen, retreating to his basement bedroom, I knew they were words that hurt. I wished I hadn't heard them. I wished I was back up in my bedroom and that the heating vent for once would blow only air.

Because we had grown up seeing the dangers of challenging our family's devotion to the church, my sister and I developed less confrontational strategies to distance ourselves from it. Kathleen was always the highest achiever of all of us—she had the best grades by far and was also the most involved in extracurricular activities—so it was only natural that dancing lessons and soccer practice began to take the place of St. William's children's choir, just as the extra attention she gave to her regular schoolwork eventually pushed her CCD lessons aside. As the years passed and she became too busy for church altogether, our mother could hardly complain. It was perfectly normal for a girl her age to be as involved as Kathleen was, and "normal" was what Mom had come to aspire to above all else.

By then, too, we were all getting tired of fighting. My mother had been genuinely surprised to be alive after her surgery and, in the years that followed, her relief seemed to lighten the mood at home. Even my father and brother made peace. As Sean reached adulthood and its inevitable trials, he discovered having a priest around was not always a bad thing. More than once, when his eldest son needed someone to talk to, Dad proved himself a man who knew how to listen.

As for me, by the time I was a teenager I had been furtively avoiding church for years. Lacking my brother's courage of conviction, instead of admitting that I didn't see the point of our weekly trip to a temple of bad singing and empty words, I looked for ways out. Some Sundays I relied on the ruse of telling my parents that instead of going to the nine o'clock Mass with them, I would go by myself later in the morning. "I'll ride my bike to the twelve o'clock," I'd tell them, "so I can catch up on sleep." Perhaps impressed by my initiative, they always agreed. Three hours later I'd ride my bike to church all right: pedaling into St. William's driveway as the singing of the children's choir drifted out through the windows, I would lean my ten-speed up against the base of the statue of Blessed Virgin, jog up the walkway to the rear entrance, and grab a bulletin from just inside the door. Then I'd run back to my bike before anyone could see me. Evidence to the contrary in hand, I'd ride another mile up Main Street and spend an hour at the arcade.

I didn't even like video games—I simply, suddenly, had come to hate church. The exact details of worship that had so entranced me five or six years before then aroused in me a physical, visceral reaction. Just the smell of the place—the sweet, stale air of incense mixed with air-conditioning—was enough to tighten my jaw and blacken my mood. Honestly, I felt no more comfortable in the arcade, where boys my age smoked cigarettes and groped big-haired girls in the parking lot, but there at least the novelty was alluring. On my way home I would always stop and read over the church bulletin to see if there was any useful information to add to my lie. Then I'd fold it up and tuck it in my pocket for my mother to find when she did the wash.

From then on church was for me little more than an occasional annoyance, something I would put up with from time to time for the sake of avoiding the kinds of blowups I'd seen between my father and brother. For the most part, though, I barely gave it a thought. When I reached high school and joined the cross-country and track teams, long Sunday morning training runs replaced my bike rides past St. William's. Jogging on the roads near our house, I suffered through the miles and suddenly felt lighter upon realizing how much worse it could be: *At least I'm not in church.*

That was the extent of my reflection on the faith at the time. When I left home for college, I thought of it even less.

My parents never asked my siblings and me why we each in our own way left the Catholic Church, and I wonder now if they feared that our answer would be that we could not have done otherwise. They'd brought us into this, after all. Had they demanded we explain our rejection, we could have quoted from an anti-drug campaign I remember from television in the early '80s, the one that targeted ex-hippies whose teenage children were beginning to behave in familiarly illicit ways: I learned it from watching you.

IN SEARCH OF

The University of Massachusetts at Amherst is the kind of large public school where a student could easily get lost, both on the sprawling grounds and in the shuffle of sixteen thousand undergraduates. Unlike a lot of the colleges New England is known for, UMass was founded not as a denominational institution but as an agricultural one; when I arrived, parts of the campus two hours west of Boston remained as rural as they were a hundred years before, with the fields and barns of what was left of "Mass Aggie" still visible from the upper levels of the high-rise dorms. A thoroughly secular institution in atmosphere and appearance, built more of midcentury concrete than Puritan brick, it was an unlikely place for a spiritual education, but ultimately that was what I received.

I entered college as an archaeology major, influenced primarily by a television program I'd watched like an addiction when I was young. Narrated by the calm, curious voice of Leonard Nimoy, *In Search Of* was a weekly investigation into the world's unsolved mysteries, from the historical to the criminal to the supernatural. I was particularly interested in the episodes that sought to find the locations of sacred objects like the Ark of the Covenant or the Holy Grail, telling the stories of these lost treasures along the way. Throw in the adventure of the *Indiana Jones* movies my father took me to when I was small, and I was hooked on the idea of digging into the earth to make contact with an unseen or forgotten world. That this seemed to me a rational, scientific approach to the questions my parents approached with faith was undoubtedly part of the attraction.

So imagine my excitement when I learned that the first class of my college career, at 10:10 on a September Wednesday morning, was Anthropology 102: Introduction to Archaeology. I walked from my dorm on the hilly east side of campus, past the man-made pond and sloping lawn that formed its brown and green heart, down to the glass, steel, and tile of Thompson Hall, all the while with the theme from *Raiders of the Lost Ark* ringing in my head.

When I reached the classroom, the same theme was playing from the lecture hall sound system. *Da da da daaaaaa, da da daaa* . . . I found a seat up front and settled in as the film score played on a loop. Apparently the professor knew what filled his enrollment every semester. Other students entered with smiles as wide as my own must have been.

After a few minutes, when the flow of students into their seats came to an end, no one resembling an instructor had yet appeared. A graduate teaching assistant rose from the front row to tell us not to go anywhere, but even she began to look around wondering if the piped-in music was all we were going to get.

Just then the door at the back of the hall swung open. A shaft of morning sun shot into the windowless lecture hall. A fedora-wearing silhouette stepped into the glare. When he moved into plain sight, we saw a bearded man in a brown leather jacket, carrying—could it be?— yes, in his left hand he carried a coiled bullwhip. He bounded down the aisle as if there were a boulder rolling behind him; holding his hat on his head, he pumped his left arm so his whip flapped against his chest. Skidding to a halt at the front of the room, he slammed his fedora down on the podium. The music stopped mid-gallop.

This was our professor. He lifted his bullwhip in the air and shook it so it writhed like a snake. *"This,"* he said, "is *not* archaeology."

I'd be hard-pressed to remember my other classes from that semester, but I couldn't have asked for a more memorable start to my college career. I also couldn't have been more disappointed.

"What archaeology *is,*" he told us, "is thorough research, painstaking attention to detail, and most of all *patience.*"

Around the room were the sounds of creaking chairs and changing majors. I didn't give up hope, though. I could be patient. I told myself this was just the intro class. We'd learn some necessary foundations, and the exciting part would come later. Hopefully soon.

The next semester seemed promising. I enrolled in a field methods course with the senior archaeologist in the department, a professor in her late sixties who looked like she had stepped from a Jane Goodall monkey documentary: khaki pants with multiple pockets, sturdy cotton shirt under a gray fishing vest, floppy canvas hat pulled low over hair the color of smoke. Whatever archaeology is, hats apparently are essential to it. This time, however, it wasn't theater; she dressed like she was ready to dig.

Sure enough, the third week of class we trooped off into the hills of Amherst, slogging through woods, mud, and cow fields to find the right spot to survey. We followed the remnants of a two-hundred-year-old fieldstone wall, mapping the area on sheets of blue-lined graphing paper—treasure maps in the making, as far as I was concerned. When we reached a location the professor deemed "promising" we slung our backpacks onto the ground and got ready to work. I held a wood-handled trowel in my hand and waited to be shown where X marked the spot.

"Won't need that," the professor said. "Just this." From her own bag she drew a long silver tube that looked like a section of polished pipe. "Core-sampling tool," she said, but she handled it like a sword. In one motion, she drove the tool into the ground, pulled up a column of dirt the diameter of a quarter, and held it out to examine in the light. She took one look and grinned beneath her hat.

"My, oh my. I think we've found something here. I really think we've found something!"

"Really? Where?"

"There! Right there!"

I leaned in to see, but all I saw was dirt.

"No, no, no." She pointed to the bottom end of the sample, to soil from about eighteen inches down. *"There!"*

I followed her finger and saw half of a wriggling worm, sliced neatly by the edge of the core sampler. It seemed to stare back at me, poking its nose into the air, though I couldn't be sure I was looking at its head. A few inches away, I saw an acorn with a green shoot breaking its husk. Only when I squinted could I make out what the professor was indicating: a deep black pebble in the red and brown earth.

She cackled with delight. "It's not a stone, I'll tell you that much. At least not a native one!" She picked it out and rolled it between her fingers, grinning as it crushed to flakes and ash. "Just as I thought."

Apparently a shard of charcoal was a major find in the picked-over universe of New England archaeology. The good stuff, I was dismayed to consider, had already been found. My classmates nodded, made notes, and plotted the site on their maps. I ended the semester depressed. *In Search Of* this was not.

To overcome my disillusionment with fieldwork, I focused on other facets of my chosen major. If I stayed with archaeology at all, and by then I was having my doubts, I had no intention of specializing in what I'd come to regard as the slim pickings of North America. In the larger world of antiquities I supposed ancient languages would be useful, so I enrolled in an introductory Greek course and worked at improving the Latin I'd learned in high school.

That I had begun to pursue a classic seminary education didn't dawn on me until I borrowed my father's Greek and Latin New Testament, which he had diligently read and underlined forty years before. I had asked to borrow the book not because I hoped Dad and I might bond over a subject he had studied when he was young, but simply because I had heard that New Testament Greek was far easier for a beginner than Homer or Plato. Soon enough, though, I was confronted by the notes and scribbles made by my father when he was a man my age. The world of his religious formation felt as alien and unknowable to me as must combat to the children of a wounded veteran, yet when I read the first words of the Gospel of John in Greek—*en arche ein ho logos,* "In the beginning was the word"—I felt a thrill I imagined Dad must have felt.

Years later I would learn about a movement in Anglican theology called "Radical Orthodoxy," one of the principal ideas of which is "the word made strange": in order to understand the Gospel, these theologians assert, you must experience something like the shock that it would have caused when it first entered the world. To encounter Scripture this way—letter by letter, sounding it out and speaking it aloud, checking and rechecking my Greek-English lexicon for all variations of meaning—was to read the text unfettered by its history, or by my own. And most importantly to me, it was to experience the Bible for the first time *as* text—as thoughts recorded by a man with a pen. Reading the Gospels in their original language was like looking through the veil; learning the skill behind the magic trick. It was also my first connection, as an adult, with my father and his faith. I still thought the latter was bunk, mind you, but I was beginning to appreciate the fascination it held for him.

As I'd been by Indiana Jones and *In Search Of,* I was hooked. Now, though, the digging I most wanted to do was not out in the wilds of Western Massachusetts but in the equally muddy ground of religious literature. I gave up archaeology and signed on for a whole new kind of education: I added Hebrew to my Greek, overreached in my short flirtations with Sanskrit and Tibetan, and took classes on comparative traditions and theories of religion.

My Hebrew teacher, Noemi Schwarz, had been a map reader in the Israeli army, studying aerial photographs for lines and dots that might mean something other than what they seemed. That was her approach to language as well: by the end of the first week of class, after we had committed the strange characters of the *alef-beyt* to memory, she put Hebrew text in front of us and challenged us to find words, to make guesses at their definitions and usage.

"You must *decipher,* people," Noemi would say in her singsong, accented English. "You look and you see this puzzle in front of you and you tell me, 'Noemi, it means nothing!' But I tell you, you must look and look until it has meaning!"

A still girlish older woman, five foot five but made to seem smaller by the oversize sweaters and floor-length skirts she wore, she was herself a gifted decipherer not just of words and maps but of her students. I had known her only a month or so when she gave me a copy of *Narcissus and Goldmund,* Herman Hesse's novel about the friendship between a cloistered monk and a man devoting his life to the pursuit of beauty, sex, and knowledge (not necessarily in that order). It's a book concerned above all else with the conflict between religious commitment and worldly experience, the hopes of the spirit and the needs of the flesh. I read it as a story about the kind of conflict that made me, as probably Noemi suspected I would. I have no idea how she knew.

"Always you are contradicting, *Peetor,*" Noemi told me once. "To every question I ask you answer *Lo, aval . . .* Do you like ice cream? Lo, aval . . . Have you done your homework? Lo, aval . . . 'No, but' 'No, but' 'No, but.' Why always so complicated? Never only yes or no, always with the qualifications! Can you explain this to us *b'ivrit*—in Hebrew?"

"Lo, aval—"

"*Oy va voy,*" she shrugged. "For some, things are simple. You? You will have many lives."

As a Hebrew speaker I never made it past an elementary level—barely as good as a bar mitzvah boy's—but Noemi's lesson of looking, deciphering, was one I took into my other classes, and it was the most important thing I learned in four years of college. Beyond *Narcissus and Goldmund,* though, I still had made little effort to understand my own religious upbringing. In my courses I was grappling with religion in general terms: competing theories, rival theologies. I was becoming well versed in texts and abstractions. But for the most part I still regarded particular belief—my parents' belief especially—with head-shaking frustration.

I remember sitting on the lawn outside my dormitory playing chess with a friend one Saturday afternoon, a beautiful day on campus. The hypnotic hippie rhythms of the jam band Phish poured out of any number of dorm room windows; the smell of pot smoke was in the air. I didn't care much for either but it was so much the sound and scent of freedom, of being so far from home, that when I looked up and saw walking down the hill a former teammate of mine from my high school cross-country team, I was as surprised as if it had been my father.

At least that's how I remember it. Really I shouldn't have been so taken aback: dozens of kids from my high school went to UMass every year. It was not at all uncommon to run into someone I'd known since the sixth grade. We'd greet each other like the old friends we were—"I didn't know you went here!"—and then go our separate ways, happy enough not to run into each other ever again. We were all pleased to have left behind who we'd been before, and at UMass it was easy to do.

That day, though, a two-minute conversation so jolted me that to this day I recall the whole encounter as a singular event. After exchanging hellos and a moment of small talk, my old running buddy Tom said he was sorry he couldn't chat; he was late.

"Where you headed?" I asked.

"The Newman Center," he said. It was the name of the university's Catholic student union, but—because the only religion that mattered to me at the time was to be found in books—I didn't know that then. Tom must have seen in my face that the name meant nothing to me.

"To church," he explained.

In the distance, we could hear the bells from the university chapel. That's not where Tom was going—despite its steeple and medieval-looking wooden doors, the chapel was not a church; it was the headquarters of the marching band. When the chapel's bells tolled they were as likely to chime the UMass fight song as whatever struck the fancy of the music majors who played them. That day the notes clanged out *Up, up and away in my beautiful balloon . . .* , but still the sound seemed to remind him to keep moving.

"Church?" I didn't know anyone my age who still went to church.

"Yeah," Tom said, "I really like the priest at the four o'clock Mass."

There was an eagerness to him that made me feel he'd had a very different Catholic upbringing than my own. He took obvious pleasure in his faith, displaying an uncomplicated ease to which I found it difficult to respond. I managed to say it was good to see him, that maybe we'd bump into each other again.

"Sure, that would be great!" he said, and it seemed like he meant it.

The bells chimed on—*my beautiful, my beautiful, ballooooon*—and Tom started to jog away. He'd been an excellent runner in high school, a fifty-two-second quarter-miler, much faster than me, and continued to have a long, bounding stride. The ease of his running, the ease of his faith: as I watched him go, I wasn't sure which was more irritating. Before he was out of earshot, I called after him, "Hey! Say hello to God for me!"

Tom looked over his shoulder smiling, but with a perplexed expression, the same he might have worn had I just reached out and slapped him. The sarcasm in my tone hung in the air between us and he squinted as if he couldn't see me through the cloud.

Immediately I felt sick. I thought of myself as a serious young man—a newly minted religion major, no less. When exactly had I become a mocker of faith? Did it make me feel better about not going to church to belittle someone who did? Here I was in my second year of college, finally free of the family and its expectations, and I was only now fighting the battle I had avoided at home. Was I still so bitter at what I took to be the church's rejection of me—*ex damnato coitu*—that I could only treat those who shared my parents' beliefs with disdain? More confusing still: if I hated church so much, when I watched Tom run off to Mass, why did part of me want to go with him?

One of the best things about the university was the Five College Consortium, which allowed UMass students to enroll in classes at the four private colleges in the area: Smith, Amherst, Mount Holyoke, and Hampshire. I took advantage whenever I could—my own school had no religion department of its own, so I had no choice but to cobble together my major from the offerings of the others. My first Greek class in fact had been at Amherst, my second at Smith. The only trouble with the arrangement was the additional time and effort involved in getting from one campus to another. So when I learned that a Smith course called Introduction to Buddhist Thought met on the same days as Greek Scriptures, I added the former to my schedule for convenience as much as anything else.

With its gothic buildings and leafy quad, Smith was far prettier than UMass, much more classically collegiate. This, combined with the fact that as a rare man on the grounds of an all-female school I earned more attention than I was used to, made me look forward to my twice-weekly visits to campus. Yet the highlight of the course turned out to be the one day we didn't meet at the school.

Near the end of the semester, having moved through the historical development of the various branches of Buddhism, the instructor decided it was time we experience Buddhist practice first hand. The class—seventeen women and me—gathered at a nearby *zendo* in Northampton. We joined the regular practitioners for a *seshin*—a meditation session—balancing cross-legged on round yellow *zafus* that I'm sure made us look like a coop full of chickens hatching giant Zen eggs. After about thirty minutes of leg-cramped sitting, the regulars went off to another room to continue their practice while the zendo's *roshi* invited the visitors to ask questions.

One of my classmates' hands shot into the air. Sitting next to me in a black top and jeans rolled to the calf, throughout the mediation period she had sighed as if she wished she were anywhere else, releasing phlegmy breaths that were either asthmatic or exaggerated to draw the attention of the class. Even more distracting had been her proclivity, every three minutes of the thirty-minute session, to reposition her feet, tucking her right heel into the crook of her left knee, pushing the toes of her left foot up toward the ceiling or down toward floor. Now her legs were stretched in front of her; one hand rested on the carpet, the other she used to knead her spine as if she was squeezing fruit.

"Yes, Mr. Roshi, I have a problem," she said. "I want to become enlightened, I really do. But you see, sitting like this, it's bad for my back . . ."

At the front of the room, the roshi's clean-shaven head hung above the drape of his robes like a moon over a dark sea. Born in Japan, he had been teaching in the U.S. for years and so spoke a crisp but still accented English: "I am sorry to hear that," he said.

The questioner continued, "So what do you do if you want enlightenment but you need lower lumbar support?"

"Yes, a difficult a problem," the roshi nodded. He began his pre-scription in a grave tone: "There is only one thing to do in such a situ-ation." He paused, then smiled broadly, his eager teeth a surprise. "Try a chair."

Soft snickers all around and he chortled at what he apparently meant as a joke. He was a classic Zen comedian, playing on the aura of his robes.

"A chair?" the girl sniffed. "That would be okay?"

"I will tell you a story. Once a student came to his master and said, 'Master it hurts when I do this.'" The roshi held his hand up, opened and closed his fingers like a baby saying bye-bye. "The student asked, 'Do you have any advice?'" He peered at the girl with the bad back. "Do you know what the master said?"

She shook her head.

"He said, 'It hurts when you do this?'" More fluttering fingers, then the roshi squawked like a bird. "'So don't do this!'"

Around the room there was more laughter. One student snorted and fell off her zafu. But still there was not a glimmer of levity in the one who had asked the question. Hearing his answer, she just said sadly, "Oh."

He tried again. "It is very simple. It hurts you to sit, don't sit! A dog with a sore bottom knows this. Yes?"

"I guess."

"Also, there is a store in town that sells a zafu with a backrest. Stay a moment after and I will tell you where. Who is next?"

Another hand went up. A redhead in the front row: bobbed hair and black plastic glasses, she sat straight as a fence post in a bulky sweater that made her neck look impossibly thin.

"I was raised Catholic," she said, and I braced for her question. My recent run-in with my high school teammate had made me more aware of my knee-jerk reactions against the church, but despite myself I rolled my eyes.

"I'm not one anymore, though," she continued. "I took this class because I'm thinking of being a Buddhist."

"Aaaah," the roshi said.

"So I was wondering: Is there a way I should start? Something I should do first?"

There must have been a few other ex-Catholics in the room because a number of women leaned forward, nodding their heads to affirm the importance of the question. They all jerked back when they heard the roshi's answer.

"Yes!" he shouted. "Go to church!"

The redhead pulled her chin down into the collar of her sweater, turtle-like, muffling the shock in her voice. *"Church?"*

"Church!"

Several faces around me pinched at the thought. The roshi rushed to explain.

"Maybe if you try too hard to be Buddhist, you won't be Buddhist. You are too worried, Am I Buddhist? Am I now Buddhist? Am I *now* Buddhist? How can you be something if you are always chasing it away? Maybe if you go to church you'll be Buddhist without meaning to."

"I don't understand."

"Good! There is a reason it is said if you meet the Buddha, kill the Buddha. Sometimes you think you understand and the thinking keeps you from understanding and the understanding keeps you from thinking. Be what you are, and then maybe you will be Buddhist. Yes?"

To the silence that followed, he asked, "Who is next?" but there were no more questions after that. We all gathered our shoes and went our separate ways.

On the bus back to UMass, I thought about what the roshi had said. With his accented English and unexpected humor, he and his challenges reminded me of my Hebrew teacher—"Decipher!"—so I had liked him right away. I'd also enjoyed the brief meditation enough to want more. Yes, I had scoffed at the ex-Catholic in the front row, but by the end of that day I too wanted, if not to become a Buddhist, then at least to start doing a few Buddhist things.

I wouldn't go so far as to follow the roshi's church-attendance advice, though. How could I? We had learned earlier in the semester about the tendency of Buddhist stories to suggest paradoxes that challenge the mind past reason. I was convinced that his words were not to be taken literally but rather as a kind of koan, a sneaky Zen riddle that tricks you into understanding. That's how far I had come since the days when I had the Mass memorized: the idea of going to church had become to me as impossible a notion as the sound of one hand clapping.

Instead of taking his suggestion at face value, I began once again to do what I had come to school to do: I dug. This time the ground was the vast collection of books on Buddhism in the basement of the Smith College library. I spent hours down there each week, pulling volumes at random, piling them on a desk I had claimed as my own, and then sitting behind them like a wall. I tired quickly of the more esoteric primary sources—the Lotus Sutra, for example, left me totally bewildered, first by its obsessive descriptions of gatherings of 1,200 stainless monks, 2,000 monks-in-training, 6,000 nuns, and 80,000 boddhisattvas, all of whom "had been intimate with many hundreds of thousands of Buddhas," then by language I found distractingly clumsy, not transcendent at all. That this was likely a regrettable by-product of translation—"Let thy voice be heard, O thou whose voice resounds like an egregious kettle-drum!"—didn't make it any easier to read.

Fortunately, I soon found a few more accessible titles, stumbling upon what I now know are the classics of Buddhist literature in English: *What the Buddha Taught, The Five Pillars of Zen, The Tibetan Book of the Dead.* My favorite was a slim paperback by the great Zen monk Shunryu Suzuki called *Zen Mind, Beginner's Mind,* for no more substantive reason than the fact that, fifty pages in, I turned the page and thought there had been a misprint: two facing pages were apparently blank in the middle of the book. Then I glanced down the page and saw printed there a fine pen drawing of a housefly, as if it had flown across the room and landed there. For a long moment I simply stared, then I laughed out loud and unself-consciously, as the roshi had laughed, drawing glares from the Smith librarians. Oh you clever Buddhists! To turn the page and find a bug where words should be, it tricked my mind to work on a different level, beyond wondering or worrying if I adequately understood the text. The simple act of reading a book made into an experience of the shock of consciousness. This was not just the *word* made strange but the whole damn world.

I had no idea then about the religious transformation my father had experienced in his own library basement forty years before, but I know now that I responded to the joy of discovery I felt much as he had. It didn't even matter whether or not what I felt seeing that fly pressed between pages was the enlightenment we were supposed to be looking for. It was a hell of a lot better than a speck of charcoal. I could've stayed in the stacks all day, not quite praying, but filled with gratitude. *Thank you, thank you, thank you.*

Wait a minute—thank *who?* I thought I'd left God back home with my parents, so that was a question I was not yet willing to answer. Lately it had begun to nag at me, though. I left the library floating every time, but the more I thought about the exciting new approach to faith I had discovered, the more I thought also of the boring old one I had left behind.

At times in fact I felt I was literally running from it. On my training runs now, I would lace up my sneakers in the evening and make my way out past the edge of the campus, to the rural roads and farmers' fields that kept Amherst insulated from the rest of the world. The sky grew dark while I ran and when the rare car roared by me I found myself reciting the prayers of my youth as spells of protection. "Our Father . . . please don't hit me . . . who art in heaven . . ." As the miles went by and I let my mind wander, the bits of Buddhist wisdom I had learned during the day slipped away as the Mass welled up inside me and left my lips as easy as breath, marking the rhythm of my stride. *Lord, I am not*—step, step—*worthy*—step, step—*to receive you*—step, step—*But only say the word*—step, step—*and I shall*—step, step—*be healed.*

Actually, receiving the Lord was the last thing I wanted, so back to the Buddhist books I'd go. Had I truly aspired to put my religious history behind me, I should have quit while I was ahead. It was on a trip to the library soon after that I came upon a book called *How the Swans Came to the Lake,* which told the story of Buddhism's journey to Amer-

ica. Within a few minutes of opening it, I learned the names of dozens
of Westerners who had made contributions to the spread of Buddhism
in the United States. In every chapter there were Christians without
whom the dharma might have been much slower in coming from
Asia, perhaps forever out of my reach. Who were these people, I wondered. Christian Buddhists? *Catholic* Buddhists? The shock of it was
like finding a fly on every page.

At the zendo I had gotten tired of sitting after about thirty minutes;
in the library the day I discovered *How the Swans Came to the Lake*, I sat
for three hours studying the index, retrieving titles by and about the
people named there as if I could find the answers I was looking for in a
list of names. I had to learn more about these Christians who had
been able to get past the rigidity of their faith.

I must have started from the bottom, because I turned first to Alan
Watts, and I found him very intriguing. Though born in Britain, Watts
had been an Episcopal chaplain at Northwestern University during
World War II, and soon after became known as the man who introduced Buddhism into the American counterculture. Blurring the divisions between Western and Eastern religious traditions, he used
words like *Supreme Identity* rather than *God* and when he did use *God*
he discussed it as a principle only and not as God per se. I wonder now
what I thought the difference was, but I certainly saw one then, and,
as was his intention, that difference made accessible a whole range of
religious ideas that otherwise would have been beyond my grasp.

From Watts I moved naturally enough to the work of his most
eager students, the writers of the Beat Generation, those great popu-
larizers and debasers of exotic traditions. Here I felt on slightly firmer
ground than I had with Watts since I knew something about them already. In high school I had read every Jack Kerouac novel they had at
the town library, and later dabbled a bit in the poetry of Allen Ginsberg. It would have been hard not to: the mid-'90s were the biggest
days the Beats had seen in thirty years—there were CD box sets, children's cartoons featuring beret-wearing hip chicks, and of course the
beatnik Gap ad: "Kerouac wore khakis." Ginsberg was even on tour.
In fact, just as I was beginning my investigation into Buddhism, he

came to UMass. I saw him read, maybe a year or so before he died. With his shaggy beard and Coke-bottle glasses, his rumpled tweed jacket and linty sweater vest, he looked like a caricature of a classics professor. Still, there was indeed an otherworldly aura about him. The old man sat up on stage and sang a few rhymes from William Blake: *Tygere tygere burning bright / in the forest of the night,* accompanying himself with a harmonium he held on his lap and squeezed as if it was an extra lung pumping air into his creaking bones. To say it was like a song from the grave would be too dark; Ginsberg shook and rasped and tweedled along like a half-dead hurdy-gurdy man leading his own funeral parade. Then came his poems, and the room sat riveted. To everyone's delight he closed with the poem that had made him famous but was rarely read in public, "Howl": *I saw the best minds of my generation destroyed by madness, starving hysterical naked . . .* After the first lines the spell was complete. I would have listened as intently to whatever he read, no matter how mundane: his grocery list; a weather report. It could've been the utterly incomprehensible Lotus Sutra for all I cared. "Let thy voice be heard, O thou whose voice resounds like an egregious kettle-drum!"

That firsthand encounter combined with the reading I'd done made me think that whatever the Beats had tapped into, it was a long way from what I had yet experienced. As I dug more deeply into their particular brand of patchwork Buddhism, however, I learned of the unshakable hold the traditions they'd been born into had on them. Shaping everything that was Beat, there was Ginsberg's Judaism—his poem *Kaddish* a memorial not just to his mother but to a whole Jewish world now gone: "as I walk down First toward the Yiddish Theater—and the place of poverty you knew . . ."—and also, maybe more so, Kerouac's Catholicism.

It was an unnerving revelation. When I was in high school Kerouac had been for me, as for many, an archetype of escape; someone who had come from similar stock and circumstances—in fact from the next town over—yet managed to completely reinvent himself. Then I read this: "It was as a Catholic," Kerouac wrote, "that I went one afternoon to the church of my childhood, Saint Jeanne d'Arc in Lowell, Mass., and had a vision of what I must have really meant with 'Beat' anyhow when I heard the holy silence in the church . . . the vision of the word *Beat* as being to mean *beatific*."

I'd always known he had been raised in the same French-Canadian enclave as my father, but I'd never imagined he was like Dad in any other way. But there it was: Kerouac was the original American dharma bum, and yet the faith had made an indelible mark on him too. Suddenly my archetype of escape stood for its opposite, and began to look more and more like my father. No matter how far either man roamed—Buddhism, excommunication, marriage—the church was there looking over his shoulder.

I went back to the index of *How the Swans Came to the Lake*. In that long list of names surely someone had made a clean break, letting the church door close behind him without a second guess—as I liked to believe I had. But even there, in my Buddhist hideout, I began to get nervous. Maybe there was no running away.

That night I joined some friends and went to a party at a farmhouse about a mile north of campus. It was a lovely old place, shaped like a barn with a lopsided porch attached. Much of the paint had chipped off but what remained was still a vibrant blue, spread across the clapboards like veins. As was the case with most of the houses on that side of town, it had once been home to a farming family—the pipes of a rusted jungle gym poked out of the brush that ringed the yard—but now was rented to a group of six or seven undergrads. I didn't know any of them. It was a friend of a friend of a friend kind of party, and it was being thrown as an exercise in collegiate transubstantiation, to turn beer into cash.

A guy with a wispy goatee and a blue baseball cap pulled low over his eyes stood at the door, charging five bucks a head, marking a big black X on every right hand that entered. In the front rooms they had covered the windows with garbage bags, to make the house look empty from the outside. If the police came to investigate a noise complaint, one of the guys who lived there would stand on the front porch and say, "What party?" while three hundred people held their breath on the other side of the door.

We drank beer from red plastic cups and then more beer. There was never any food at a party like this, but the fear that it would be shut down was always present, so from the moment you stepped inside the race was on to get your money's worth. Cup after cup, we got drunk beside the keg on the frozen back porch, drunk crammed in a hallway waiting for the bathroom, drunk leaning against the counter in a kitchen with no furniture but a microwave balanced on a folding chair.

I was doing just that when a girl I didn't know bumped into me. Black hair cropped short, pale skin the color of sandbox sand, she wore thick-soled shoes, high up the ankle, almost boots, that marked her as too cool for this frattish keg party. My soles were thinner by an inch but still she asked me, "Didn't I see you on the bus to Northampton?"

Her name was Maggie, she said, and we started talking. It began with the inevitable question of who studied what, the quick summing up and sizing up, the instant of hoping you've been stuck beside someone interesting.

"Religion," I told her.

She tilted her cup back, taking a big gulp. "Are you?"

"Am I?"

"Religious?"

I took a drink myself. "A long story," I answered, and I must have made a face that said I didn't want to tell it.

"So which ones do you study, all of them or what?"

I might have said that I had spent three hours that afternoon in the Smith library's Buddhist section; or that I was becoming interested in Judaism because of my Hebrew class; or perhaps something about being interested not so much in religions per se as in general theories about them, how they work, why people need them. All of which was true, but suddenly felt inconsequential. Instead, I found myself talking about my parents, about the priest who met the nun and the paradox of their religious vows leading to the creation of their family; about how the promise never to have children made children possible; about *ex damnato coitu* and the unlikely set of circumstances that added up to the koan that is my life.

All the while Maggie nodded and sipped. Then she said, "What's that thing they say? About how he writes?"

"How who writes?"

"God."

"How God writes?"

"Yeah. Shit, what *is* that thing?" She tilted her beer way back, the red cup's white bottom pointing to the ceiling. When she swallowed, her throat bulbed like a hose with a golf ball forced through. Then she smiled and held the cup upside down to show it was empty. "Tip of my tongue," she said, putting her free hand to her forehead. She seemed to wobble a bit.

"Are you okay?"

"Shh! Thinking." She squeezed the skin at the top of her nose. Finally she looked up and shouted triumphantly, like she was on a game show, "Straight with crooked lines! Straight with crooked lines!"

"What?"

"God writes straight with crooked lines. That's your family."

I tried to focus on her. It wasn't easy: the room was spinning, all those red cups lifted to all those red faces. I had been there maybe ninety minutes and was on my fourth or fifth drink. But then there she was: dark-haired and freckled, Boston Irish for sure. Who was she trying to fool with this *Maggie* business? She was a Margaret Mary if ever I saw one. She would have fit right in with all those Dorchester girls forty years ago, climbing aboard a convent-bound train at North Station. I looked down and noticed again her thick-soled boots, their square black toes. Nun's shoes. They made me dizzy.

When I glanced toward my hands I realized they were shaking, and also that I was holding my beer with my thumb in the cup, foam up to my knuckle.

"Are you Catholic?" I asked.

"I was," she said. She lifted her empty cup in a toast. "But fuck that, right?"

"Right," I said, then pulled my thumb out of the beer, reached over to her, and made a wet cross on her forehead, down from her hairline to the space between her eyebrows, then from left to right, a latitude line on the globe of her skull. The movement of it felt like the most natural thing in the world.

"It doesn't wash off," I told her, and she laughed like I was kidding.

After another half hour or so I wandered away from the party—alone. Whether or not the anointing in beer had anything to do with it, at a certain point Maggie decided it was not the time or place to discuss theology. At least not with me.

Just as well. I was done talking, anyway. I somehow managed to cover the mile or so back to campus and stumbled into my dorm room around 2 A.M. When I fell into bed, I remembered the index I had studied that day, all those Christian names, blurry now, as if the paper had been soaked through and dried in the sun.

As I drifted off to sleep I dreamed I was at home, in my parents' kitchen. No one else was around but there on the table were my father's glasses. I picked them up and put them on, then looked at my reflection in the window above the sink. In the dream I had Dad's lips and his chin, as I do when I'm awake, and as I studied the reflection it looked like I had his collar as well—his Roman collar, black and white and choking. I backed away from the window and tried to pull the glasses from my face but could not. They'd become a part of me, joined to the skin.

I woke up with a start. When I opened my eyes I could see the index of that American Buddhist book again, not just remembering it this time, but actually *seeing* it, still blurry, floating in front of me. Then I saw one name as clearly as if it had been written by a lightning strike in the air. I read it aloud, *Thomas Merton*. The name meant nothing to me, but something made me sit up straight and shout it, *Thomas Merton!* Scrounging for a pen, I wrote the name on the back of my hand, just below the thick black X from the party. Then I dropped back onto the bed and let sleep cover me, wondering as my eyes fell shut, *Who?*

The next day I took a detour on my way to the library and went instead to the Smith College bookstore. Playing a hunch, I asked if they had anything by this Thomas Merton, the man who had troubled my sleep and whose name was now an ink stain on my hand.

"Back of the store," the clerk told me. "Religion section."

After a quick scan of the shelves, I saw his name again. It was printed in a dozen different fonts on a score of titles, eight or ten copies of each; a wall of Merton from ceiling to floor. Either his books were being taught in some Smith class that semester or the store had just received a shipment of remainders and was having a two-for-one sale. The first two I looked at—*The Asian Journal of Thomas Merton*, which featured a giant stone Buddha on its cover; then an elegant little volume cryptically titled *Zen and the Birds of Appetite*—made me realize that, of course, I had seen Merton's name not just in the index of *How the Swans Came to the Lake*, but mentioned in a number of books I'd perused those past few weeks in the Buddhism section. When I read the back covers, I learned he was a Catholic priest and that he had lived for twenty-seven years in a monastery in Kentucky, writing books that made him probably the most famous monk since St. Benedict.

Facing that wall of words, I was struck by the sudden realization—struck like a wave slamming into me, almost knocking me down—of my own ignorance. Here I was the son of a priest, the son of a nun, and I thought I knew everything about the church, as if such knowledge came genetically. And yet I knew nothing of this man. It made me wonder: when I rejected my parents' faith, did I even know what I was trying not to be?

I flipped through the *Asian Journal*, Merton's account of the trip he took through India, en route to an international, interreligious monastic conference in Bangkok. In the book's preface I learned he had been propelled on this journey by the spirit of Vatican II and that it was his first and last long trip from his monastery; he died before he was able to return. Then I came to an appendix, the text of a talk he gave in Calcutta, October 1968. Elsewhere in the Catholic world, I thought, my mother had just left her convent, my father his rectory. They were negotiating the need for change in their faith, their lives. So was Merton. Speaking to a gathering of Buddhist and Catholic monks he said:

> The deepest level of communication is not communication, but communion. It is wordless. It is beyond words, and it is beyond speech, and it is beyond concept. Not that we discover new unity. We discover older unity. My dear brothers, we are already one. But we imagine that we are not. What we have to recover is our original unity. What we have to be is what we already are.

I looked again at the Buddha on the cover, then at the pictures throughout. One showed Merton, bald and barrel-chested in his white and black habit, posed with a young and smiling Tenzin Gyatso, the Dalai Lama, who called his new American friend "a Catholic *geshe,*" a learned lama. Then I picked up *Zen and the Birds of Appetite* and read that another Eastern sage, D. T. Suzuki, had said Merton was one of the few Westerners who understood Buddhism at all. *This* was a priest?

When I left the bookstore that day it was not with either of these later Merton books (both written in the 1960s, toward the end of his life), but with his first: *The Seven Storey Mountain.* A thick paperback with a medieval-looking picture on its cover (naked figures hiking a spiral path up a rocky incline shaped like a wedding cake, climbing from purgatory to paradise), it tells the story of his conversion, from agnostic intellectual to baptized believer, and finally to a cloistered monk and writer. I began reading Merton supposing he must be a kind of Catholic Alan Watts—Christian in name only, more a secret Buddhist who just didn't feel like formally switching teams—and so I played the kind of substitution game Watts encouraged: When Merton wrote about "God" I would simply insert Supreme Identity or Ultimate Reality into the sentence, depending on context. When he wrote "church" I would say to myself, "Community, he means community." When he wrote "Christ" I would just put the book down and go for a run.

Yet Merton wrote so well and with so much love—for writing, for living, for God—that I could not turn away for long. And the more I read, the more I realized my substitution game didn't work. Unlike some of the spiritual dabblers I'd been reading, Merton understood that the way to understand another religious tradition was to be fully engaged with his own. I came to accept that when he wrote G O D he meant God and when he wrote C H U R C H he really did mean the church. And the fact that I could not easily dismiss him challenged me to wonder for the first time what those words meant when I used them. Had I been rebelling against God the Father, or merely my father? Were my struggles with the faith theological or psychological, not Christ who was the problem, but Freud? Or could it be that these feelings were not so distinct as I imagined them to be; that questions about God are always questions about family? I wasn't so sure anymore.

I'm still not sure—I write this ten years later and still the best I can do to make sense of the person I was becoming then is to call upon the archaeologist I might have been, to piece together scraps of evidence. They are not hard to find: beside my desk there is the shelf full of Merton's books, most of them bought in the weeks following that initial discovery; their pages folded and falling out; their spines cracked, taped together. Digging deeper, there is the bookmark tucked into the first one purchased, when I was nineteen years old. On the back, there is scrawled handwriting, barely legible though it is my own. While reading this memoir of a monk who died the year my parents met, the story of a convert to the faith I had tried to leave behind, I wrote on that paperboard bookmark words I would have found naïve or laughable only a few months before: "I feel like I've swallowed a hook," I wrote, "like God has got me by a sharp point and a strong line . . ."

Suddenly I was caught, and something was reeling me in. But to where?

THE WORD MADE STRANGE

It is sometimes the sign of a vocation when a person fears
that God may call him; when he prays not to have it and
cannot banish the thought from his mind . . .

—*Signs of a Vocation to Religious Life,* 1955

St. Joseph's Abbey in Spencer, Mas-
sachusetts, is a former dairy farm turned into one of the largest
Catholic monasteries in the country. The monks of Spencer are Cis-
tercians, also known as Trappists, which means their religious observance is among the most strict in the Catholic Church. They live by
the 6th century Rule of St. Benedict, valuing silence, prayer, and obedience above all else. Their monastery is a bastion of the kind of Old
World faith my parents have spent their lives trying to reform, and it is
a place I felt drawn to as if it was a homeland I had never seen.

Late in November of my senior year, I rode a bus from Northampton to Worcester, which was as close as one could get to Spencer without a car. It was Thanksgiving week; most of my friends would be
spending the holiday with their families, but that year I preferred to
avoid the trip back to Tewksbury. I had reached the point at which the
town where I grew up felt entirely foreign to me. From my first
semester on, I had been working my way through school with various
odd jobs around campus—repainting dorm rooms in the summer; in-

stalling exhibits for the university's art galleries in the spring and fall—
so it had been three years since I'd spent more than a week at home.
By then my brother had moved to San Francisco, my sister to Port-
land, Oregon; our parents were alone together for the first time since
those golden days when they were newly married and they believed
the church and the world were changing around them. During my occasional visits, I would often walk into the kitchen and find the two of
them standing in an embrace beside the sink, rocking lightly side to
side, my mother's face against my father's chest. I was pleased to see
it, but it didn't lessen my feeling of not belonging there anymore.

It wasn't just them. Suddenly I felt I didn't want to see anyone who
had known me before I'd been on my own. Maybe I had been spending too much time in library basements; among my hometown
friends, I found it difficult to talk about the things that had become important to me since I had seen them last. My girlfriend at the time was
a woman I had grown up with—in fact, the first time I was aware how
I felt about her was the day of our confirmation. I remember watching
her walk through the church, one girl among dozens in identical flowing robes as we lined up to be blessed by the bishop. I was behind her
in line, and when she turned around after receiving the blessing, a
cross of oil applied just below the hairline, all I could think of was
moving her curls off her forehead to have a fuller view of her newly
anointed face. After high school, we had gone off to different colleges
but had managed to stay together, in part because we were always
sure to be home for holidays. Yet neither to her, nor to my oldest
friends, nor to my parents was I prepared to offer an honest explanation of what I was doing on my way to a monastery, so I was glad I
would not have to see any of them.

It was much easier to sit anonymously and watch the traffic as my
Worcester-bound bus rolled along the Massachusetts Turnpike. The
highway was clogged with travelers heading east, and we didn't reach
the terminal until early in the evening.

When I stepped off, I saw a man standing in the glow of the Peter
Pan/Trailways sign, his silver hair tinted green by the neon. Despite
the chill in the air, he wore his light fall jacket unzipped, holding it

open like a flasher, showing off his black shirt and white plastic collar to everyone who walked by.

"I never wear this getup," he told me when I introduced myself. "But I wanted to be sure you'd recognize me, and the habit can be a bit of a spectacle away from the abbey."

His name was Father David and up until then we had spoken only by phone. A month before, I'd written a letter to St. Joseph's telling whoever received it that I was a Catholic and a student of religion. I explained that reading Thomas Merton had led me to study monasticism, and now I was interested in learning more. I did not say that since that first encounter with Merton a year previous I had felt alternately charmed by and doomed to the life he described, but that was what I thought as I dropped the letter in the mail. My excitement on the way to the mailbox turned to dread the instant the metal slot slammed shut. It could've been the clang of a jail cell. Father David called a week later.

"So what would you like to know?"

"It's not so much what I'd like to *know*," I said, "as what I'm supposed to *be*."

"To be?"

I took a long breath. "I think I might have—a voc—a vocat—."

The possibility that I had a calling to the religious life was an idea I had not spoken aloud before that moment, and even then it felt softened by distance, as if speaking it into a cordless phone—into the mouthpiece, into the air—somehow made me less accountable to all that it implied. Yet the thought that God had something in store for me had lodged in my brain and spread like a cancer, pushing against the walls of my skull. Now the need to say it impaired my ability to form the word. I had to concentrate to get my lips and my teeth and tongue to work together. "*Vo. Ca. Tion.*"

"Of course!" Father David laughed. "That's why I called. I'm the abbey's vocation director."

It was a short, simple, dizzying conversation. I was living by then in a cracked-walled three-story rental with five friends in Northampton. Speaking to a cloistered monk while sitting in my ramshackle collegiate housing, I felt connected to another world. Only the slow calm of his voice reminded me that for him answering questions about the monastic life was an everyday occurrence. It was his job, in fact. With a businesslike manner, he explained the options open to a man who wanted to become a Trappist. Never have I been so aware of free will, or so frightened by it, as when I realized that dropping everything and disappearing behind the cloister wall would be as easy as deciding to do so.

"You'll need to visit for a few days to get started. Do you have any time off from school in the coming weeks?"

That was all it took. Some small part of me had expected the clouds to part, the heavens to open, when I planned my entrance to the monastery, but I might as well have been talking to a travel agent. We settled on an arrival date, the weeks passed, and I boarded the bus. Before I knew it, I was sitting in a monk's Oldsmobile in the green light of the Worcester Peter Pan bus terminal. Next stop Never-Never Land.

To anyone who asked, it was "research."

I never uttered a word about my vocation, neither to my friends nor my family, but my interest in extreme forms of religious life was well known, so my trip to the monastery was taken in stride. My room in Northampton was decorated with macabre medieval paintings and unlikely pictures of the pope: John Paul II in an Indian headdress, in a Mexican mariachi hat, blessing his favorite cycling team. A gaudy Sacred Heart hung above the bed. Three feet tall, in a gilded frame, it was like a parody of the kind that once hung in my grandparents' kitchen in Lowell. In the picture, Jesus' hair hung in flouncy curls; his pink cheeks and long lashes made him look like a drag queen. A heart like a pomegranate dripped blood on his blue blouse. Everyone thought it was a joke, and, in a way, it was. Except that I was completely sincere in my desire to understand devotion to such an image. When I looked at it I wondered, how can something so laughable be deadly serious at the same time?

It was no accident that it was around this time that I began writing.

My head felt full to bursting and there seemed no other way to relieve the pressure. Nor was it a surprise that the idea of vocation—the meaning of it, the fear it inspired—came through in whatever I wrote. In a creative writing class, I began a poem about a priest with the line "Father, your collar too choking-tight . . ." Later in the semester I wrote a short story about a nun called away from her convent when she hears her name in a winter storm's whistle of wind. The first story I published was about a teenage boy in the 1950s attending his prom on the last night before he leaves for seminary. His high school sweetheart traces a cross on the back of his neck as they dance; soft music plays as a thunderstorm rages outside; *earth angel, earth angel, please be mine* . . . It was a story as much about what I imagined of my father's past as what I secretly thought about my future. Writing fiction was good cover for exploring such things.

At the university, I had begun working on my writing with the novelist Julius Lester. I'd sought him out initially not just because I respected his books, but because I'd heard he was a Baptist preacher's son turned Black Power radical who later converted to Judaism. Such a man, I supposed, might understand something of my own work-in-progress spiritual life. When I read in the memoir of his conversion, *Lovesong*, about his early fascination with Merton, I guessed he might also help me make sense of my overlapping interest in writing and religion. He had spent some time in Merton's monastery in Kentucky, in fact, and it was he who told me there was an abbey of the same order only about an hour from Amherst.

"Go out and have a look at the place," Professor Lester told me. "You might not learn anything new about Merton, but you may learn something new about yourself. When you get there just remember that the man's greatness didn't spring just from his *Catholicism* but his *catholicity* . . ."

Professor Lester helped me see that Merton's faith—not the piety of his conversion but the faith that remained unaltered from his years as an atheist intellectual through his baptism to his monastic profession to his death—was a writer's faith; an understanding of divine creation formed by his own acts of creation; a belief that, yes, *en arche ein ho logos,* in the beginning was the word, because for a writer what else could it have been? As I'd learned in my Greek Scriptures class, *logos* does not just mean "word" but "story." In the beginning was the story. That was becoming the creed of my faith as well.

Yet the more I learned about how stories work, the more it seemed to me that the story that was my beginning was now rushing inexorably to a single end. Chekhov once said that if there is a rifle on the wall of a stage set in the first act, it had better go off by the third. That lives are not governed by the logic of plot had not yet occurred to me; because of who and what my parents had been, I was certain I felt the loaded gun of vocation pushed up against my chest. The mark it left became a secret, shameful affliction. Among my friends—philosophy, journalism, and history majors—to have literary aspirations was a well-worn and respected path. But to announce I felt called—fated, condemned—to be a priest? It would have been social suicide.

And so: research. At the time I went to Spencer, I was taking my first stab at writing a long piece of fiction, a novel set in a 14th-century convent. Over beers or in the student lounge, I would explain that monastic life hadn't changed all that much since the Middle Ages, so of course I had to go to a modern monastery to get a feel for it.

"For the book," I would say.

As a child, pedaling my bike past St. William's to spend my collection plate money at the arcade, I had lied to get away from my family's faith. Now I was lying again, trying to find my way back.

We drove past the city limits, into the sleepy town of Spencer and through what felt like twenty miles of trees. The road dipped and we entered a thick fog, as if the forest all around us had been set on fire. I could only see ten feet in front of the windshield in the beam of the headlights, but I knew we were getting close. Over the hum of the engine I heard a church bell toll.

The car pulled to a stop before a stone building with wooden doors and a great tower rising from the fog like a castle in the clouds. My escort dropped me before a darkened doorway and then rushed off with the assurance he would find me later. "Those bells are for Compline," Father David said. "I'm glad we made it in time."

The monks of Spencer gathered for prayer seven times throughout the day—seven "offices"—beginning in the middle of the night, then continuing every three hours, when all activity stopped for the chanting of psalms and the reading of Scripture. For centuries this schedule of intensive prayer has been known as the Liturgy of the Hours, the goal of which is to experience each day as a retelling of the life of Christ. At the Vigil, they wait and watch for the promised coming of the Savior; at daybreak, Lauds, they give thanks for the Incarnation: at the third, sixth, and ninth hours of daylight—Terce, Sext, and None—they recall Jesus' life and works; at Vespers they remember the Crucifixion; and at Compline they resign themselves to sleep, their God to His grave, and wait again for the Resurrection.

I entered the church alone, wandering through one twisting hallway and then another, following voices. With the medieval dark of the place it felt like I was trying to find my way out of a cave, only I was going deeper in. Finally the passageway opened to a high raftered hall. Inside, thirty monks sat across from one another in wooden choir stalls. They were just beginning to chant: *O Lord come to my assistance . . . O God make haste to help me . . .*

Standing close by one of the few candles that lit the nave, Father David adjusted his glasses. In the time it took me to find my way down the hallway, he had apparently parked the car, changed his clothes, and taken his position among the other monks. He was dressed now, as they all were, in a Cistercian choir robe: a floor-length smock like a linen tablecloth, hooded at the top, wide enough in the arms to shoplift a pumpkin. As he and his monastic brothers sang, a draft shook the flames of the candles and the room's only light flickered, making their shadows jump on the walls. Many of the monks kept hoods pulled over their heads, and the cold of the place made the whole getup seem quite reasonable. I took a seat in the visitors' gallery but kept my coat buttoned, pulled my head into the collar, and wished for a hood of my own.

It was over in about twenty minutes: a few sober Gregorian

chants, psalms proclaiming our helplessness and inevitable end, pleas for God to remain steadfast when all else falls away. At times it took the form of a dialogue, one section of monks beseeching their maker *(Hear me when I call, O God of my righteousness . . .)* while the other answered with a divine rebuke *(O you sons of men, How long will you turn my glory into shame?).* Then they all joined together again to sing the Salve Regina, their voices growing louder though the tones sunk low, thirty voices producing a rumble of praise that sounded like the stones of the walls were breathing through them. *Hail, holy Queen, Mother of Mercy . . . our life, our sweetness, and our hope . . .*

When the hymn ended, the lights were extinguished one by one, until there was just a single candle lighting the church. The monks filed past it, each bowing to the altar before disappearing through a door behind the choir stalls.

I began to follow them, and bowed awkwardly at the candle, touching my fingers to my knees, making a right angle at the waist. As I rose up, a hooded figure caught my arm. In the dim light he looked like a grim reaper, towering above me in that thick robe, a bony hand outstretched. Darkness where a face should be.

"Come with me," he said. Only when I peered into the hood did I see that the darkness wore wire-rimmed glasses. It was Father David. "You'll be staying in the postulants' cottage."

He led me out of the church to the cloister walk, a glass-walled hallway that looked over the garden at the heart of the abbey. From there we crossed a small yard with white crosses standing like saplings under the limbs of an ancient oak tree. Then we reached the small stone cottage I would call home for the next few days.

"Vigils are at 3:30; reading and meditation until Lauds at 6:30, then Mass, then breakfast," Father David said. "Brother Chris will be by about eight o'clock to put you to work."

With that, he started back toward the cloister. No moon that night, no stars, his white robe seemed the only source of light. He was ten paces away when he turned and grinned under his hood.

"God bless you, brother," he said. "We're glad you're here."

• • •

For the week that followed I lived by their schedule. Every morning after Mass, Brother Chris appeared at the door of the postulants' cottage with my assignment for the day. He was a burly man with a boy's face that hadn't seen much of the world; he had entered the monastery as a teenager thirty years before. Six foot four, ruddy Irish cheeks, it was easy to imagine him turning a field back in the Old Sod. When the abbot decided early on he would not study for the priesthood, he became the de facto manager of the grounds. He knew every square foot of the place, and kept in his square blond head a running list of repairs and maintenance that needed attending to.

As on the farm the abbey had been, the day's work at Spencer was often determined by the weather. That first morning, the fog of the evening before had turned to rain, so when I met him he was waiting for me with a mop in hand and a cheery grin bulbing his cheeks.

"Morning, brother! Today we mop!" Whenever he opened his mouth a voice as big as he was boomed into the room. He blushed at the sound of it, as if he kept forgetting about the vow of silence that preserved the monastic calm.

Inside the cloister, Brother Chris pointed down the long glass-walled walkway to the church. "There are four halls like this, then the chapter room, then the refectory, the kitchen, and the infirmary. Shouldn't take but a couple of hours."

"What should I do then?"

"Don't worry about that. By the time you're done, it will all need doing again!" He walked away chortling at the inevitability of it all. This much was certain of life at the abbey: there would be bells and there would be work.

I was mopping all week. With a wheeled bucket and a wet-floor sign I made my way up the length of one cloister walk, then another. The monks, now dressed in the daytime habit—white robe with black hooded apron and cape attached, all held together by thick leather belt—passed by en route to the library, the church, or the kitchen. They nodded and grinned their greetings, never using actual words, since technically, according to the Rule, they were not permitted to speak. Occasionally one monk or another would pass with a puzzling hand signal and a wink. They had an elaborate sign language system consisting of several hundred gestures. A hand swiped over the face meant, "Beautiful." Fingers tapped together and pulled apart meant, "Stop."

When I finished the cloister, I moved into the chapter room, where meetings of the full community convened. It resembled a hotel banquet hall, just four walls and an empty floor roughly the size of a basketball court. Next, it was on to the refectory, where the monks took their meals, and the kitchen, in which a dozen brothers manned giant steel vats producing Trappist Preserves, the jams and jellies they shipped around the world and sold in supermarkets across the country. Complete with a logo showing a monk mixing a cauldron over a fire, the little jars were the abbey's main source of income, and, with jam available at every meal, an obvious source of pride.

Finally it was on to the infirmary, where a number of the most senior monks now lived full-time. They shuffled down the hall in slippers and winter hats, cardigan sweaters pulled over their habits. I mopped thin stripes along the floor, careful to let one dry before beginning another.

The work was mind-numbingly monotonous, but that was the point. *Laborare est orare,* the monks like to say. To work is to pray. Wetting the mop, wringing the mop, slathering the mop around the tile floor, a line from Scripture kept coming to mind: *Wash me and I will be whiter than snow, wash me and I will be whiter than snow . . .* Even when the water in my bucket was less snow-white than beef-stew-brown, I mopped to the cadence of this biblical mantra, my rhythm disturbed only by the bell that announced Terce, the midmorning prayer session also known as "a monastic coffee break."

Around the abbey all work stopped and I joined eight monks in the common room for plainchant and jelly sandwiches. A brother passed out photocopied pages worn soft as satin from daily use, and we chanted psalms with the tools of our various labors—oven mitts, tape measures, hammers, drills—waiting on the table or against the wall. When the prayers were finished, I grabbed my mop and took the long way back through the cloister, letting the words of a closing hymn guide me to my bucket:

> Love, light up our mortal frame
> till others catch the living flame . . .

The days slipped by. Few choices to make, no need for conversation, I was a cell of a larger organism with only automatic functions to perform. Wake pray eat pray work pray sleep pray, all of it as natural as breathing.

The only break from the routine came on Thursday: Thanksgiving.

I took my meals in the guesthouse, which was booked solid all year long by visitors making retreats of several days to a week. There was a usual crowd who had been making a retreat over Thanksgiving weekend for the past few years—most of them were priests affiliated with colleges back in Boston, so they had a long fall break just as I did.

In the refectory the abbey's full-time residents were strictly vegetarian, but for their guests they cooked a big fat bird, brown as molasses, as well as the usual holiday fare: yams and stuffing, beer and wine, fresh baked rolls and every variety of jam imaginable. A couple of the monks joined us, and judging by their meatless plates it was more for hospitality's sake than for turkey, though one did pop open a can of Budweiser and admit with a wink that his brothers didn't know what they were missing.

At dinner, when my tablemates heard what I studied we talked of Merton and poetry and vocations, how and when each knew he should be a priest. They were older men, close to my father's age, though all of them were religious order clergy rather than diocesan, so they didn't know his name. Talking with these men I could understand something of the collegiality, the brotherly attachment my father to this day feels toward men still in the priesthood. And, in me, they seemed to see both a bolsterer of the decisions they had made and an embodiment of the road not taken: a would-be monk and the son who never was.

At one point in the conversation, a bearded literature professor from Boston College left the table briefly and came back with a small volume of poems by Gerard Manley Hopkins, the 19th-century English Jesuit. He flipped it to a poem called "The Woodlark," in which the poet listens to the call of a bird and imagines he can make out words in the sounds. "Sweet-joy," he hears in the birdsong:

> With a sweet joy of a sweet joy,
> Sweet, of a sweet, of a sweet
> Of a sweet—a sweet-sweet—joy.

"That's what it's like," the priest said as he put the book in my hand. "You'll love it like I do." I wasn't sure if he meant the poetry or the priesthood until he added, "It's quite a life. Sweet joy. It really is."

Despite my fears that the monastery would be a prison from which I would never escape, "sweet joy" is just what I felt there. I savored every moment in the cold of the cloister, even while mopping. Each night I woke eagerly at 3 A.M. to make it to Vigils. And in the morning, having prayed in darkness until exiting the church following Communion, it was easy to believe that God had brought the dawn. Later in the day, I would sit down and write in my spiral notebook, trying to preserve on paper the peace I felt there, so I would not forget it when I was back in the world.

Only once did I try to express as much to someone else. In the short interval between dinner and Vespers one evening, I borrowed a few pages of St. Joseph's stationery from Father David and sat down to write what I intended to be a love letter to my girlfriend. I was sorry we hadn't seen each other over the holiday, I wrote, but something had brought me to the abbey that I couldn't explain to myself, let alone to her. I wrote that though I didn't know exactly what I meant when I used such words, I thanked God for her. I did not write that I did so mainly because I believed she was the one thing keeping me tethered to the life I had known. Without her, I was certain, I would slip away into the silence of this place, and I was not yet sure I could survive the loneliness that would follow.

Then the church bell rang and all such feelings fell away. It was time to pray again, and that was what mattered. The simple recitation of psalms had become almost narcotic, lulling and addictive. To sit in the cold of the monastery church with my attention focused only on saying the words was to forget, for as long as I could keep the syllables coming, that I had people and responsibilities waiting for me back in the world. In my Greek class I had recently learned the difference between *chronos* and *kairos:* time measured in minutes and hours, and time experienced as moments of revelation. This life, it seemed to me, was *kairos* all the time.

The days passed quickly. I missed the abbey before it was time to go.

As we set off to the bus terminal Sunday afternoon, Father David asked me how I liked my first taste of monastic life.

"It's been wonderful," I said. "I thought when I left I wouldn't have any romantic notions about being a monk. But really it's been everything I hoped for."

As soon as I said it, I doubted myself. Was it really? In my mind, I could hear my Hebrew teacher teasing me: *Lo, aval! Why always so complicated?* But this *was* complicated. I had been raised to think of the celibate religious life as an unhealthy perversion of the Christian ideal—an artifact of medieval politics, a papal power play designed to keep subordinates in line—and yet the attraction I felt to it was real. Wasn't it? Watching the trees roll by, moving through the no-man's-land between the monastery and the world, for the first time I felt something of the conflict my parents have known every day of their lives.

We drove on through the woods, wending the tidy streets of Spencer. After a few minutes of silence, Father David spoke of the events that had led him to the abbey. Before taking his monastic vows, he told me, he'd been a missionary priest in Japan. He had a friend there, a young man who had died young and whom he missed dearly. "Oh boy I can't wait to get to heaven," Father David said, grinning like a child. "Then I'll get to see him again." The way pleasure in the memory turned to wistfulness in his voice made me think of lost love.

When we reached the station, I forced myself to admit what I'd been pondering since we passed through the monastery gate. "Honestly, being at the abbey felt so right I don't think I trust it."

Father David tilted his head and stared at me like I had just questioned the existence of the sun; a look that said, how could you not trust something so obviously true?

"All is grace," he said. Then he smiled sadly, as if he felt sorry for my unbelief.

When I got back to Northampton everything had changed. The town was louder and brighter, the shops and bars and coffee shops I had frequented now seemed overcrowded and unnecessary. Even at home there I couldn't escape the sense of excess. The house had always been louder, brighter, and more crowded than necessary. Six of us lived there, all of us undergraduates; fairly often we had raucous parties that broke furniture and left beer bottles filled with cigarettes in every room. Now, though, it seemed a world into which I no longer fit.

It was unlikely there had been a party while I was away, but still the place was a mess. The sink was full of dishes; the kitchen wastebasket overflowed onto the floor. A week previous, I might have left the trash there, but fresh from the monastery, glowing with the "sweet joy" of communal life, I washed plates and scrubbed pans, humming the tune to which the monks had sung the last lines of Compline: *Into your hands, O Lord, I commend my spirit* . . . They were Jesus' last words, and also a line from the Book of Psalms. I wiped down the counter and swept the floor, thinking about the way one story becomes another, each changing the other's meaning. Jesus' death becomes the blueprint for a monk's life. Words spoken at an execution in the burning sun are sung two thousand years later in the cold of a monastery church. I sang them to myself as I gathered empty cans of Pabst Blue Ribbon, rinsed them with water, and chucked them into the recycling bin.

That night I woke before dawn, afflicted with a kind of spiritual jet lag. I had classes the next morning, but for an hour or more I lay awake staring at the bloody Sacred Heart on the wall above me. I didn't bother now with musings about the tension between the seriousness and the silliness of religious kitsch. Instead I thought only, *The monks are singing; why am I in bed?*

From then on, I tried my best to follow the prayer schedule I had internalized at the abbey. A few weeks before, for my twenty-first birthday, my father had given me the breviary his parents had presented to him at his ordination. The breviary is a portable Liturgy of the Hours, a four-volume prayer manual that breaks the day down into hymns and Scripture appropriate for the hour and the season. Priests used to call it "the wife"—because it nagged you, kept you in line, and yes, even provided a little comfort now and then. When my father was my age, priests and seminarians were required to pray with it. For me it became a compulsion. Each day on campus, I snuck away between classes to read aloud from its onionskin pages. Filled with Latin in black and red type, it was an ancient text in which all answers might be revealed.

One day in December I came home early from campus, recited the prayers for the ninth hour, None, and stretched out on a couch in the living room, the only warm spot in the house. It was turning to winter in New England, and inside it was as cold as out. Already that season a plastic bottle of olive oil had frozen to paste in the pantry; coffee went cool after two minutes on the kitchen table. Beside the couch there was a waist-high metal box that was the one source of heat for three floors, a gas heater whose pilot light flickered and died at the slightest draft. Every night my housemates and I would crowd around it to warm our hands over the flame before going to bed.

No one else was home yet that afternoon so I drifted in and out of sleep in the room's rare quiet, thinking about the monastery and my parents. I wondered if they had made some kind of devil's deal when they married, if when they took a priest and a nun from the church, God had demanded something in return. Only then did the full weight of what I was considering hit me: if I was going to be a monk, I realized, I would never be a father.

I looked up at the ceiling and said, "Is that what you want from me?"

In the silence, I heard nothing but the heater's oily hiss. It sounded like an answer.

Yes.

I put a hand over my mouth as the feeling washed over me—*I will never be a father*—and hurt with the loss of children I could not even imagine. Later, I would tell my girlfriend God wanted me to be alone. Lying on the couch, I tried to find a way of expressing the idea that might make sense to her. It barely made sense to me, though; making her understand seemed so impossible I decided not to try. Instead, I just ended up staring into space in that cold room. I watched as the window light shifted from the floor to the walls and then was gone, until there was only the heater's blue glow.

I returned to Spencer that January, to spend the month between semesters inside the monastic enclosure. This time, there for a longer stay, I would be more fully part of the place, working with the novices, allowed to sit and pray with the monks in their choir stalls.

When Merton entered his monastery fifty years before, in the shadow of the war, there were thousands of young men leaving the world to pursue religious life. In the mid-'90s at Spencer, there was just a handful. I had seen them during my previous stay, noticing the crisp way they bowed to the altar as they left the church after Compline. They were all a few years older than me but with their shaved heads and hoodless white novice robes they looked like overgrown altar boys with summer haircuts.

In truth they were far more experienced than me. Each of them had gone to college and then supported himself in the world: Brother Thomas had worked on Wall Street. Brother Sebastian had been a pharmacist in Louisiana. Brother Moses sported a beatnik's Vandyke beard and kept his own counsel; I never learned a thing about him other than the quality of his silence, but there was a solemnity to his devotion that felt formed by knowledge beyond his years. They were all men certain in their faith and their vocations. Meeting them my first day back, I felt like an impostor.

Nevertheless I fell easily into the monastic routine. Up before dawn, two hours of plainchant in church, an hour of reading, back to church for Lauds and Mass, then I tended to Brother Chris's work assignment—"Today we rake!" "Today we dig!" "Today we move five hundred folding chairs!"—until the bell rang out and it was time to chant again.

For the first few days I had company in the cottage, a man of about twenty-nine preparing to enter the monastery the following month. Inside the cloister and out he wore a New England Patriots' jacket, which combined with his crew-cut round head and jockish goatee would have pegged him for a meathead fratboy had I met him under any other circumstances. When he formally became a postulant he would take a new religious identity, but for the time being the monks simply added "Brother" to his given name: Brother Larry.

Brother Larry told me he worked as a short-order cook in one of the struggling former mill towns not far from Worcester. All that was left to do before he became a monk was to sell or give away his remaining possessions, close out his apartment, and work a few more shifts—not for the extra money, of course, but because the restaurant would be stuck without him. I asked him how he knew, how he had become certain, that the monastery was right for him. Whether he'd misheard the question or had simply tried to read between the lines I can't be sure, but mustering all the intensity his cherub cheeks would allow, he locked his eyes on mine and intoned, "Just. Pray."

Later, when Father David asked Brother Larry if he was happy that the date of his entry to the abbey was fast approaching, he grinned and squinted, nodding as he searched for words adequate to express his feelings. Finally he said, "Oh, I'm happy-happy," and the uncomplicated glee in his face made me wonder if I had ever felt happy-happy about anything in my life.

A week after my arrival, a Nor'easter came in before Vespers and blew hard against the windows of the postulants' cottage, dumping ten inches of snow in a matter of hours, with chest-deep drifts collecting in the odd angles of the monastic architecture. It had blown itself out by Vigils, so we all gathered as usual in the church and dedicated our psalms to those who might have been caught in the storm. At daybreak, the sun glared on the icy fields that sloped away from the abbey.

The crosses in the monks' graveyard stood buried to their heads; the cloister windows were so well covered we might have been inside an ant farm, looking out from a narrow tunnel behind the glass.

Just after breakfast, Brother Chris appeared in the cottage doorway with a sharp-edged icebreaker and a metal snow scoop in hand.

"Morning, brother! Today we shovel!"

"I had a feeling," I said.

He kept the icebreaker for himself and gave the shovel to me. "North side of the abbey's all plugged up. Gotta clear the exits. Fire codes, brother. Fire codes!"

When I reached the back entrance to the cloister, Brother Sebastian was already hard at work. No longer in his novice's hoodless robe, he wore deep blue dungarees, baggy in the seat and the knees, with a quilted black jacket zipped to the chin. From the moment he saw me he talked nonstop. The sun kept me warm though the wind blew squalls around us, and all the while came this great gush of words from my workmate's mouth. He talked mainly about not talking.

"Some of the brothers make a big deal about the silence here but jeez that's something I've never been able to get a hold of you just experience so much there's always something bubbling up . . .

"Like on Good Friday," he said. "On Good Friday we have a procession through the cloister you know like Our Lord's march to Golgotha all of us in our bare feet—" His eyes widened behind his glasses. "Our bare feet! Can you imagine! Nobody and I mean nobody sees my feet.

"I did it like everybody else and it wasn't so bad but still how do you go through something like that and not talk to somebody about it . . ."

I focused on my shoveling but didn't want my future monastic brother to think I was ignoring him, so I found a rhythm of scrape and scoop and nod to Sebastian, scrape and scoop and nod to Sebastian, which kept me working at a steady pace and seemed to add punctuation to his sentences.

"It's a good thing we have spiritual directors" scrape and scoop and nod "boy if I couldn't talk to Reverend Father about that kind of stuff wooo" scrape and scoop and nod "I'd just about burst last week he

told me my interior life was like a big clump of overcooked spaghetti"
scrape and scoop and nod "all these strands boiled too long they got
all stuck together" scrape and scoop and nod "he told me I need to get
them separated to figure out what it is that has got me in such a
knot . . .

"You know trying to make sense of what God wants from me is a
bit like shoveling in the wind," he said. "I work and I work and I feel
like I've cleared a path only to look back and see that it's all covered
over again it's like I think I've gotten somewhere but then there's
nothing but white behind me like I'm right where I started . . ."

I scraped and scooped and nodded through two hours of this, cutting across a field of snow up to my knees. By the time the bell rang
for Terce, we had dug a trench as long as the shadow of the bell tower.
When we reached the iron and wood door to the cloister and brushed
away the last powdered inches, Brother Sebastian finally stopped talking for a moment and looked at me.

"Hey you know I probably shouldn't say this"—he paused again
and we both stood helpless as a snowdrift fell like an avalanche, bury-
ing our boots, the doorway, the stairs—"but you have got *priest* written all over your face."

That seemed to be the general consensus. With vocations to the
priesthood at an all-time low, I was treated at the monastery like an
NBA draft pick. The brothers made me feel welcome, even loved, but
I suspect this reception had less to do with me than with the fact that
any new interest in monasticism was celebrated as an affirmation of it.
It was not for nothing that whenever I mopped the floor in the infirmary one of the elderly monks would pat me on the arm as he walked
by. As it had been for the priests and nuns my parents knew in their
adolescence, there was only one way these men could be sure that the
life they had chosen would not die with them.

And like my father before me, I discovered that when it came to
priests, I was eager to please. As a group, the men of Spencer were the
kindest, most sincere and honest I had ever met. They also seemed
genuinely pleased with their circumstances—pleased in a daily, glad-

to-be-alive way. To share, even for a short time, in the life they lived was a gift; it made me believe, despite my knee-jerk skepticism, what Father David had told me, that all is grace.

Yet the longer I stayed at the abbey, the more difficult it became to ignore the obvious. The more I thought about what it was I was experiencing there, the more everything that made this place different from my life back in Northampton began to feel like a lie—perhaps not a deception, but certainly not the whole truth. At one point I walked down the hill from the monastic enclosure to the abbey gift shop—there is, of course, a gift shop, which sells all manner of Catholic tchotchkes and two dozen kinds of jam—and I bought a postcard to send to my mother. It was only when I wrote her first name in the address line that I realized the only times I had heard women spoken of while I was there had been during the nightly singing of the Salve Regina.

> *Hail, Holy Queen, Mother of Mercy . . .*
> *To you do we cry we poor banished children of Eve.*
> *To you do we send up our sighs, mourning and*
> *weeping in this valley of tears . . .*

That, it seemed, was what this kind of religious life came down to: trying to get from Eve to Mary, original sin to impossible perfection. For all the beauty of the abbey and the sincere efforts of the men I had met there, it rested on divisions born of the idea that this world is nothing but a waiting room. The old catechetical bifurcations—man and woman, spirit and flesh, the Kingdom of Heaven and "this valley of tears"—had been played down by the Catholics since the reforms of Vatican II, but still they could be seen in the young monk's embarrassment at the thought of showing his feet, in Father David's eagerness to reach the hereafter to be reunited with his friend. Everywhere I looked I was reminded that as far as the church was concerned, life is merely a trial that must be endured in all its fleshy indignities—naked toes, untimely death—for the sake of the eternal, spiritual reward.

Not only were the monks' days divided, I began to think, so were their lives. Within the monastery walls it was possible to maintain the illusion that the world of women and bodies and sex didn't exist, yet the only true break occurred within the men themselves. Perhaps someone with unambiguous, unfailing faith could explore such a rift and find a divine spark hiding inside. My faith was neither. What would happen if I stayed?

On one of my last nights in Spencer, I prayed for a sign. Something that would make me feel, if not "happy-happy" like Brother Larry, then at least not frozen by ambivalence about this place and what being there meant to me. If I was ever going to make sense of it, I decided, it would be at Compline. In my weeks at the abbey, the last office had become my favorite. The peace of the darkened church felt like falling backward into God's arms. And when we sang together, *"Into Your hands, O Lord, I commend my spirit . . ."* it was a moment at which anything seemed possible.

It may have been the tricks darkness can play on the eye sometimes, or else the peculiar monastic sleep schedule, or perhaps the cumulative effect of what by then had been hundreds of hours spent chanting psalms and hymns, but I had begun to see things while we prayed. There was something to the movement of the candlelight, the way it jumped in the drafty church, that made images appear in the shadows like flickering silent films. Sometimes it was a vision of myself dancing, moving like some sort of tai chi master or a slowly whirling dervish, both arms outstretched, spinning like the earth around the sun over the shining tile floor. Other times I saw a hooded face in the splash of light against the polished wood of the choir stall. At first it looked like a figure straight from the comic books that were my earliest scripture, sunken eyes in a skull barely covered with skin, but as I stared and as the psalms rolled on—"Teach us to number our days . . ." "The bones you have crushed will rejoice . . ."—I saw that the face was my own as it might be if I became a monk and remained in this place forty years or more.

That evening I looked away from the glow of candle flame, afraid of what I might see. Instead, I stared up at the crucifix that hung above the altar, at the tortured man who had brought my parents together, making my life possible. How was it, I wondered, that a church with a body at its very beginning, a faith with a body as its most potent symbol, could come to so distrust the flesh?

Studying the cross as best I could in the dim light, my mind wandered and I imagined I was running across a desert. I could see a figure in the distance. As I approached, I saw it was Christ, down from the cross but still half-naked, as if he had just emerged from the tomb. I ran on and soon I was standing in front of him, not the frilly blushing Jesus of the Sacred Heart that hung above my bed; a bleeding, beaten man. He reached toward me, but before his hand met mine, he had become an infant, and I was holding him in my arms. He grabbed my finger with a fat baby fist.

At my side the monks began stirring. Compline was over. I hadn't noticed when the psalms ended and the Salve Regina began. Now the church bell was bonging and bonging, telling us it was the start of the Great Silence, time for the monks to return to their cells.

One by one they stood and formed a line leading toward the altar. I took my place behind them and saw that at the front each man was bowing to the abbot, a mustachioed monk wearing a large pectoral cross. Holding a holy water dispenser that looked like a gold-plated ice-cream scoop, he splashed a few drops on each brother as they passed, and then on me, the end of the line.

I was about to leave, to head back through the cloister to my cottage, but something stopped me. I had felt close to something the moment before the bell rang, and like someone desperately trying to get back to sleep to finish a happy dream, I figured all I had to do to experience it again was go back where I had been. I returned to my spot at the rear of the church, knelt, crossed myself, and prayed. To understand what I was doing there. To know what it was that I was supposed to learn. How could I feel called to be something that would shut me off from half of life, from women, from fatherhood, from sex? I thought of my mother and my father and my Great-Uncle Fred. Of all the failed priests and runaway nuns who had passed through our home. Of faith and hope and bodies tied in a knot. Dear God, I prayed, couldn't you for once make something simple?

"Please," I said.

For a moment there was only silence, but then I heard a voice above me, an answer to all my prayers. The biblical cliché for such pronouncements is that it comes in the kind of "still, small voice" heard by the prophet Elijah. This one rang out like an Irish whisper.

"You don't belong here," it said.

Just a simple, obvious statement, but I felt a flood of relief wash over me.

No, I thought, I don't.

Then I felt a hand on my shoulder. I opened my eyes. White and black habit, thick leather belt, big blond head. It was Brother Chris.

"Yeah really sorry, brother," he said, "but no one allowed in the church after Compline." He shrugged, lifting his thick arms into the air. "It's the rules."

I stood and walked with him out of the church. When we reached the cloister, he put a hand to his mouth and tried to speak softly, without much success. "Weather report says more snow tonight, brother. Tomorrow we shovel again!"

Part Five

REVELATION

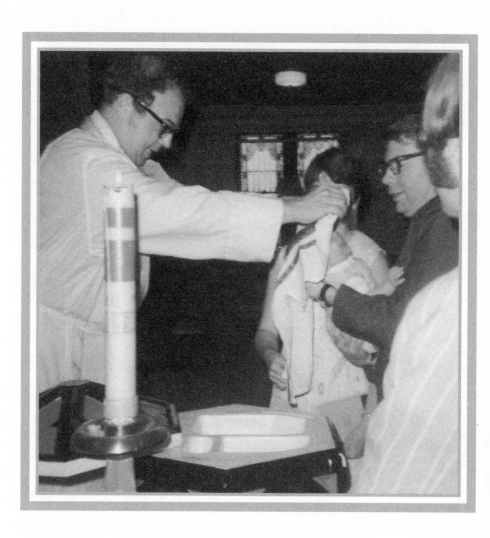

SMOKE AND MIRRORS

One Christmas soon after college, I went with my parents to Midnight Mass at St. Patrick's in Lowell, not too far from where my father grew up. Lowell is a perpetually recovering mill town, never quite getting it right, in its churches or anywhere else. Recently, though, an old friend of theirs had taken over as pastor at St. Patrick's and had begun to turn the place around.

Father Dominic George Spagnolia—my parents' fellow traveler in the Roxbury days; one of the priests who married them, damn the consequences—had returned to active ministry after a twenty-year leave of absence. He had left the priesthood in 1974 over a disagreement with the archdiocese and had been happy enough to pursue second and third careers—managing nursing homes, owning an inn on Cape Cod—until the higher-ups saw things his way. That he had spent a year fighting cancer in the early '90s and had to close his inn as a result made the decision to return to the church an easier one, but mainly he'd just felt it was time to come back.

I had been hearing Father Spagnolia's name for years. My parents referred to him only by the single syllable, "Spag." They said it with a grin or a nod, satisfied by the very sound of it. Dinner table discussion of an out-of-touch papal decree or any other sort of ecclesiastical arrogance would always hit the same note: *I'd like to see what old Spag would do about this.* His name alone was a quick jab at the church hierarchy, sticking it to them but getting away with it, as he always did, like slapping a bull on the ass and then jumping over the fence.

I'd met him for the first time a few years before, at the party held for my parents' twenty-fifth wedding anniversary. In a room full of ex-priests and their wives, Spag stood out in his Roman collar and black clericals as if he were wearing a suit of armor. But that's not what made him the center of attention.

He was midstory when I sat down at his table. I'd heard some of it before: starting in the late '60s, Spag had pressed the archdiocese to demolish and replace the falling-down parochial school in the lot behind St. Francis de Sales.

"Cardinal Cushing was going to do it," Spag said. "He was a liar and a thief, of course, but we had an understanding. You'd go to see him, make your pitch, and he'd say 'That's a wonderful idea, George. Just go down the hill to the business office and tell them what you need.' The minute you're out the door, he'd be on the phone, 'Hey, Spagnolia's coming down to see you. The guy's a nut! Don't give him anything.' But at least you *knew* it. You knew Cushing wanted to give you the run-around. You knew that down the hill was where the pitch mattered, so you could still get things done.

"But then Cushing died," Spag said. Years went by, bricks fell into the driveway, and the new archbishop, Cardinal Humberto Medeiros, did nothing.

"So I just pitched a tent out there on the cardinal's lawn," Spag said. He notified the press that he had begun a protest and fast in front of the Archbishop's Residence, just up the hill from the seminary where he had taken his vow of obedience. Before the photographers arrived, a couple of kids from the parish joined him in his tent. It was for their sake he was there, after all, and even if the cardinal could ignore the nut in the Roman collar, how could he ignore them?

"Whenever Medeiros walked by I stuck my hand through the flap to let him know I was still there," Spag said. "I wanted to remind him how I felt about prelates who wouldn't build new schools in Roxbury because the landscaping bill in Brighton was too high. I think he thought I was waving."

Spag was the kind of priest I always imagined my father would have been had he been able to return to the active ministry; the kind of priest willing to work within the system, but never afraid to speak his mind. Twenty years before, for example, during his last confrontation with the cardinal, Spag was told he would be removed from St. Francis de Sales. He could have any other position he wanted, Medeiros insisted, but in Roxbury Spag was making too much trouble. Forget it, Spag said. If he had to leave Roxbury, he would leave altogether. "I am very sorry to hear that, my brother," the cardinal told him. He reached to shake Spag's hand, to wish him well and give his blessing, but Spag backed away. "Your Eminence," he said, "the world is full enough with empty signs and gestures without us adding to them." He'd left the Archbishop's Residence, and the priesthood, with the cardinal's hand hanging in the air.

Now that he was back, I was anxious to see him in action, to see if the man I'd been hearing about my whole life still had left in him some of the same old fire. I went to the Christmas Eve service eager to see him preach.

That he knew a thing or two about exile came in handy at St. Patrick's. It was a parish made up of refugees, of the formerly stateless, the formerly powerless, now gladly filling to capacity a depressed city and a church emptied by white flight to the suburbs. Of the several hundred families that made up St. Patrick's, 350 were Vietnamese and Cambodian, the newest immigrant groups to occupy the section of Lowell called the Acre, which used to be where the Greeks lived, before them the Irish; always it had been a part of town outsiders knew to steer clear of. Not Spag: his first summer there, he had walked through the housing projects that ringed the church wearing shorts and sandals like some kind of beach bum St. Francis. Trash blew in from every direction, stuck to the low fence that enclosed the churchyard like bugs on a screen, but as far as Spag was concerned he was home. As soon as he arrived he set about raising money for a $1.4 million renovation.

By Christmas, it had begun to show. Outside, the church displayed the same drab stonework set in place eighty years ago by Irish labor-

ers; but inside, patches of Southeast Asian pastels brightened the surrounding gray. Jesus was saffron yellow at the start of the half-relief
Stations of the Cross on the wall of a small side chapel. Moving
through the palette with his torment, he was painted green as jade on
the Via Dolorosa. By Golgotha he was Krishna blue. It was not the
usual *Via Crucis,* and it would not be the usual Mass.

In white cassocks like bathrobes with hoods, Vietnamese and Cambodian deacons, lectors, and altar servers led the procession to the
altar. Spag followed, swinging a censer on a silver chain, filling the
aisle and then the pews with the chalky smoke of incense. Bald and
spotty-headed, pudgy beneath his vestments, he seemed every few
paces to step from the clouds. All the while, like a chorus of polyglot
angels, he, his servers, his deacons, and the whole of St. Patrick's sang
Gloria in Excelsis Deo in Latin, English, and Vietnamese.

Next to me a teenager pointed a video camera toward the center
aisle. His free eye shut tight, his camera arm steady, he seemed to be
concentrating on the job at hand. But his mother wouldn't leave him
alone. Talking nonstop, standing on the kneeler to reach the boy's ear,
the tiny woman sputtered in Khmer, a rush of sounds with just one
discernible word: *Spag, Spag.*

"Make sure you get Father Spag," I supposed she was saying, as my
own mother might. "Can you see him? Is he there? Make sure you get
Spag in the picture."

Her son's answer came in clear, impatient English. "Shhh. I'm
trying."

His mother cut him off, with sharpened whispers now. Nagging
sounds the same in any language. Naturally, he back-talked, really asking for it, but within these walls he was safe from a smack in the head.

"Sorry, but the light sucks," he snapped. "And there's too much
smoke!"

When they reached the altar, members of the procession turned to
face the crowd, then fanned out diagonally to Spag's left and right,
making the old priest the tip of a human arrow. For a moment, he
stared out at his congregation, then called to them, simply, nasal-
voiced: "Hello!"

"Hello Father Spag!" the church answered.

He raised a hand in front of his face as if to sign a cross, then waved it comically instead, coughing and pushing the smoke from his face. It was classic Spag: using the incense to make an entrance, then tweaking it once he'd arrived; a mix of irreverence and devotion.

"Ah!" I heard from all sides. You could feel the place smile.

"It's Christmas!" Spag laughed. "Let's pray!"

And we did. The smoke of incense has a way of transforming the world. Changing the smell, the texture, the substance of the air, it can inspire piety even in the godless. Breathe it in deeply; it's bittersweet and thick as exhaust, nearly like the clouds of pot smoke I remember walking through in my dormitory days, and nearly as narcotic. Around me six hundred heads bowed as one, six hundred heads as synchronized as two eyes falling shut.

The Mass's first reading was given in Vietnamese, the second in Khmer, the gospel in English, and then came Spag's turn, rising from his throne and walking into the center aisle to preach.

He gave the kind of sermons people hold on to. The gist of it had been printed up in bright orange sheets stacked at the back, next to church bulletins, color-coded by language—hot pink for Khmer, lime green for Vietnamese, English on plain white. The words were no less perfect for being standard tropes.

"Christmas fills us with an attitude of joy and peace which you and I as a Christian people try to capture all year long. The very air is filled with all those good things which if made a part of our everyday living would not only change us but, in truth, would change the world.

"One of the names given to Jesus at Christmastime is Emmanuel, which means 'God with us.' Yet God's presence is not an external reality pulling strings, cajoling, and pushing us in one direction rather than another. No, our God's presence is an internal power in which He gently moves us with the gift of His life to a deeper union with Himself and each other.

"In the midst of a world which does not know the Gospel of Jesus, the Christian is to stand as a sign of contradiction. In the midst of a world filled with lies and deceit, the Christian is to stand for Truth. In a world which is unable to see beyond its own selfish interest, the Christian stands as a light leading to a love which the world refuses to make its own."

New life, new light, new love, a new world; in the Gospel according to Spag, that was the meaning of Christmas, that was the heart of Christ. It didn't matter so much how or why Jesus got here, he told us, what mattered most at Christmas was what always matters most to God: *What now?*

All eyes were on him. All ears too. Simultaneous translations began all around me; the camera boy whispered to his mother as he filmed.

When the sermon ended, Spag turned and walked silently to the front of the church. He sat for a moment in the oversized chair behind the altar, slumped like a prizefighter, victorious but spent. Soon he was up with his censer once more, swinging it forward and back, left to right, consecrating the air for Communion. Smoke-and-mirrors time again; a spell of transformation.

Next to me my father's eyes closed slowly. His right index finger slid up under the rim of his glasses and traced a line across the top of his cheek. Maybe just an itch, maybe smoke in his eye, but the finger moved lightly, more a wipe than a scratch. His chest rose with a long inhale, then dropped lower than it had been, breath released like air from a tire. When his eyes opened again, they settled on Spag, now standing in a fog at the focal point of the church. The two priests seemed to nod to each other through the haze, across the rows of pews that separated them, across the altar that had come to mark the boundary between the choices they had made.

It was that moment, and moments like it, that sharpened my interest in telling stories about faith. Seeing the ways in which tradition— always mediated, often scripted, by definition formulaic—could serve as context for interactions that were spontaneous, unexpected, ultimately mysterious, I became more aware of the paradox of belief, of the ways lives and stories with no apparent connection to our own can nonetheless shape who we are. Since my time in Spencer I had gradually come to the conclusion that I might make a better writer than a priest, and it was those stories I wanted to tell.

Which is more or less how I found myself, two years later, driving across the country gathering material for a book about spiritual life in America. For months on end I lived out of a rusted old Ford, meeting people of every faith and of no faith, getting to know them well enough to tell their stories. With only the search for the varieties of religious experience to guide the journey, those were heady, hectic days; the kind of classic cross-country trip that proceeds as if its sole object is the road ahead.

As it happened, it wasn't so easy to distance myself from where I'd come. Just after I had left town that winter, January 2002, the *Boston Globe* revealed how pervasive sexual abuse had become in the Catholic Church, unleashing an enormous scandal. In a series of reports, the *Globe* showed that Cardinal Bernard Law had approved of the transfer of a known pedophile, Father John Geoghan, from one parish to another, where inevitably new abuses took place. Even as the evidence mounted, Law lied about it repeatedly, until finally the entire church seemed implicated. Archdiocese records showed there had been similar abuses and cover-ups going back sixty years or more, to the episcopacies of Cardinals Cushing and O'Connell. Some of the alleged abusers had been high-profile clergy like Father Paul Shanley, who had been Boston's media-friendly "hippie priest" in the 1960s; most had been less well known. In some ways, the latter were the more troubling cases. In the papers they were just jowly men with Roman collars, anonymous in their vocations, hiding in plain sight.

I couldn't believe my bad luck. There I was knocking on church doors a thousand miles away when the biggest religion story in the country was unfolding back at home. Everywhere I went people wanted to talk about "the Catholics" and "those priests." In some of the smaller towns in the evangelical South, many had never met an actual Catholic before—one from Boston, no less—and wanted to hear what I had to say about the scandal. But what was there to say? Father

Geoghan? Clearly a sick man. Father Shanley? A monster. Cardinal Law? A self-serving criminal, no doubt about it.

I didn't come to see my personal connection to all these men until the day I picked up a local paper at a truck stop outside Memphis. Flipping through the pages for anything that would distract me from the fact that I'd been on the road for two months, I turned to the news from around the nation. Sure enough, there was more trouble for "the Catholics": ANOTHER PRIEST REMOVED FROM HIS CHURCH, the headline read. I scanned the article quickly.

Then I stopped cold.

"Father D. George Spagnolia denies all allegations of abuse . . ."

It was like the story had been chasing me across the country. Now it finally had me, grabbing hold of my collar in the harsh light and dirty air of a Memphis truck stop.

I read on. It had happened, Spag's accuser said, thirty-one years ago, when he was fourteen years old. Father Spag had groped him, he claimed, while they were camping.

Camping? I found that detail a little hard to believe. I wanted— needed—to find something impossible in this; something that would allow me still to believe in the priest who seemed to embody my parents' principles completely, the priest who had married them and baptized their firstborn, for godsake; the priest who had made my family possible. And so I reasoned it away: Spag was a lifelong city boy; he was as likely to be found in a pup tent as he was orbiting the moon. Camping? Not Spag. I shook my head at the paper. Sorry kid, you've got the wrong priest.

Then I remembered: the cardinal's lawn. Spag with his hand through the tent flap. *I think he thought I was waving . . .*

Out there in the middle of nowhere my cell phone had poor reception; I found a pay phone by the gas pumps and called my parents.

"Hello?"

Mom sounded so tired I had to look at my watch to make sure I hadn't called too late. It was only 8:30, but still her voice shook wearily.

"Hello?" Dad picked up on the extension, coughing into the receiver.

Hearing them, I wondered first if I had woken them up, then if they were sick, then if maybe someone had died. It was nothing like that, they said. "It's just all this with Spag," my mother explained. "So awful what he's going through."

Dad sighed in agreement.

"Have you talked with him about it?"

"Oh sure. He says he remembers the night they're talking about," Mom said. "In the tent with the boy."

"We knew him, too, the boy," Dad said.

"Spag remembers that they were both in their sleeping bags—"

"Zipped in," my father added.

"Right, zipped in. And in the middle of the night the boy wakes up Spag, saying, 'Don't do that! Don't do that, Father. Why did you do that?' And Spag didn't know what he was talking about."

"They were zipped in," my father said again.

"And you know Spag," my mother said, "how he jokes and all. Well, he said maybe he was dreaming of some sweet young thing, and maybe while he was asleep he turned over without thinking and . . ." Her voice lightened, as if on the other end of the line she was smiling at the innocence of it all.

"Jesus. He *said* that?" I nearly shouted into the phone. I repeated myself in disbelief, trying to work out whether it was the content of his words or the act of speaking them that bothered me more. "He said *that*?"

"Well, maybe he didn't say exactly that."

"He was dreaming? Is that supposed to be an excuse?"

"Well, that's what he told us," my father said. "And we believe him."

My mother saw what I was getting at, and retreated. "No, no. He must not have said that then . . ."

"But something like it?"

"Oh I don't remember what he said."

Could there have been two Catholic worlds in the tent that night? One for the radical priest pestering the cardinal to rebuild a school; the other for this one, the Spag left out of all my parents' stories?

"Spag remembers the night," Dad repeated, "and it wasn't like what the boy says at all." He seemed drained by the conversation, and hoped to wrap it up. But Mom wanted the last word.

"How could it have happened that way?" she asked. "On the cardinal's lawn? Really, would anyone be so stupid?"

A faith of inversions: find eternal truth and everyday truth becomes a work in progress. I needed to talk to someone less Catholic than my parents, less Catholic even than me. I said a quick goodbye, then called my brother in San Francisco. Thrown out of two Catholic schools by age sixteen, he had never looked back.

"You hear about Spag?" I asked.

"Yeah. You think he did it?"

"I don't know what to think."

Fifteen years after the fights that threatened the family, my brother still hated the church as much as my parents loved it. I, as always, was somewhere in between. *You think he did it?* The answer, whatever it was, was not so simple as one man and one act. Whether he did it or not, in that tent on the cardinal's lawn was the entire Catholic universe in miniature; a universe moved by power, love, and abuses of both.

"I think I'm going to write a book about all this," I said.

"Oh yeah? Why's that?"

"Because Spag has always been the priest I thought Dad would be if he stayed in—the priest he *still* wants to be sometimes. And now this. It makes me wonder if they're all infected, and if they are, how they got that way."

"It's the institution, man. It breaks people, warps them."

"Maybe, but it's more than that. It makes me wonder if we're infected too."

Silence on the phone now. The silence of the sons of a priest and a nun, two thousand miles apart. Two brothers wondering about the lives that made them, and the larger forces that have made them who they are.

"Got a title?"

"Yeah, I've got one," I said, and then I thought for a minute. The pervasiveness of all this; the layers of lies and half-truths; the excuses; the implications. I cradled the receiver between my shoulder and my ear and rubbed truck-stop exhaust from my eyes. Maybe God wrote straight with crooked lines for other people; for my family he seemed to scribble all over the page.

"So what is it?"

"*What a Fucking Mess,*" I said.

Lowell pastor agrees to leave rectory

Admits to having 2d gay relationship

By Shelley Murphy
GLOBE STAFF

and Caroline Louise Cole
GLOBE CORRESPONDENT

A day after admitting he had lied about being celibate and acknowledging a long homosexual relationship during a leave from the priesthood, the Rev. D. George Spagnolia yesterday gave up his fight to remain in the rectory he had been ordered to leave after he was accused of sexually abusing a teenage boy 31 years ago.

During a rambling press conference at which he admitted to a second gay relationship, Spagnolia acknowledged that he is gay but denied molesting any child.

"Being gay doesn't mean you're a pedophile, being gay does not mean you cross-dress. They're apples and oranges," said Spagnolia, who was removed as pastor of St. Patrick's parish last month by Cardinal Bernard F. Law and ordered to leave the rectory after he was accused of molesting a 14-year-old

GLOBE STAFF PHOTO/BILL GREENE

Parishioner Irene Harris listening to the Rev. D. George Spagnolia yesterday.

boy in 1971. He denies the charge and had refused to move out of the rectory while he challenges the allegation.

"So I am saying, 'Yes, I've had gay relationships.' But I have never harmed a child," Spagnolia said.

Spagnolia also disclosed that in

addition to his nearly four-year relationship with Winston F. Reed after leaving the priesthood in 1973, which was reported by the Globe yesterday, he also had a year-long relationship with another man in 1981 or 1982 before resuming a life of celibacy. He had previously said that he had no other sexual relationships after parting with Reed in 1980.

He apologized to his supporters, insisting that he never meant to deceive anyone and lied to protect the privacy of himself and his partners. However it was Spagnolia who brought up the issue of celibacy during an interview with the Globe on Tuesday, insisting that he had lived a celibate life during his 20 years away from the priesthood.

But the lawyer representing Spagnolia's alleged victim fired back, arguing that credibility, not sexuality, is the issue and the priest's lack of candor and conflicting statements supports her argument that he's also lying when he denies abusing her client.

"No one should disbelieve him because he's gay, but everybody should disbelieve him because he's

a liar," said lawyer Wendy Murphy, who represents the unidentified man who claims Spagnolia sexually abused him twice during 1971 in Roxbury and Brighton.

During an interview with the Globe on Tuesday, Spagnolia volunteered, without being asked, that he had been celibate during his leave from the priesthood, noting, "It's a special gift of the Holy Spirit and it's not meant for everybody. I am comfortable with it and, therefore, I can say I have the gift of celibacy."

But, on Thursday night, when questioned about his relationship with Reed, Spagnolia acknowledged that he had lied about being celibate and had a multiyear relationship with Reed. But he said that he had no other sexual relationships after they parted in 1980.

"I will not try to defend it, except to say that there was no conscious decision to deceive, but rather in my naive effort to protect my own privacy and that of others, I made the decision that these were times which were private in nature and I saw no need to reveal them," Spagnolia said.

PRODIGAL SONS

I had no idea. By the time I got back to Boston, the scandal had exploded. In the press, in parishes around the country, even at home.

My first indication of the grip it had on my parents came when I saw Dad sitting night after night in front of the local TV news. That alone let me know something was amiss. My father had never been much for television. Evenings when I was young, while I lay in front of our big wooden Zenith doing my homework, he would sit in the living room, an open prayer book in his lap, holding his hand to his forehead as if he were blocking the sun.

Back then, prayer was all I really knew of him. He always worked late hours and had no hobbies to speak of, so praying was the one thing I actually saw him do on a regular basis. Each night after washing the dinner dishes he'd say the psalms for the evening—book open, eyes closed, lips moving silently—praying the Liturgy of the Hours as I would later learn to do with the Trappists: *Into your hands, oh Lord, I commend my spirit . . .*

That season of scandal, though, his prayers were troubled. Just as he settled into his spot by the fireplace, my mother would call from the other room—"William, they're on!"—and he would hustle in to see the news.

The cardinal was on again: denying, explaining, then denying again. And the priests were on too: in handcuffs, in courtrooms, in smiling photographs taken before they had reason to run.

Dad watched and shook his head. He had known all these guys
once, knew some of them still. Together they'd grown from altar boys
into men of God. Father John Geoghan, who once remarked that he
preferred the children of poor families because they were more affec-
tionate, more needy, was a year ahead of my father at the archdiocese
seminary. Paul Shanley, accused of raping a Catholic schoolboy in a
confessional, ministered to the worst parts of Boston all through the
'60s. So did Dad.

There was Shanley now: just off the plane from San Diego, extra-
dited to Boston to face multiple charges of assault on a minor. Surrounded by a small army of Massachusetts state troopers, his head
down as though he was walking through a hard rain, he wore a bul-
letproof vest and baseball cap with an unbent brim. Back in the '60s,
he had worn thick black locks down to the shoulders of his clerical
suit; now he was white-haired and balding: he could have been
someone's grandfather. Since his story broke, the newspapers and
television anchors had been referring to him disgustedly, damningly, as
"the so-called street priest," as if the notion of it—a priest in the
streets—had always been a sham. It was a label my father once wore
with pride.

"Poor old bugger," Dad sighed.

My mother couldn't help but smile. "Are you sure that's the word
you want?"

They both mustered a small laugh. It was not a joke that I would
have expected either of them to make or be amused by, but in those
days they laughed when they could. This was their life they were watching on television each night. Heartbroken though they were, they could
not turn away from this latest chapter in the long history of sex, love,
and the Catholic Church. Love might seem a strange factor to include
between those others, yet love was at the muddled heart of it: love for
the church; love for each other; the challenges and limits of each.

On the screen the news moved on from Shanley to an overview of
the scandal. A grid of images now, priest after priest in still frame, each
face above a name in harsh yellow letters and, in parentheses, a one-
or two-digit number. The number had something to do with the ac-

cusations made against them; whether it referred to the number of children abused or the number of alleged acts of abuse was unclear. Either way, there was something to the parenthetical quantification that made me think of indulgences, all those endless days off from purgatory the catechism once encouraged children to collect with their prayers.

In the corner of the grid was a familiar face: glasses on his nose, mouth open midsentence. "Rev. D. G. Spagnolia," the caption read, "(1)." It was the first I had seen him since that Christmas Eve two years before. He looked just as he had after his homily, exhausted from the effort of being both an old man and a priest.

My father closed his prayer book and set it aside. Watching the news those nights, nodding at and naming the priests he knew, he seemed to see clearly what he had feared for some time. The sun was setting on his church and no one knew what the night would bring. *Into your hands, oh Lord, I commend my spirit . . .*

He asked me to turn up the volume on the television. "But not too much," he said. My mother had fallen asleep on the couch beside him, and he didn't want to wake her.

In the months I'd been away, Spag's story had played out not just on the front pages of the local papers but in the national media. It wasn't kids with camcorders filming him now; TV news trucks sat outside St. Patrick's with their satellite dishes pointed to the sky; a black limo showed up one morning to take him to New York to appear on *Good Morning America*. He was the first priest to speak out about what, as far as the clergy of Boston were concerned, had become a witch hunt. Having finally admitted wrongdoing, the Catholic hierarchy stood behind a shield of "zero tolerance," cleaning house of anyone remotely involved in the scandal. The moment a charge of abuse was made, the accused priest was suspended from his position, evicted from his rectory home with no regard for where he would end up. Many priests removed from service accepted their fate, guilty or not, staying with relatives and trusting the bishops to take care of it, as they always had before.

The climate was such that another of my parents' old friends from Roxbury, Father Jack White, who in the '60s had presided over the experimental ministry center called Warwick House, left the country and refused to return. He was not charged with any crime, but years before he had made what in retrospect must have seemed one of the worst real estate investments in history: he had purchased a hotel in Palm Springs, California, with Paul Shanley. When the press began referring to this property as Shanley's "sex hotel," Father White's attorney advised him to stay away until the scandal and the scrutiny came to an end.

For him it never did. Jack White died in exile late in 2003. *There but for the grace of God go I,* many priests of his generation might have said, but grace by then had come to seem less than reliable.

Even those who had not been accused began to brace themselves when they sorted their mail or answered the phone, wondering if some misinterpreted word or pat on the back forty years before would today bring a lawyer's letter or a message from the cardinal's hatchet man.

For Spag, news that an accusation had been made came in a phone call in February 2002. He was told to be out of the rectory that evening and stay away until the matter was cleared up. He refused to go, first insisting on his innocence to archdiocese officials, then, ever the rabble-rouser, calling a press conference to do so publicly.

It seemed as if all of Lowell turned out to support him. Eleven hundred people packed into St. Patrick's to hear Spag refute the charges made against him. Signs of support in a half-dozen languages waved from the pews, all of them saying, more or less, what one up front declared: *We stand by you.*

"I have done nothing wrong," Spag said from the pulpit. The congregation cheered, filling the church with applause so loud it shook the stained glass in its frames. He spoke over the noise.

"I was told on Saturday, February 16, that I had been accused of an incident which was alleged to have taken place thirty-one years ago while I was serving as parochial vicar at St. Francis de Sales Church in Roxbury. It was then that I realized the full impact of the cardinal's zero-tolerance policy. I was told that I must be out of St. Patrick's rectory that very day and that my ability to exercise priestly ministry was taken away. But even more devastating was the knowledge that I will never be assigned to minister as a priest in the Archdiocese of Boston. All of this without due process.

"The events of this past week have affected more than just me and the exercise of my priesthood. No action is taken in isolation. What is done by anyone for good goes to build up the Body of Christ. Whatever is done that is evil goes to tear down the Body of Christ. This policy of no tolerance as it is being implemented does not arrive at justice, but cloaks fear and arrogance in the mantle of righteousness.

"For my reputation, for my brother priests serving the people of God in the archdiocese, and for the people, I cannot stand by mute and allow this injustice to continue unchecked.

"It has been, and will always be, an honor for me to exercise the priesthood of Jesus Christ, and as St. Paul said, 'I can do all things in Christ who strengthens me.'"

Up until then, the press had taken part gleefully in the exposure of abuser-priests. Offered up a scandal, they had covered it as if a century's worth of Catholic dirty laundry had been soiled overnight. After three months, though, the story was losing steam. Now, with Spag's last stand, it seemed a new angle had emerged: the charismatic, unjustly accused priest; the man of the people fighting against both the abusers and the cardinal who tried to hide the truth. "We've been betrayed by our brother priests who commit sexual abuse on children," Spag announced from his pulpit, "and we've been betrayed by our bishop because of the way he has handled it and the secrecy." Making him all the more compelling was his long history of run-ins with the hierarchy. As one reporter put it, "He has been here before."

Later that week, the *Globe* ran a long profile depicting Spag as a wrongly suspected truth-teller. In the article, he spoke of his life in the church and out, of his time in Roxbury and of the quarrel with Cardinal Medeiros that began his two decades of exile from the ministry. Through it all, he said, even while working in the world he had lived as a priest.

"My faith in Christ was very strong," Spag told the *Globe*. "I was still a man of prayer." Without being asked, he filled in the one detail it seemed everyone wonders about fallen clergy. "Celibacy was for me," he said. "I felt called to that."

The abuse scandal had been a saga with villains and victims to spare; what it had lacked was a hero. With Spag's defiant yet affable face on the front pages and the evening news, it had one now: a life-long fighter who had always remained faithful to his vocation. It made for a great story.

Trouble was, it wasn't true. The lie was not his innocence, but his celibacy. During his twenty-year leave of absence, he'd had two rela-tionships; two relationships—and this is why he lied—with men.

Like every other Catholic within five hundred miles of Boston, Spag had been following the scandal in the press for months. He'd seen how conservative columnists and television commentators and, worst of all, the talk-radio hosts quickly made specific acts of sexual abuse into broad questions of the number of homosexuals in the clergy. The easy math of it—gay priest equals Paul Shanley equals rapist of altar boys—left Spag no room for hope that the truth would be accepted in all its human complexity. When he had lived and worked as a priest he had done so completely. When he was not living as a priest, well, he had done his best to be happy. He had shared his bed with a lover for two years; they'd made a home together, thrown dinner parties, laughed, fought, grew bored of each other. It didn't work out, but that's life, right? What did any of it have to do with hurting a child?

And so he said he had always been celibate. He'd known he was gay as long as he'd known he was Catholic; fifty years spent living a dou-ble life told him that at this point, with the cameras rolling and the na-tion watching, if he was going to admit that he'd had sex with men he might as well tie his own noose. "Honestly," he later told me. "I didn't even think of it as a lie. You get so used to telling the same story about yourself, it starts to have its own truth."

But our truths are inevitably entwined with the truths of others. The morning the *Globe* profile ran, an e-mail came to the paper from a man calling Spag a liar. How did the man know? Easy: he had been there, at the dinner parties, in the celibate's bed.

As fast as the press took up Spag's cause, it turned on him. The editorial and Page 1 headlines came in quick succession over the next few days: "Pastor Admits Lie on Celibacy." "Lowell Pastor Agrees to Leave Rectory." "Spagnolia Vacates St. Patrick's." "Lost Credibility is Not Easily Regained."

The last press conference Spag held was not from the pulpit but on the church steps, the door locked behind him. The packed-pews support he had enjoyed a week before was nowhere to be seen. Eleven hundred people proclaiming *We stand by you* had dwindled to a small huddle of lawyers and reporters. The next day my parents read in the *Lowell Sun,* the same paper that had splashed "Lowell Priest Marries Boston Nun" across its front page thirty-three years before, that the friend who helped make their marriage possible had stood alone in the rain.

From the St. Patrick's rectory, Spag moved to a walk-up apartment in Boston. Barely unpacked, boxes piled in the living room, he stayed close by the phone for news that it all was over and he could get back to work. He was informed, as my father had been, that an ecclesial court would rule on the status of his priesthood, so he got himself a canon lawyer and waited. As the months went by, though, it became clear that nothing more was going to happen, at least not any time soon.

In the meantime, Cardinal Law resigned—a late response to the general outrage at the extent of his involvement in covering up decades of abuse. An interim administrator, Bishop Richard Lennon, came and went, and the new Archbishop, Sean O'Malley, took his place. Across the country, the heads of various scandal-shaken dioceses held meetings, voiced concern, and got on with the business of trying to put it all in the past. As for the priests removed from their parishes, the guilty and the innocent alike, the church simply washed its hands of them. They were the scandal made flesh; better these particular "other Christs" stay dead than force the hierarchy to deal with the ambiguities of resurrection.

With nothing to be gained by remaining in Boston (and much to be lost; not a day went by when he wasn't recognized and stopped on the street), Spag moved to the home of a new friend in coastal Rhode Island. The mysteries of faith are endless: they had met as a direct result of all the bad press Spag was receiving. One day a call came in and a kind voice told Spag he had seen him on television. He believed him, the voice said, and just wanted him to know. A few days later, the phone rang again. He still believed him, the voice said. Would he like to have coffee?

I visited Spag at his new house a few months later. Just as I'd been eager to hear him preach to see if he measured up to my parents' memories, I was now anxious to talk with him to judge for myself whether or not he was worth their continued credulity. They believed him as if to do so was another tenet of their faith. I had no such bias, but was willing to give him the benefit of the doubt.

It was early autumn by then, a day even cooler than I expected so close to the ocean, but Spag still wore the uniform that had let his former parishioners know he would not be the usual pastor: beige shorts and gray T-shirt, sandals at the bottom of pale legs without much hair.

The house was crammed with furniture; its every surface covered with bric-a-brac gathered at flea markets, barn sales, and estate liquidations. "Richard dabbles in the antique business," Spag said as soon as I'd walked through the door. "I'm getting into it a bit myself, but he's the real expert."

He had only lived there a short time by then, but already he seemed settled in and comfortable. He guided me through the rooms like a museum docent, walking backwards across the hardwood floor, giving capsule histories of each item we passed. On every wall five or six large paintings butted up against each other in heavy wooden frames. The place was mostly dark; when Spag turned on a light, it was only a wall-mounted gallery lamp, shining directly on a three-foot-tall canvas, casting severe shadows around the room.

"That's a French painter Richard really likes," Spag said. The style of the painting seemed to be photorealist, but it depicted a place that never was: the waterfront ruins of a castle that looked far too new, like a gothic cathedral wrecked by a hurricane.

"Only a little bit of the art is mine," Spag said. "I like one fellow, an engraver whose work I first saw in the pages of the *Catholic Worker.*"

I knew the artist he meant: Fritz Eichenberg. His work could be found not just in Dorothy Day's leftist magazine but in many a liberal Catholic household, including my parents'. His most famous print, *Christ of the Breadline,* shows a hooded figure standing among gaunt figures of the Depression.

"I've got that one over here," Spag said.

When I was young it was among the first images I saw that helped me understand what separated my parents' idea of faith from the opulence of Rome. In the print Christ stands in the middle of six ragged men, not facing them, not dispensing wisdom or healing their wounds, but just waiting with them on the grimy street, as if the miraculous was a slow, dirty business. It was a rendering of the kind of religious ideal that had sent all three of them—Spag, my father, my mother—to Roxbury forty years before. Seeing it hanging in a room full of obscure art and dusty antiques seemed both fitting and sad.

"What do you say we have a look at the town, maybe find a bite to eat," Spag said, and we went out to the driveway and climbed into his Tracker.

Spag's new home was in a picturesque little seaside village, pretty houses kept apart by big yards ringed with horse fences. Leafy branches arched over the roads, letting orange and yellow light filter through the trees. By choice or not, it seemed to me Spag had certainly moved up in the world from his crumbling rectory in Lowell; the views there were only of the projects and the trash in the churchyard. From his new home, he told me, he could be at the ocean in about five minutes. I asked him if he was still in touch with anyone at St. Patrick's.

"Oh sure," he said, "next week I'll be up there to cook for a fundraising dinner. Just like old times. We have to do it in a rented hall, though, because I'm not allowed to step foot on church grounds." He shook his head as he drove. He didn't miss being a priest, he insisted, but this business of only being an occasional part of people's lives, that was something different. "It's all so fucked," he said with a crooked smile. "Forgive the language, but it is."

He seemed in remarkably good spirits for a man accused of being a child molester, but as far as he was concerned what he was going through was just business as usual for the church. The shifting of blame from men of power to a man committed to helping the power-less—how could he be upset by it, when he was barely surprised?

"This whole abuse thing, the disregard with which the people in-volved are being treated, it has reaffirmed my total disdain for bureau-cracy," Spag said. He drove and talked fast, looking at me as much as at the road. "But it's not like it's a shock. The way the church is deal-ing with this has a lot in common with the nonsense that we went through in the seminary. Your father, me, everybody who went through it."

"Like what?"

"Oh, all of it. There was this whole attitude toward personality and character that led to the lack of sexual development. We had to wear our cassocks down to the shower. After lights-out we had to get per-mission even to go to the bathroom.

"I remember once a few of us got letters from one guy's mother. She was a great lady, a real joker. She signed the letters '*la femme de vos pensées.*' Well, within a day we were all marched in to see the rector who demanded to know what woman we all knew. It was somebody's mother! But that was the neurosis, this fear of the body, fear of the feminine, fear of anything remotely sexual.

"Looking back I see how ridiculous it was. At the time it was some-thing we felt we just had to get through. If you wanted to be in you had to use the means they gave you. Maybe I was better off than most—I knew what my deal was going in. My classmates were even more sexually retarded than I was. But that was also the toughest thing about it for me, knowing I was a homosexual and being in sem-inary. It was torturous. Only by the grace of God did I fight off what I was feeling.

"We all swallowed the idea that celibacy was a sacrifice. That if you lived by this you wouldn't have these other distractions that would keep you from being a good priest. But what you did have, and they never taught this, were all these sublimations.

"You know, the only thing of use I learned in seminary was Scripture. Everything else was bullshit. And in Scripture it is very clear that celibacy is a charisma, it's a gift of the Holy Spirit. It is specialized. But what the church has done is they've universalized it, they've put the Holy Spirit in a box, like a pigeon. You know what happens to a bird in a box?"

Rhetorical or not, he didn't give me a chance to answer, or to say much at all. "You getting hungry?" he asked. "I thought we'd swing by this diner up here."

At lunch, Spag recounted the details of the case against him. His tone was lower now; he was less excited and irate than he'd been in the privacy of his car. He was starting over in Rhode Island, he had explained, and though his former life was not a secret, he also seemed wary of it becoming gossip at the local coffee and sandwich shop.

"Basically when I was out in the tent on the cardinal's lawn in Brighton, a lot of people from the parish were coming out, giving their support. We'd hold prayer vigils, call out to Medeiros when he went by—you know, generally making a nuisance of ourselves. Two of the kids from Roxbury asked if they could stay out overnight with me, as part of the demonstration. One of them was the kid who made the accusation that I fondled him.

"So there we are in front of the Archbishop's Residence, and what I remember is waking up in that small tent, and I'm facing the kid, and he was pushing me away, saying, 'Don't do that, Father.'

"That was the basis of the allegation.

"You know what the kid also said? How much I made a difference in his life, what a great help I was to the community. When they sent the file on me to Rome they didn't include that part, just the tent. He was a screwed-up kid then, what he's like now I have no idea. Why he has said what he's said I have no idea.

"The thing that bothers me so much in all this is through it all you think of all the people over thirty years that you've met and had relationships with, and where are they? You were there for them, but where are they now?

"It reminds me of a situation when I left my first parish in West Bridgewater. I was at a new church but I used to go back there because there was this barber—" Spag ran a hand over his scalp and smirked. "I used to have hair. So I used to go back there because this guy had this hair stuff I liked.

"It was my day off so I walked in there pretty much like I'm dressed now. And there was a kid sitting in the barber's chair, his mother waiting in the corner. I knew them both very well. There was not a family in town that I spent more man-hours with. One problem after another, I was always helping them out with this or that. I gave a big hello and got blank faces in return. Finally, Louie the barber says, Oh Mrs. So-and-So you remember Father Spag . . .

" 'Oh Father!' the lady says, 'I didn't recognize you without your collar.'

"That was a great lesson. When you're a priest, people see you only relative to their need; they don't see you in any other context. I'm sure your father could say the same thing: they don't see beyond the collar. It's like you're not human."

Spag shook his head, sipped his coffee, called for the check.

"So where does it all stand now?" I asked.

"Just waiting to hear from Rome," he said. "It doesn't look good. The board that decides which cases to pursue has declared that my accuser is credible but I am not. And you know the reason they cited for declaring me not credible? Because I lied about celibacy to the *Boston Globe*. Because I said something stupid that has nothing to do with this case, they decide I'm not credible. Because I lied about having sex. Makes me wonder what the real issue here is."

When we returned to the house, Spag continued his tour as if we'd never left. There was a whole room full of art that I hadn't seen. As soon as we were through the threshold, he made a beeline for a large canvas surrounded by an ornate, weathered frame.

"This one over here is mine," Spag announced. "I got it at an art auction, pretty cheap." It was a colorful but dark portrayal of a man with a pack on his back, reaching out to open a door.

"It's called *The Prodigal*," he said. Hearing the name, I realized it was a contemporary depiction of what is perhaps Jesus' most famous parable. As it's told in the Gospel of Luke, it's the story of a rich man's son who takes his share of his father's fortune and leaves home to squander it in the world. The son comes back contrite, expecting to beg for forgiveness, but the father greets him with a celebration.

"The thing I like about it is it's the only portrayal of the prodigal son I've seen in which he's opening the door himself. Usually you see the father or his servants rushing out to meet him, but here—" Spag waved a hand over the painting, indicating the spot where the man grasped a doorknob. "You see? He does the work. What it says to me is you've got to make your own way in this life, even if you think God is watching out for you. Maybe especially then."

We stood silently for a moment, just studying the painting.

"And look at his hands," Spag said, "how they're out of proportion with the rest of the picture." I looked where he was pointing and saw he was right. The prodigal's hands were like thick gloves on a starved body, callused and meaty, a worker's hands, as if returning took more effort than simply leaving and dealing with the consequences.

I looked more closely at the painting and saw very faintly the word ROOMS beside the door the prodigal was opening. A motel? A flophouse? My interpretation, I realized, differed from Spag's. The man in the painting had not gone home at all. Or else, like Spag himself, he had gone home only to leave again.

Spag nodded at the painting in sad appreciation. "It's hard work, going back where you came from."

Back where I came from, my parents were still watching the news. I'd had about as much as I could take of priests and sex scandals and the ambiguities of who touched whom where thirty years before, so instead of joining them for the latest report on clerical misconduct, I went about my usual routine. Whenever I visited my parents' house, I

did piles of laundry and checked my e-mail compulsively, moving between one task and the other as if on a track from the washing machine in the basement to the computer room on the first floor.

With all my clothes in various stages of the washing cycle, I had
gone up into my old room to find something to wear while the pants
I'd shown up in tumbled in the dryer. The best I could do was a pair of
old sweatpants from my high school track days. They had been gray
when I bought them, but I'd washed them so many times they now
were faded white, shrunken to three-quarters their original length,
with permanent mud stains splattered across the seat.

So it was in these ill-fitting white pants that I sat at my parents'
computer, making use of the computer's CD burner, copying some
music I'd borrowed from a friend, when, from the other room, I heard
my parents talking over the television.

"It's not good to have secrets," Dad said.

"I know, I know," Mom sighed. "It's just—"

"He's an adult. He'll understand."

"I suppose you're right."

I uncapped a black Sharpie marker, took the compact disc out of
the machine, and was about to label it when my father appeared in
the doorway.

"Pete, could you come in here for a minute? Your mother has
something to tell you."

"Right now?"

"If you're not in the middle of anything."

"Well . . ."

"She'd like to tell you now."

Sitting on the couch, the TV glowing in front of her, my mother
looked as if she'd been waiting there for hours with her hands in her
lap. She scrunched up her face like she'd just tasted something sour.

I sat down in the rocking chair across from her, the uncapped
marker still in hand.

"Well," Mom said. "There's going to be something in the news
about it one of these days, so I wanted you to hear it from me first."

My father sat down beside her, nodding in encouragement.

With what seemed like great effort, Mom went on. "You've been reading in the papers of course about all the—the—you know—the Troubles." For months now, Mom had been using the word often associated with religious violence in Northern Ireland as shorthand for the abuse crisis. For as long as I'd been alive, the Troubles had been the defining issue for many Irish Catholics; now here we were living through another one. To me it seemed fitting to use the same collective name: both cases dealt with something awful involving God and man; each was like a force of nature, even if men were to blame.

"When I was young," my mother said, "before I entered the convent. I was sixteen or so and I was involved in the CYO and the church softball team and you know how kids are and . . ."

Dad squeezed her shoulder. "It's okay, Mary."

Mom closed her eyes. She took a breath. As I remember it now, it was a breath that lasted long enough for me to realize she was about to tell me something she had carried with her for quite some time. Her breath was so long, in fact, so deep and heavy with what seemed to me a gathering of strength, that I glanced down at the black marker in my hand and the white pants I was wearing, stretched across my leg like a empty page, and even before I heard what she had to tell me, I can remember thinking, and simultaneously feeling ashamed of the thought, *I should be writing this down.*

"I was abused by a priest," Mom said.

Dedicates Life to Glory of God

Kneeling in prayer, Mary Doherty, of Roseclair st., Dorchester who is joining Order of Sisters of St. Joseph, receives blessing of Rev. Gerard Creighton, St. Margaret's Church. L. to r., family, Francis, Mr. and Mrs. Michael Doherty, Joseph, Sister Mary, Danny, Rita, Paul, and John, rear.

(Record-American Photo, Frank V. Mahoney)

"MY LIFE HAS ALWAYS BEEN SECRET"

"This is what happened." With a thud, Mom dropped a stack of white office paper on the table in front of me. "These pages go back to the fifties," she explained. "All the complaints made about him through the years."

My eyes widened at the size of the pile. It was easily as tall as a shoebox; a thousand pages or more. I hefted it in my hands; it weighed as much as a baby, and I held it just as carefully, uncertain what it contained.

"That's a lot of complaints," I said. "He must have been a real piece of work."

Mom nodded, yes, but then said only, "I'm afraid of what you will think." Standing over me, looking down with her lips tightened to a worried frown, she seemed to be studying my face for a reaction. "I was just so young. So stupid."

"Don't worry, Mom." I wished I had more consoling or convincing words for her, but I still didn't really know what I was looking at, and I couldn't think of anything else to say. After a moment, she turned and walked out of the room, leaving me sitting in front of a mound of pages that apparently said something about my mother, something that made her afraid of what her son would think.

In truth, I didn't know what to think. Until that moment, I had believed our family had been shaped first and foremost by the fact of my father's vocation. The idea that he had been called by God, and the fact that he continued, against all good reason, his quest to serve the faith, seemed the origin of all our ongoing concerns. Until then, I had believed that the simultaneously simple and paradoxical statement "My father is a Catholic priest" was the best way to sum up who we were. Yet just as the world had recently discovered the hidden life of the church, I was now discovering my own hidden history. *My mother was abused by a priest.* This fact also had been there from the beginning; it had formed us as much as had my father's priesthood. To love the church and to be hurt by it: we were a family with two prime movers.

I dug my fingers into the pile and spread it across the table. The pages were documents; all second- or third-generation photocopies by the looks of them, the typefaces blurred, the longhand jottings barely legible. I shuffled through letters, memos, handwritten notes, not sure what I was looking for; a page that would explain it all, maybe; one slip of paper that would make clear the significance of all the others. Every sheet was stamped in the lower corner with a name and a number: CREIGHTON 2-421, CREIGHTON 2-422 . . . Evidence, I realized. Exhibits A–Z, fifty times over.

The file was that of Reverend Gerard E. Creighton, a priest of the Archdiocese of Boston. Until recently, every document before me had been part of a confidential file kept by the church's personnel office. Along with the files of every other priest accused of abuse, it had been made public earlier that year. And now here it was in front of me: a combination scrapbook and timeline of one man's gradual perversion of the "perfect life" to which he'd been called. Picking through at random, I came across an announcement from 1951 declaring that he had been ordained by Cardinal Cushing. On another page, I read a letter from a group of altar boys naming him "the best priest we ever had." As I dug deeper into the pile, I read letters between the chancery and various parishes around the city, letters in which one pastor or another pleaded with the cardinal's assistants to have Father Creighton transferred. The man was dangerous, the pastors complained; he threatened parishioners; he took money from women; he kept a gun in his bedside table in the rectory, and made no secret of his ability to use it.

I couldn't believe what I was reading. Even after months of daily revelations of abuse in the news, to see it all laid out before me this way was to understand the extent to which a bad priest could terrorize those around him without fear of punishment. On one occasion after a complaint had been made, Father Creighton received a letter from the chancery warning him that "as priests, we are all susceptible to these kinds of attacks."

Not even complaints made by fellow clergy were acted upon. In one internal memo, a priest who shared a rectory with Father Creighton made a visit to the church offices in Brighton to voice his concerns. As on every page of the file, the name of Father Creighton's accuser had been concealed before the documents were made public.

8/4/69
[REDACTED] was in re: Fr Creighton

[REDACTED] quite visibly upset and tense about the situation. Many "small" things: work Creighton will not do, foul language in presence of girls' softball team, moods of depression, etc.

But—big item—his homicidal tendencies. Creighton told a Jesuit who is there for a time that some night he was going to <u>kill</u> [REDACTED]

He still has the gun—His presence and attitude have also seriously upset [REDACTED]

Creighton now on vacation—due back Aug 13—[REDACTED] does not want him back—even to clean out his room. [REDACTED] talks about police protection etc.

Extremely dangerous.
Will probably kill someone

"Relieve of duty," this note says in closing. In fact, Father Creighton went on serving the archdiocese for another fifteen years, transferred to and from a list of parishes rivaled in length only by the number of complaints made against him.

Quite a piece of work, indeed. So what exactly did such a man have to do with my family? Mom had told me this was the file of the priest she had known when she was young. She had said this was the priest who had sent her to become a Sister of St. Joseph, and that he had somehow hurt her before she left. Yet she remained guarded as to what had actually happened. Understandably so, I thought. I am, after all, her son. Just as she would have hoped to protect me from abuse when I was a child, it seemed her instincts led her to shield me even from the fact of it now.

But her story, too, was waiting in the pile of pages. I soon came across a letter helpfully labeled "THE FACTS." It had been written by a lawyer and sent to the offices of the Archdiocese of Boston in 1995. Like every other page, it was covered with the redactor's thick black lines, inking out names and identifying details such as age and address. From what remained, however, I had no trouble determining that each thick black mark stood for my mother.

THE FACTS

[REDACTED] was a cheerful and energetic child who enjoyed dancing and sports. She was also actively involved in her church and with the nuns who taught the children in the parish parochial school. She and her friends would often walk the nuns from the convent to the school, often carrying their books for them . . . [REDACTED] was a good girl. Soon after entering her senior year of high school in September 1957, [REDACTED] decided to become a nun after graduation.

[REDACTED] first came into contact with Father Creighton in 1958 when Father Creighton was assigned to the Parish CYO. At that time, [REDACTED] was only 16 years old. After Father Creighton was assigned to the Parish CYO, he recruited [REDACTED] to help in planning CYO events. He quickly assumed a special relationship with her and for her 17th birthday bought her a baseball glove.

Father Creighton began inviting [REDACTED] to join him in his activities. The CYO had record hops. Father Creighton told [REDACTED] to come down to the rectory basement to tape music with him. On one occasion, he just had his cassock on without any pants underneath, and asked her to rub his backside. This happened a few times. Then at another time at a record hop, he brought her into the boiler room and began touching her breasts and genital area and had her touch him.

He began taking [REDACTED] away for sexual encounters. He would take her to the beach in his car and would touch her breasts as they drove. Then he would touch her in the water including her genital area. During the summer of 1958, he took her to Cohasset and to Nantasket Beach several times. Along the way, he would pull off the road and tell her to go into the back seat. Then he would tell her to pull on his penis.

On the way back to Dorchester, he would stop at St. William's Parish Church to visit Father Peter Hart who apparently was a friend of his. First, Father Creighton would speak privately with Father Hart and then Father Hart would call [REDACTED] in to confess the sins she had committed with Father Creighton. She remembers that her impression was that Father Hart already knew what she was telling him before she told him. His only response was to tell her not to do it again.

After confessing twice to Father Hart in this manner after sexual encounters, Father Creighton told her to go to the Arch Street Shrine in downtown Boston to confess their further sexual encounters. [REDACTED] recalls going into the confessional at the Arch Street Shrine and telling the priest she had touched another priest and saying that she was sorry.

While on an encounter at Cape Cod, Father Creighton took [REDACTED] to a cottage to which he had access. To this day, [REDACTED] has scattered memories of what happened in that cottage. She remembers Father Creighton coming over to her while she was sitting on a couch and suggesting that the bed in the other room would be more comfortable, but her remaining memories of what happened in that cottage are still repressed. She is working on that with her psychiatrist.

Father Creighton felt the need to control [REDACTED]. She had originally intended to join and had been accepted into the Sisters of Charity in Halifax, Nova Scotia. But, Father Creighton started pressuring her to instead join the Sisters of Saint Joseph in Framingham, Massachusetts. It was the Order to which his Aunt belonged. Ultimately, she could not resist him and agreed to his plans—a change which meant she would also not be join- ing the same convent as her small circle of close friends. I have enclosed a photocopy of a newspaper photo of [REDACTED], her family and Father Creighton at the time. With what we now know of Father Creighton's actions, this photograph becomes repulsive.

In late August as that fateful summer was ending, and shortly before she was to enter the convent [REDACTED] told Father Creighton she had a toothache and needed to see her dentist be- fore she entered the convent. He insisted instead that she go to a dentist whom he knew in Dorchester. She complied. That den- tist told her that she must have all of her upper teeth pulled so that her dental problems would not delay her entrance into the convent of the Sisters of Saint Joseph to which Father Creighton was so anxious for her to enter. She complied. When she woke up in the hospital, a helpless 17-year-old girl with no upper teeth, Father Creighton came to visit her and touched her sexually be- neath the sheets. This was the state in which she entered the convent.

As a result of this abuse, [REDACTED] entered the convent grieving and broken in spirit, seized in emotional pain and grief. She felt as though the shame of her deeds was transparent and visible. She was terrified that she was pregnant. She was grief stricken and her lack of teeth and her mutilation was like a badge of shame. She was seventeen years old, and without her dentures she looked like an old lady. Her agony was very acute and very intense. She felt a deep sense of shame and loss and could share it with no one. Dr. Grassian, her psychiatrist, in his report states that "inevitably she became severely depressed." She could not eat, or sleep, and cried almost daily.

[REDACTED] remained a nun for the next ten years but she never recovered from the agony of shame and grief with which she had entered the convent. She lived with an overpowering sense of shame, fear and defectiveness and she suffered from a pervasive and at times immobilizing depression. Fleeting thoughts and images of herself with Father Creighton and of her mutilation plagued her daily but she could not tell a soul about these demons. There were days when she did not know how she could go on. She lived in constant fear that there was something visibly bad in her—some defect, some dirtiness.

Eventually, she left the convent and married [REDACTED]. But, even this brought [REDACTED] little relief from her feelings of depression and defectiveness. She reported to Dr. Grassian that "It was very bad to [REDACTED]"

She could never tell her husband about her history of sexual abuse. She cried all the time, but hid it from her husband. She reported to Dr. Grassian: "With this hanging over me, I couldn't share myself. Since the abuse, my life has always been secret . . ."

From other documents in the pile, I learned what happened next. Early on a Thursday in August 1995, months before the above summary of events was written, Mom got into her car and drove toward Boston. That much was common enough; several times each month, she would make a similar trip to see my grandmother, who still lived in the Dorchester neighborhood where as a little girl my mother had wandered off and gotten herself lost. This time, though, she wouldn't stop there.

Mom had noticed recently that Reverend Gerard E. Creighton was still listed in the archdiocese directory, the annually published listing of all parishes, clergy, and Catholic organizations in and around Boston.

Creighton would have been just over seventy by then; the directory let her know he was retired from ministry and living in Dennis, one of Cape Cod's picturesque coastal villages, a well-heeled community complete with lighthouses and a quaint shopping district for the seasonal influx of vacationers from the city. The thought of it—of old, crude Creighton puttering around the beaches, playing the part of the respectable elderly priest—sharpened all the feelings that had been pressing in on her for decades. The Cape, after all, was where he had often taken her; it was the destination of those awful, groping drives in his car; the scene of the crime that had left her terrified she was pregnant even as she prepared to make her vows. Because of him, the Cape was the place where the life she had planned had ended and another had begun. So that's where she was going now.

She wasn't sure what she would say to him. Through the years, she had spoken to no one about this—to no one, that is, except for a series of confessors: the priests Creighton had taken her to see after each time he abused her; and, just a few days before setting to off to find him, an old family friend both she and my father had known since the Roxbury days. He had become her confidant and confessor over the last ten years. It was to him she had admitted that she sometimes imagined confronting Father Creighton, and it was he had who encouraged her to do so. "Confrontation can be good," he'd said.

With that in mind as she made her way to the Cape, she felt perfectly calm for the first time she could remember. Before then, she had thought of all that had happened with Father Creighton as *her* fault, *her* sin, and the feeling of it, like a black spot on her soul, had left her permanently anxious. Now, though, driving in from the northern suburbs, past Medford and Somerville, the outlying towns where she had first worked as a nun, down through the half-dark of the South Station Tunnel and up into the light as the expressway emerged on the south side of Boston, the weight of that imagined sin left her. She listened to taped Irish music and drove without thinking, not worried about the confrontation to come, not the least bit afraid. When the highway rose over the streets of her childhood, she could see the redbrick tower of St. Margaret's Church out the passenger side window. No longer the highest point in the neighborhood, but still perfectly visible from a mile away, it reminded her again, half a century on, of who and what she was: Mary Doherty from Dorchester, a girl who had lived her whole life in the shadow of the church.

She reached Dennis ninety minutes later. With the help of a map, she found the house she'd come looking for, but was dismayed to realize the address in the directory was out of date. Father Creighton had moved to Falmouth, a neighbor told her. Though she still was not sure exactly why she wanted to see him, she knew enough about herself to know she would always regret it if she'd come this far only to let this chance slip away. So she headed for Falmouth. It was less than thirty miles away, but in the summer traffic it took well over an hour. When she reached the town limits, she stopped into a gas station and borrowed their phone book. She asked a few directions and was on her way.

Ten minutes later, she discovered that Creighton lived in one of Falmouth's newer developments. A gatehouse at the entrance looked as though it might slow her down, but there was no guard on duty, no one to ask which resident she was there to see. It didn't make much difference; had anyone asked, she would have said "Gerard Creighton" without hesitation. She'd kept his name a secret far too long.

It was a strange place for someone who had played such a singular role in her life to live: identical houses, identical lawns, all neatly manicured; a community made up of the kind of quiet residential roads to nowhere that fill up with landscapers' trucks as soon as all the Volvos and BMWs have gone off for the day. With a new address written in the notebook beside her, she drove past streets with names like Bumblebee and Wigwam and then turned on to Bob White Lane. Driving with one hand, leaning to the right to see out the passenger-side window, she studied the numbers on the houses as they rolled by. When she saw one with an enormous blue and white statue of the Blessed Virgin out front, she looked at the number on the mailbox and was not surprised it was the one she'd come to find.

But again she was disappointed. She rang the bell, gave a good rap on the door, even peeked in the living room window. Inside, she saw more statues of the Virgin, a Sacred Heart image hanging on the wall, various other religious bric-a-brac, mainly tiny statues of the saints: Francis, Patrick, the usual suspects. It was all very tidy; not at all what she had expected. The way the place was kept up, she wondered who lived there with him—some woman, probably—though other than the decorative saints the place was deserted.

She knocked on a neighbor's door.

"Sorry to bother you," Mary told the woman who answered. "I'm looking for the Creightons. Do you know what time they come home?"

"Usually a little later," the neighbor said. "Did you try the store?"

"The store?"

"His furniture shop. If he's not here, he's there."

Of course, she thought; what else would he be doing with his retirement? Even as far back as when he was stationed at St. Margaret's, Father Creighton had been infamous for his elaborate business schemes: real estate speculation, construction deals, stock tips; anything that would let him make some extra money on the sly. His favorite sideline had always been selling furniture out of the rectory garage. Now that he was free to pursue such work without the encumbrance of his pastoral responsibilities, he had opened a couple of furniture stores nearby.

"It's not far," the neighbor said. "You can probably catch him before closing time."

Closing time? She looked at her watch. Suddenly it was getting near five o'clock. She had been driving up and down the Cape for most of the day.

She got more directions, got back in the car, and in no time she was there: a big barn of a place just off Route 28. Furniture shopping is one of the Cape's preferred pastimes; a tourist could have spent a full week browsing in the shops Mary had driven by in a single day. This one looked like any other. But, still, sitting in the parking lot, knowing who owned it, knowing that he might be waiting on the other side of the door, how could it not give her a chill?

Inside, there were several people milling about among a warehouse worth of sofas and coffee tables, floor lamps and easy chairs, beds and sideboards and bookcases, all arranged as if they were a dozen separate rooms packed in around each other like a house without walls. In an office connected to the showroom, Mary saw a young man unpacking boxes. A woman about her age, plump and harried-looking, popped up in front of her. "Can I help you?" she asked.

Mary just walked right by. Her eyes were drawn immediately to the rear of the store, to an elderly man with gray hair swooped across his head. He was dressed in baggy pants and canvas sneakers; his big glasses fell down his nose. He was talking and nodding his head perfunctorily to a customer, but when he looked up and saw who was walking toward him, his eyes flashed with pleased recognition.

"Mary Doherty!" he shouted. "What are you doing here?"

Quickly excusing himself from his conversation with the customer, he moved in her direction. The young man in the office looked up to see what the commotion was about; the woman by the door looked on smiling at this apparent reunion. They both seemed to study the situation as if curious to know who this lady was who could inspire such spontaneous affection in their usually gruff employer. Even the customer appeared interested, trying not to watch while she pretended to inspect her purchase.

Mary didn't know what to do. The last thing she wanted was to cause a scene. Had she really imagined that would be possible? Then suddenly Creighton was in front of her, an old man smiling with his arms outstretched.

She hadn't seen him in almost forty years. There was no doubt he was the man she had known, though. He still had the same smirking grin; the same jocular tone to his voice that barely concealed a deeper anger. There was still something careless to the way he put himself together, his shirt rumpled, half tucked-in; his pants so loose they swept the floor. The last time she had been touched by him, she was lying in a bed at Carney Hospital, her upper teeth removed earlier in the day. He had slid his hand under the bedsheet, found an opening in her hospital johnny, and told her she would be fine. Four decades later, despite herself, she gave him the kind of hug she usually reserved for old friends. It was then she knew the real difference between her memory and the old man before her. He seemed smaller now in every way. When he wrapped his arms around her she could feel how he had shrunken in the shoulders. It felt like she was holding the bones of the priest he had been.

A public embrace inevitably draws attention and Mary felt it now: all those eyes on them, on her, somehow making the ugly fact of touching him again all the worse. She had not intended to create such a spectacle. She asked if they could speak privately, and so they sat down in a living room set on the other side of the showroom. Creighton told her he didn't understand why she insisted on sitting so far from the front of the store. "That's just my niece and the black kid who works here," he said, shrugging innocently. What did they have to talk about that they shouldn't stay out in the open?

"I came to ask you why you hurt me," Mary said.

Creighton's eyes narrowed behind his glasses.

"Hurt you? I never hurt you."

"What you did to me was wrong," she said. "I came to ask you why you did it."

He stared blankly. He had instantly remembered her face, her name. Though he was an elderly man now, and maybe his memory was fading, there was no way he would not remember this. Finally he said, "Well, you were eighteen."

"No," she said. "I was sixteen and then I was seventeen, and you were my priest."

"This is why you came here? To throw rocks at me in my own store?"

"I came here for answers."

She sat steaming. What had she expected? Remorse? A tearful apology? She was willing to forgive him and put it all behind her, but first he would have to admit he had done something wrong; that the things he had instructed her to confess all those years ago were not her sins but his.

"Everything all right over there Gerry?" The woman who had greeted Mary moved closer to the living room set. "I'm going to get my hair done. Do you need a ride home?"

"My niece," Creighton said.

His *niece*—this time the word caught Mary's attention. As far as she knew, he was an only child; he had always complained of being the only one who could take care of his mother. She supposed this was the woman who lived with him. Did *she* have any idea what he had done?

Not that it mattered now. Mary could feel her chance slipping away. He would leave the store and who knows if she would ever find the courage to drive down here a second time and demand answers to his face. Then she recalled her friend's advice: *Confrontation can be good.*

"Why don't I drive you home?" she asked.

Creighton looked warily at Mary, then at the woman he called his niece. He stepped away from the living room set for a moment and had a word with her. When he came back to Mary he agreed she could drive him home. "But I need to close up first," he told her, and shuffled off in the direction of the office.

Waiting by the door, Mary watched as overhead lights clicked off in blocks around the store: lights out over the living rooms; lights out over the bedrooms; lights out over the dining rooms and a gathering of miscellaneous ladder-back chairs. Soon every section of furniture sat in darkness. She was glad to be standing by the windowed entry-way, with August evening light still shining in.

From somewhere in the showroom, Creighton called out, "You know how I got this place?"

"No."

He stepped out of the shadows and again stood directly in front of her. "With the help of my mafia friends."

"Is that supposed to scare me?" she asked, but Jesus it did. As they stepped out into the parking lot and made their way to her car, she wondered if someday soon it was going to explode around her.

For the entirety of the drive back to Bob White Lane, Father Creighton talked about his thriving business and his failing health. As much as she wanted to return to the discussion she had begun in the store, he wouldn't let her get a word in. Another car was already in the driveway when they reached his home.

"My niece," Creighton said again. Either she had had a very speedy haircut, or he had warned her this lady was trouble, had asked her to be waiting there.

Mary knew immediately she would not get any more answers out of him today. Even when she agreed to go inside, she knew it was not to talk over all the questions she had raised. For all the effect it had on him, she might as well have said nothing at all. Inside, he showed her around, pointed out the statues of saints she had seen through the window, told the tales of how and where he'd come across each. He made sure she saw the Sacred Heart hanging on the wall.

"I'm in good standing," he said, using the canonical term meaning that he was still considered a priest. Mary did not yet know about the years of complaints made against him, but she knew what he had done to her, and she could not reconcile her memories of the man with the fact that, as far as the church was concerned, Father Creighton's faith and his life were as pristine as the day he was ordained.

They sat together with glasses of ginger ale. The old man and his niece seemed so pleasant, so normal, at their kitchen table. He was rumpled and gray-faced, no different from any man of seventy; she was apparently happy to entertain an old acquaintance of his. Whether she was actually a niece or not, they were a kind of family. They obviously cared for each other. It was almost difficult to remember what he had done, who he had been, so long ago. The three of them chatted more about the house; Mary mentioned briefly her job, her husband, and her children. After an hour or more, no further opportunity to discuss the issue at hand had presented itself. She'd spent the day hoping for some kind of satisfaction, and suddenly it was time to go. Moving toward the door, addled by the awkwardness of leaving with a task half-done, with all she had meant to say still lodged in her head, she hugged him goodbye.

Back out in the car, she was no longer as peaceful of mind as she had been that morning. She was as upset about what had happened to her as she had ever been. Now, though, she was not angry at herself, but at him. It was not some defect in her that had caused her all those years of depression and pain; it was not God that had forced himself on her, groped her and molested her not far from where this tidy Cape Cod home now stood; it was not she herself who had pulled out her teeth and sent her to the convent confused and grieving. No, it was not her fault. It was his. After thirty-seven years, it was about time she did something about it.

That night, my mother told my father where she had been. She told him the whole story of what had happened to her, said all she might have said thirty years before, when she'd told him that a priest had tried to kiss her. Among many of the priests of Dad's generation, Father Creighton—"Pops" Creighton, as he was sometimes known—had been notorious for being impossible to work with and an occasional threat to parishioners. Dad had never met him, but he knew the type. Together, they sat down and wrote a letter.

> Gerard,
>
> I'm sending this letter to express my dismay, disappointment, upset and anger over the responses I received from you during our meeting of Thursday, August 24, 1995. It took me over thirty-five years of emotional and psychological upset to finally tell someone about the things that you did to me. My next step was to seek you out and confront you with the facts. I expected answers to the questions of why and expressions of remorse and apology. Instead I received denials and protests of not remembering. You treated the issues I talked about as nonexistent.
>
> It was not my intent to have some kind of angry, emotional scene. I believe that was the proper course of action to take especially in light of the fact that your employee and niece were present in the store. At the time I thought it was better to be friendly and courteous in order not to upset her. I wanted to discuss the matter further on the ride to your house but you totally avoided the issues.
>
> The statues of Mary you have in and outside the house and the pictures of the Sacred Heart do not cover up or erase the fact that you used

and abused me for your own sexual gratification when I was a high
school student. Until you acknowledge that fact, being in "good stand-
ing" has no real meaning.

Your protestations of denial do not close the book on the matter for me.
I intend to pursue the answers to my questions about your behavior to-
ward me and then I will decide what further steps to take.

She hoped a strongly worded letter would bring about some kind
of response; he could not simply go on denying actions that were
among the formative events of her life. But weeks went by and she
heard nothing from him. It began to seem little else would happen
with it, which would mean the courage she had found to confront
him had been wasted. The more she thought about their meeting,
though, about the way he was able to act and talk as if he had done
nothing wrong, she began to wonder if perhaps he was so casual
about her accusations because she was just one of many. If he hurt
her, maybe he hurt others.

She went to the library at the archdiocesan seminary—to St. John's,
where my father, Creighton, Spag, and every other priest in this story
was trained. Keeping her intentions to herself, she asked to see all the
directories of parishes and personnel for the last forty years. Then she
sat by a window with a pen and a notebook, and leafed through every
directory until she found the information she was looking for:
Creighton's assignments; more than twenty churches, from which she
could glean all the places he had been, all the people he had known
before and since the dark day when he walked into her life. She built a
list: St. Joseph's, St. Margaret's, Our Lady of Lourdes . . . Somewhere,
she thought, someone else had to have seen this man for what he was.

Obviously she couldn't just call the current pastors. He'd been
transferred so many times it was unlikely anyone in the rectory or the
church office would have been there at the same time. But, she knew,
the people in the pews have long memories, and they see more than
the pastor and priests ever imagine. Back at home she checked the
phone book, found the local papers in each of the towns Creighton
had been stationed, and made a phone call.

"Classifieds, please. Yes, I would like to place an ad."

The following week, classified sections in newspapers around the state asked the question:

DO YOU REMEMBER FATHER CREIGHTON?

Beneath she included only a P.O. box number; as far as she was concerned, nothing more needed to be said. If anyone remembered him, they would have an idea why someone was asking.

Almost immediately she began to hear from people who had seen the ad. One man said that he believed Father Creighton was the priest who had married him; the bride was a few minutes late and Creighton had ruined the ceremony by scolding the couple even as they took their vows. Another person wrote to say Father Creighton had once helped him move some furniture. Others had a complaint found throughout the priest's personnel file, that he was more interested in making money than in serving God. A woman who worked as a parish secretary provided no further details but asked, "This is about abuse, isn't it?" Through another tip, Mom learned the story of a recently married woman who'd had a run-in with Creighton once when she was having trouble with her husband. Good Catholic that she was, the newlywed went to the rectory of St. Bridget's in Abington to find a sympathetic ear. She was inside just a minute or two when Father Creighton appeared in the parlor wearing only his boxer shorts. As the story goes, he looked down, announced that his shorts were on backwards, and proceeded to strip them off in front of her. The woman left in hysterics and reported him to the police.

Nothing Mom learned about Creighton through her investigation was a surprise, and none of it made her feel any better. The thing that gnawed at her was that, as far as she could tell, Father Creighton was just going on with his life as if she had not confronted him at all.

What she did not know at the time, what she learned only from the pile of documents she later dropped before me, was that, far from being unaffected by her accusations, Creighton immediately contacted the archdiocese for advice and assistance. In the chancery office in

Brighton, Reverend Brian Flatley, assistant to the secretary for ministerial priesthood, made notes on their subsequent conversations, in which Father Creighton gave his account of all that happened between Mary Doherty and himself.

"Father Creighton swears that he never molested her or any other woman," Flatley wrote. "He said something to the effect that he has his own urges, but that they don't involve women." As far as his interactions with young Mary in the spring and summer of 1958, Creighton claimed they were limited to a Red Sox game the two attended with St. Margaret's pastor, Father Farrell; a field trip to the movies—"I think it was *The Ten Commandments,*" Creighton said—and once or twice when he went to Carson Beach with the CYO.

"He is very upset," Flatley continued. "His narrative was very agitated and 'earthy.' He did reference a couple of times that he would like to kill her. (His file has numerous references to his owning a gun, and the fear of pastors and others that he would use it.)"

When my mother contacted the archdiocese herself to inquire how to make a complaint of abuse by a priest, no mention was made that Creighton had threatened her life. In fact, for several months it was difficult to get any response at all. It was not until she had a lawyer make contact that things began to happen. Along with "The Facts," her lawyer sent to Brighton formal statements of liability against Father Creighton; Father Farrell, his direct superior at St. Margaret's; Father Peter Hart, the priest to whom Creighton had taken Mary to confession; and the archdiocese itself, which, through its refusal to do something about a notoriously "dangerous," "sick," and "homicidal" priest, put Mary Doherty and countless others in harm's way.

Creighton's file spanned four decades and more than twenty parishes, but it would not have taken long to find indications of what a menace he had been. Nor did it take long for the archdiocese to make an offer of settlement. For the sum of $150,000 and payment of her therapy fees, lawyers for the archbishop of Boston asked Mom to drop all claims against the church. She signed a release that, in the quasi-religious language of the law, "forever discharges" the office of the archbishop and all its "agents, servants, employees, officers, trustees,

directors and independent contractors, of and from all debts, demands, causes of action, suits, accounts, covenants, contracts, agree-
ments, damages, and any and all claims . . . I now have or ever had
from the beginning of the world to this date, including but in no way
limited to events which occurred in approximately 1958." As part of
the settlement, she also agreed, as was the church's policy in such
matters, that she would not reveal the details or the nature of her
claim to anyone.

Though the release she signed made clear that, legally, the church admitted no culpability through its settlement, Mom was pleased to have
received from the church something like an apology, if not in fact then
in kind. However, she had still received nothing of the sort from Father
Creighton, and it was his apology she wanted most of all. Her agreement with the archdiocese did leave room for her to pursue a civil case
against Creighton himself, and that was just what she planned to do.

Upon hearing of the settlement, Creighton called the chancery
again. It's conceivable he truly had no idea of the case his own file
made against him, for he was apparently bewildered why the church
would choose to settle, which he saw as a move that aided her cause
by casting doubt on him. Among the things he said about my mother,
all recorded by various officers of the archdiocese: "I don't want to
hear from this bitch the rest of my life"; "She downplayed her kids
when she was here, not proud of them. Disappointed with her husband. Looking for annulment grounds"; and perhaps most damningly
as far as he was concerned: "She's anti-pope, wants a married clergy."

When the secretary for the ministerial priesthood wrote to Father
Creighton summarizing the pending case against him, he could barely
contain his rage: "Someone will pay for my anger." "I get a letter like
this it's like waving a red flag in front of a bull." "My father said the
only way to deal with a rattlesnake is to get away from it and crush its
head with a stone."

By the time I learned all this, sitting at my parents' kitchen table with
hundreds of pages of documents spread out before me, the civil case
my mother initiated had already been through a cycle of decisions and

appeals. It had begun, I realized, during my last year of college. I'd noticed at the time that my parents had seemed closer, more affection-
ate. I can still see my father holding my mother in the kitchen, and I
can hear her sighing in his arms. I know now that he was consoling
her through a troubling time. While I was considering and then re-
jecting the notion of disappearing into the monastery, I was oblivious
to the story unfolding at home.

Had it ended there, I may never have heard a word about it. As Mom
said, they had told me only because "it was going to be in the news."

When a comprehensive history of the scandal of sexual abuse and
cover-up in the Roman Catholic Church is written, the case of *Jane Doe
v. Gerard Creighton* will be at most a footnote, but an important one. As
fate would have it, *Doe v. Creighton* reached the highest court in the
state just as the long history of the church's protection of dangerous
priests became known.

In the years since Mom had begun her case—she confronted
Creighton in 1995, filed suit in 1998, lost an initial judgment in 2001,
and won an appeal in 2002—everything about the way the church
dealt with abuse, and the way the world dealt with the church, had
changed. Before the abuse crisis and the intense media scrutiny it
brought, claims of injuries caused by members of the Catholic clergy
were settled as quietly as possible. The confidentiality agreement my
mother signed is one example of this; another occurred several years
before, when the then-archbishop of Boston, Bernard Cardinal Law,
told a young man abused by a priest that he was bound "by the power
of the confessional" to never again speak of the crimes committed
against him. The church found it easy to silence such people: many
victims were shamed by what they had survived; hence the
pseudonym with which my mother filed her suit. For everyone else, it
was just as easy to look the other way.

All of that changed significantly with the revelation, at the start of
2002, of the hierarchy's protection of Father John Geoghan. My
mother began her case in a pre-Geoghan era of silence, but she was
ending it in a post-Geoghan world hungry for news of priests and sex.

With more than five hundred civil actions against abusive clergy pending in the state's courts, and the prospect of many more to come if the first wave proved successful, the Supreme Judicial Court of Massachusetts sought to make a statement about an issue that would inevitably be central to every case that would follow: the statute of limitations. The vast majority of allegations were being made ten, twenty, thirty years after the acts of abuse. Because Mom's trouble with Creighton had occurred a full forty years before, it represented to the court the outer limit of possible claims. It was a perfect test case for answering the question on which many of the lawsuits would rest: how late is too late to take action in response to harm done to a child?

In Massachusetts, the statute of limitations to prosecute someone for rape of a minor runs out fifteen years from the time the crime was committed. In civil cases, however, charges of childhood sexual abuse are handled differently. At the time of this writing, the law states that action must be taken up to three years after the victim has reached eighteen years of age, or three years after the victim "discovered or reasonably should have discovered" that the abuse had caused lingering psychological injuries or conditions which may not have been evident at the time the crime was committed. This clause in the statute obviously leaves considerable room for interpretation; it was into this gray area that *Doe v. Creighton* fell.

Mom's contention, and that of her lawyers, was that she did not fully appreciate the extent to which Creighton's actions had been the cause of her ongoing depression and emotional trauma until she had made the decision to confront him. Only then, only after the recognition that it was the aftereffects of his sin, not hers, she had been aching with all these years, was she able to see a causal connection between the dark feelings she still had and the abuse she had suffered so long ago. In discussions of the case and the statute of limitations in the media around Boston, "When does the clock start ticking?" became a constant refrain. To her there was no doubt about it: the three-year clock set by the statute of limitations did not start ticking until the day she drove to the Cape, looked him in the eye, and asked for answers.

Needless to say, Creighton and his lawyers had a different opinion. Early on in the case, his attorneys seemed intent on damaging my mother's credibility. In their deposition of her, they seem to imply several times that she had a long-standing sexual obsession with priests, asking questions as if at sixteen years old she'd been the Lolita of the Archdiocese of Boston. Her answers are exactly as worldly as you'd expect from a woman who spent her first decade of adulthood in a convent.

> Lawyer: Have you ever been sexually attracted to any priest or former priest other than your own husband?
>
> Mom: I'm not really sure about sexual attraction. I—you know, I need to know what you think of that. I don't—do you mean you see somebody and you say oh, he's nice. Do you call that sexual attraction?
>
> Lawyer: Why don't we go by your definition of sexual attraction. What do you understand that term to mean?
>
> Mom: That I could see somebody and say "Oh, he's nice."
>
> Lawyer: Somebody's a physically attractive person?
>
> Mom: Sure.
>
> Lawyer: And you've had that feeling or experience with respect to other priests or former priests throughout your adult lifetime, is that correct?
>
> Mom: Yes.
>
> Lawyer: And other than the occasion with respect to your husband, have you ever acted on your feelings of sexual attraction towards any priest or former priest?
>
> Mom: No.

A second front of this strategy seems to have been to make Creighton seem as righteous and priestly as possible. Because of the release Mom had signed as part of her settlement with the archdiocese, no church records could be obtained by discovery in *Doe v. Creighton*. No part of his complaint-ridden personnel file could be used to refute his claims of all-around innocence. Without the most damning evidence against him, Mom's lawyers challenged him as best they could.

Lawyer: Mr. Creighton, are you still a priest today?

Creighton: Yes, it's an indelible mark on the soul.

Lawyer: An indelible mark on the soul?

Creighton: Yes. I am a priest as long as I am in this world. I have kept my vows.

Lawyer: What were those vows?

Creighton: What were those vows?

Lawyer: Yes.

Creighton: Chastity and obedience. Poverty we didn't have a vow to.

Lawyer: Anything besides chastity and obedience?

Creighton: No, not really. That's enough.

Lawyer: What does chastity mean to you?

Creighton: What does chastity mean to me?

Lawyer: Yes.

Creighton: It means you lead a good life, we don't marry, we don't cavort with women and we do what we are supposed to do—

Lawyer: What does cavort mean?

Creighton: —observe the Ten Commandments of God.

Lawyer: You said you don't cavort with women. What do you mean when you use the word *cavort*?

Creighton: Well I don't know. You can interpret that any way you want.

Lawyer: How do you interpret it? What is it that you don't do with women?

Creighton: I don't do anything with women.

Lawyer: Your interpretation of the vow of chastity means to you that you don't do what with women?

Creighton: We're celibate, we don't marry. That is basically the vow of chastity.

Lawyer: You don't marry. Are you allowed to have sexual relations with women?

Creighton: No, we are not.

Lawyer: So your vow of chastity includes not having sexual
             relations with women?
Creighton: Correct.
Lawyer: When you use the word *sexual relations* do you
             interpret that to mean sexual intercourse?
Creighton: It can be wider than that.
Lawyer: What is the breadth of that?
Creighton: It is a very difficult question to answer. Anything that
             is against the commandments of Jesus Christ.
Lawyer: Let me be more specific. Is it encompassed within
             your vow of chastity to not touch a woman on her
             breasts?
Creighton: Sure. Absolutely.
Lawyer: Is it within your vow of chastity not to touch a woman
             on her ass? Excuse the word.
Creighton: Yes.
Lawyer: Is it within your vow of chastity not to touch a woman
             on her crotch?
Creighton: Right.
Lawyer: Is it within your vow of chastity to not comment to a
             woman about her body?
Creighton: Yes. I would say yes.
Lawyer: Is it within your vow of chastity to not expose your
             genitals to a woman?
Creighton: Absolutely.
Lawyer: Have you been faithful to your vow of chastity since
             you took that vow when you first became a priest?
Creighton: Yes.
Lawyer: And is that true to this present day?
Creighton: Yes.

As was her right as plaintiff, Mom sat in on Father Creighton's deposition and found his performance on the whole as scripted as his
first lines had been. Despite the fact that he had recognized Mom immediately at the time of her visit to his furniture shop, when he en-

tered the law office conference room and saw her seated at the table, he turned to his lawyer and asked "Who's that?" as if he was just a guileless old man who'd doddered in off the street.

The morning the SJC was scheduled to hear the case, Mom, Dad, and I rode down together to the courthouse in Boston. As Spag had said of their wedding, it seemed like the whole world was packed in there. With so many clergy abuse cases pending, every one of them possibly affected by what was said in the courtroom that day, the visitors' gallery was filled with lawyers and reporters. We settled in among them, no one knowing that the short-haired woman in the third row from the back was the Jane Doe who had set all this in motion.

Having read through the depositions and other court documents, I was surprised when Creighton's lawyer addressed the court. The lawyer's approach was not one of arguing against my mother's credibility. In fact, her argument, though peppered with the word "alleged," seemed to take for granted the guilt of her client. What was at issue here was not the what or the when of the abuse, but the what and when of its effects on the victim.

I scanned the room. At the front of the court, five judges sat staring down the attorneys, one of whom was speaking at a podium while the rest were seated behind her, taking copious notes. Behind the lawyers were a gaggle of court workers, and then there were the observers' benches, strangely like pews, in which everyone sat with an ear cocked toward the front; with the awkward acoustics of the high-ceilinged room, it was otherwise impossible to hear.

Creighton was nowhere to be seen, and who could blame him. Because of the peculiar wording of the statute of limitations, I realized, his guilt in a perverse way actually helped his case. His lawyer quoted from an evaluation written by Mom's psychologist that told of her memories of the awful feelings she'd had upon entering the convent; of the debilitating depression she suffered because of what Creighton had done. The lawyer argued that especially in "so pure and chaste an environment" as the Sisters of St. Joseph novitiate, Jane Doe surely would have known that it was Creighton who had made her feel this way. That she saw a causal connection between the incidents of physical abuse and the lingering mental trauma was all Creighton's lawyers needed to demonstrate, and nothing suggested such a connection like the facts of what he had done and how it had made her feel.

Mom's lawyer countered with expert testimony about post-traumatic stress disorders and the ways in which victims create psychological barriers that prevent them from fully recognizing the root causes of their injuries. The particular trauma the lawyer hoped to discuss he referred to as "the mutilation," Father Creighton's role in the removal of Jane Doe's teeth. The judges, however, kept asking about the fear and the sadness she felt in the convent. If she knew then, in 1958, that she had been wronged and it made her feel bad, how could she contend she saw no connection between Father Creighton and her long-term suffering until 1995? Try as he might, the lawyer could not come up with an answer that satisfied the court.

"If I may add a word about the mutilation," Mom's lawyer said.

"I'm sorry," one of the judges responded. "You're out of time."

Three months later, the front page of the *Boston Globe* announced the end of a chapter of my mother's life.

SJC Rejects Abuse Suit Reaching Back to '50s.

In a significant victory for church officials in the clergy sex abuse cases, the Supreme Judicial Court yesterday dismissed a suit by a woman who said she had been molested by a priest in the 1950s, ruling that she had waited too long to sue.

The unanimous decision may provide the Archdiocese of Boston with new ammunition in fighting many of the roughly 500 civil lawsuits filed by people who say they were sexually abused by priests decades ago.

As the court ruling had it: "While we recognize that, in some circumstances, sexual abuse victims may develop coping mechanisms that might obscure the source of their injuries, a plaintiff who brings suit beyond the normal statutory limitations period may not reach a jury simply by presenting evidence that sexual abuse took place . . . There is, in short, no evidence tending to support the plaintiff's contention that an ordinary, reasonable person in her position would fail to realize, for almost four decades, that her injuries were caused by the defendant."

That's what it came down to: not what Mom knew, but what should have been known by "an ordinary, reasonable person."

The "reasonable person standard" invoked here is a commonly used device in legal thinking that purports to allow objectivity in forming opinions of human actions. It holds that there is a proper response to any circumstance that would be identical to the response of a person motivated only by reason.

I was not surprised to learn that this is what is called a "legal fiction." Using something as slippery as reasonableness to judge what someone should have known or done seems flawed in any situation. In this case, with the facts of *Doe v. Creighton* tied up as they were in matters of faith, it seems all the more so. If a "reasonable person" is meant to be understood as one who has shared the experience of the individual in question, then in my mother's case I wonder if the reasonable person the justices had in mind was someone who grew up dutifully saying her prayers each night to shorten her stay in purgatory; or perhaps their reasonable person was someone raised to believe priests are stand-ins for Jesus Christ. I wonder if the justices could explain how such a reasonable person could continue to love her church, despite it all.

Mom sulked for a week following the SJC's decision. Since her days on the Monsignor Ryan Memorial varsity basketball team, she had always been a fierce competitor. The worst of it was knowing that Creighton would think he had won. He would go on selling furniture and basking in the light of the Cape as if he had never troubled a soul in his life. It was all she could to do to resist the temptation of trying to stick it to him one more time. "I just want to *get* him," she would say; by which she meant, I think, that she wished she could force him, somehow, to acknowledge what he had done.

Through the months of media coverage of the court rulings, she had been saving clippings, every newspaper article she came across that mentioned his name. "It doesn't matter," she would say of the court decision. "At least his name will always be associated with abuse. Maybe someday the case will end up in the law books, right? Then everyone will know."

She thought about photocopying her collection of clippings and sending them to him, along with the page of the new archdiocese directory that showed the church no longer listed him among its retired clergy. To Mom, that was as good as saying they no longer considered him a priest; she wanted to be sure he knew it. She held back from contacting him, though, finally content that a small measure of justice had been served when she found one last article about the case, this one from the famously opinionated editorial page of the *Boston Herald*.

In a punchy column headlined "Statute Runs Out, Pain of Abuse Stays," the *Herald* recounted the story behind *Doe v. Creighton:* the girl who wanted to be a nun; the priest who had been chased from one parish to another for more than thirty years. It told of what he had done to her, and of all the complaints made against him. It told also what the church and the bishops had failed to do to stop him. Then the columnist quoted a letter, which I had already read in the case file; a letter sent to Cardinal Humberto Medeiros by the same pastor who had worried that Creighton might kill someone someday:

"Why must we always place the immediate accommodation of the priest above the good of the church?" he wrote. "Why should so many people have to be abused and insulted and alienated just so that we can give this man a place to sleep? We seem to have our values confused."

Mom thought the column was the best thing she'd read in years. One line especially made her hoot with satisfaction: "In short, the man was a pig," it said, "a pig in a clerical collar but a pig just the same."

Grinning ear to ear, the paper still spread out in front of her, she reached for the phone and called the *Herald*.

"Editorial department, please," she said, and then asked to be connected to the columnist directly.

Five years before, when she had decided to press forward with her case, she had done so concerned about maintaining her privacy, her anonymity, and so she'd hidden herself behind a pseudonym as opaque as her habit had been. Today, though, she felt a need to claim what she had accomplished and who she had become. Maybe the case had been dismissed, but nonetheless she had made it happen. She was no longer the lost little girl looking to the church tower to guide her home; she was a woman stepping out of the shadows at last.

"Hello, I have a comment about your column today," she said. "I just wanted to say thank you. This is Jane Doe."

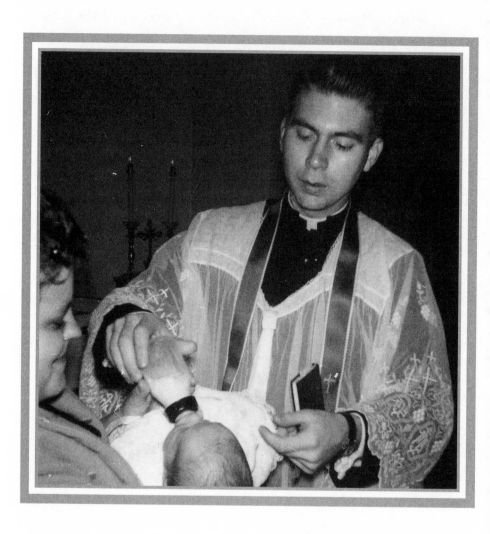

IN THE BEGINNING
WAS THE WORD

Though my mother wished the
SJC's decision had been different, at least she had her day in court. In
time she came to appreciate that, win or lose, the process had created
a forum in which to sort through all she had struggled with through
the years. For my father, a similar reckoning never came.

It was against the backdrop of Mom's ongoing abuse case that Dad
and I first visited the archdiocese offices in Brighton. It was toward the
end of *Doe v. Creighton*'s roller coaster of dismissals and appeals in the
state judiciary that he was informed an ecclesial court would be convened to rule on the status of his priesthood. As instructed by a sympathetic canon lawyer serving the archdiocese, Dad gathered a team
of canonists of his own, led by the Jesuit Father John McIntyre we'd
met with at Boston College, to provide his defense. His argument
would rest on the notion that marriage, in the words of the Vatican itself, was a fundamental human right. The thought that it could be
sanctified for some of the church's members and denied to others
seemed to Dad so much double-talk, concealing the fact that on this
issue the church had changed little since the Middle Ages. Sex still was
on the wrong side of the rift between spirit and flesh, sanctity and sin.
In the church's view, it was to be tolerated among lesser souls; the
truly holy were those who did not stoop so low as to bother with
something so base, so basic, as the concerns of the body.

With his canon lawyers assembled, Dad readied himself for the hierarchy's next move. When no further instructions came, Father McIntyre told him to sit tight, the Catholic bureaucracy is as slow as any bureaucracy. So he waited. And waited. He had been told that church law requires such matters to be settled, start to finish, in a period not longer than a year. At the time of this writing, he has waited twice that and still has not heard another word about it.

As a student of religion, I've come to wonder if the seed of belief might be a hopeful interpretation of silence. Appropriately enough, that is precisely how Dad has tried to understand the hierarchy's lack of follow-through with the process it began. By delaying, or merely forgetting, the passage of formal judgment on my father's dissident priesthood, perhaps the bishops are leaving the door open to change. Perhaps, as far as this issue is concerned, not doing the wrong thing is as close to right as the church can get.

More likely it has simply had other matters to attend to. In the aftermath of the abuse scandal, with the shortage of priests growing ever more dire, the Archdiocese of Boston began making the most extensive changes it had seen since its "brick and mortar" days. Back then, the changes in the church had all been about growth: through the years of my parents' youth, there were parochial schools and Catholic hospitals going up in almost every parish; convents and seminaries, filled past capacity, raced to acquire more land, to build more dormitories, preparing the way for what would surely be an American Catholic renaissance. Now, though, it was brick and mortar in reverse. With legal fees and settlements of cases related to the abuse crisis surpassing $100 million, the grand Archbishop's Residence and a portion of the grounds of St. John's Seminary were sold to Boston College. The new archbishop, the brown-robed Franciscan Sean O'Malley, moved his offices from the lush Brighton campus to a spot in the heart of the city, a small warren of rooms that Cardinals Cushing, Medeiros, and Law had regarded as beneath their dignity. Further tightening his hemp belt, O'Malley set about closing dozens of parishes. Twenty churches were to be sold immediately. Across the diocese, the locks were changed on church doors. Distraught parishioners protested and held vigils. The police arrested a handful, taking the faithful from the sites of their baptisms in squad cars.

When the list of parishes to be shut down was published in the *Globe*, we saw that my mother's beloved St. Margaret's was among them, as well as her high school, Monsignor Ryan Memorial. It seemed fitting: all of this, after all, was the direct result of sexual abuse committed by Father Creighton and scores of other priests. The immediate need for the closings was created by the $20 million deficit the archdiocese had amassed since the crisis began, but the deeper cause went back much further than that. Eight hundred years before, property had been one of the issues that led to the imposition of the rule of celibacy for Catholic clergy; if priests had no heirs, there would be no questions of inheritance of church buildings and thus no challenges to the centralized authority of the bishops. While this helped to make the Roman Catholic Church the single largest landowner in the world, it also instituted damaging ideas of sexuality as law.

Bodies and buildings, now as ever, tied in a knot. For those with a sense of history and an eye for poetic justice, it was not hard to see the church closings in Boston—and indeed all around the country, where similar chapters in this centuries-in-the-making saga were coming to an end—as a flock of celibate chickens coming home to roost.

Like Catholics everywhere, my parents looked on this with sadness. Churches are not just brick and mortar but the accumulated hopes and histories of the families who attend them. To see them shuttered, vacant, razed—or worse, converted into condominiums—was a tragedy such as they had never seen.

But a tragedy can also be a possibility. What Christian lesson is older than that? Who but the most die-hard true believer could have looked on Jesus' empty tomb and seen not the quick work of grave robbers but the mystery of faith? Similarly, when Archbishop O'Malley announced the church closings and said he wished there was another way, Dad thought it was a good time to offer one.

October 24, 2004

Dear Archbishop Sean:

You recently stated that you wished there was a way to avoid the current closings of parishes. I write to you as a representative of the hundreds of Roman Catholic priests who have married and who reside within the Archdiocese of Boston. We are never mentioned by you or your colleagues in the episcopacy as being ready, willing and able to assist the Church, but many of us are. Some of us may even live in the parishes which you and your advisors have chosen to close, saying that there are not enough priests to serve the needs of God's people. Yet, we are here.

Your predecessor, Cardinal Bernard Law, to his credit, attempted to bridge the divide which exists between the married priests and the institutional Church. He hosted several collegial social and spiritual gatherings for married priests and their spouses and other resigned priests. He was unwilling, however, to say that he could do anything to try to seek a change in the papal policy which dictates exclusion for us from the priestly ministry to which we were ordained. He knew that many of us stand ready to offer the nourishment of the Word of God and the Sacraments to God's people. He said that his hands were tied. We said, "Yes, but you have a voice, please use it."

You, Archbishop Sean, have a voice. Pope John Paul II has recently called upon the United States bishops to be more open with each other in seeking solutions to the problems which our Church is facing. Across the country Catholics are reeling from the policies of cover-up and the exclusion of the people from the administration of our Church.

It is time for you and your colleagues to wash the feet of all of God's people and serve our human and spiritual needs, not those of an agenda we never had a hand in formulating. We are your co-workers in the Faith. Please, use your voice to talk with us and tell the Pope and his advisors what you hear. We are here as sharers in the ministerial priesthood as well as in the baptismal priesthood of all believers in Christ Jesus. No disciplinary law can nullify those facts. We are here to help rebuild our Church.

> *Fraternally,*
> *William J. Manseau*

• • •

Sometime during that season of church closings and court cases and threats of ecclesial trials, Dad and I were in his car, and I asked him as he drove to tell me why maintaining his priesthood was so important to him. Why had he devoted the past forty years to trying to reform a church that clearly did not want to change?

Just as I finished the question, a traffic light went red in front us. Dad rolled to a stop, turned in his seat, and launched into what seemed to me to be notes on a sermon he had been waiting to deliver.

"It's not just about the church," he said. "How the Catholic hierarchy views marriage, sex, the body, it's a much bigger question than what they allow priests to do. It has to do with the original mystery of the incarnation. It has to do with what the Gospel of John means when it says, 'In the beginning was the word . . . and the word became flesh.'

"Just imagine if we stopped treating this life as a stepping stone to something greater, a doormat to wipe our feet on before we get to paradise. Imagine what would happen if we took seriously the idea the church is based upon, that the world really is redeemed, that, as Jesus told us, the Kingdom of Heaven is at hand.

"Think about that. Jesus didn't say tomorrow or next week or in a thousand years, but 'at hand.' Imagine if we truly believed and acted on the revelation that we are living—*right now!*—in the world God created for us as reward. Imagine if we lived as if all the promises of the Gospel would come true, if only we would make it so."

Behind us a car horn blared. Dad had been speaking with such excitement he hadn't noticed the light had changed from red to green. I had only been listening, but, in fact, neither had I.

The car jerked forward and we rolled along with a line of impatient drivers behind us. Dad looked flustered at having been beeped at with me in the car, and I remembered that he'd told me he had recently had a nightmare about driving. It had come to him just after his fiftieth high school reunion, at which he'd seen old pals from Lowell he hadn't spoken to in decades. So many of them had lived what seemed to him such satisfying, accomplished, normal lives. They'd become lawyers and accountants, or they had started their own businesses and watched them prosper. They all seemed so satisfied and well aged, as if all their fights, if they had had any at all, were behind them. That night Dad had dreamed he was driving down the wrong side of the highway. There were cars rushing at him, horns blaring and headlights blinding. A driver with his head out the window shouted, *Hey, you idiot, you're going the wrong way!*

Seeing Dad's face now, glowing red as the light had been at the sound of the horn behind him, I wondered if that nightmare had come back to him in a flash; if he was feeling now in his waking life as he had in his dream, a man clogging up the system by going his own way.

I should've known better. As flustered as he looked, he hadn't lost his train of thought. Blaring horn be damned; he hadn't forgotten the point of all this, his life.

"The world redeemed," Dad said. "Imagine!"

EXILES AT REST

At the bottom of a steep hill that is still called Bethany in Framingham, Massachusetts, there sits a little cottage that at one time was the recreation center for the Sisters of St. Joseph novitiate. The rust-colored mansion at the top of the hill, where my mother lived from age seventeen until twenty, has been converted into low-income housing. The only nuns at Bethany now reside in the novitiate's infirmary, which has been transformed into an elder-care center open to the sick and retired religious for whom it was built as well as their families.

These days, the former rec center serves primarily as the meeting place for the Catholic Deaf Community. With folding chairs and tables stacked in the back, and a kitchen with plenty of paper plates and ten-gallon coffee urns to go around, it's a nice location for other organizations to use informally, the Deaf Community's schedule permitting. It is occasionally the site of gatherings of my parents and their friends, the married priests and former nuns I have known all my life. Fellow travelers for the last four decades, they still get together every few months for planning meetings, brown-bag luncheons, and workshops in innovative approaches to the spiritual life. The day I joined my parents for one of these reunions, the offering was liturgical dance.

My mother was not thrilled to be attending. She was worn-out by the court business, tired of thinking about it even though it remained an obsession. In the weeks following the SJC's ruling, she spent hours searching the Internet for *Doe v. Creighton,* just to see if any other news items had cropped up. Every Web page she found was a vindication; she would print each article and put it in a manila folder with all her other notes on the proceedings. So doing, she had amassed a file the thickness of a dictionary, a file filled with evidence that she had been in the right all along, never mind the court's decision.

Yet a successful search for citations of *Doe v. Creighton* also meant she would think about it all for another day. Even with the case dismissed, even with the scandal for the most part gone from the papers, the story for her would go on, she was sure, until the day she died.

Or he did. As it happened, just as I was nearing the end of the writing of my parents' story, Mom received word from one of the connections she had made during her investigation of Father Creighton. He was dead, she was told. Died suddenly but peacefully stretched out on his sofa while the woman he had called his niece was out taking their dog for a walk. I do not quite understand and so it would be difficult to explain the pull the man's death seemed to have on us, my mother and me. And yet we both felt it strongly enough to make the trip down to the Cape Cod funeral home his obituary had listed as the site of his wake. Down through Boston and beyond, we retraced the route of Mom's confrontation with him almost ten years before. Inside the home, Mom signed the guestbook and together we approached the casket.

If he had seemed shrunken when she last set eyes on him, he seemed now almost fully faded away. The gray-yellow makeup covering the dead man's skin blended into the silver of his hair so that it seemed his whole body had been dipped in a single paint. A whitewash? No, the task of putting a good face on the man he'd been was left to the costume the funeral home had dressed him in: full priestly finery draped from his Roman collar to the bottom of his withered legs. Two little canvas sneakers poked out from the hem of his vestments. His hands had been made to clasp a rosary of orange stones. I knelt with my mother and said a prayer.

We left the wake with no better understanding of why we had gone, but we were glad we had made the effort. For Mom perhaps it had to do with a word she disliked, closure. Even if that is what she felt in some small measure, she didn't have much use for the idea. What could closure mean to a believer in an eternal soul? What could closure mean in the shadow of an all-seeing, all-remembering God? Even to someone whose faith is as shaky as mine, it seems simply common sense that true stories do not end.

Which perhaps is why, that day in Framingham a year or more before, she didn't have much interest in liturgical dance. The church of old may have been complicit in the pain she felt, but still it was *her* church. It was the one she knew and loved and recognized, and so she was often unenthusiastic about surface changes to Catholic practice. She was all for good music and lay participation in the liturgy, of course, but some things were just too foreign-seeming for her to enjoy. "I'm still just Mary Doherty from Dorchester," she liked to say; to her that fact offered explanation enough why today's workshop did not hold particular appeal.

On the other hand, in this and all manner of religious experimentation, my father was an unflappable true believer. Before they left the house for the morning workshop, he had asked her, "Why assume you won't like it? How do you know until you try?"

My mother rolled her eyes. "Dancing should be fun," the onetime champion Irish step-dancer said, "it shouldn't be"—she stretched the last word out until it sounded like work—"*liturgical.*"

"Well that's just it," Dad said. "Liturgy doesn't have to be work. It should be fun, too. It's about bringing something vital to worship, something exciting." The glint in his eye made it seem he was about to launch into the kind of stump speech you'd expect from someone running to be the next Martin Luther. "It's about renewal of the sacramental experience. It's about bridging the artificial gulf between body and spirit. It's about—"

Before he could really get rolling, Mom cut him off.

"I didn't say I wasn't going," she explained. "Just don't expect me to spend the whole day at the workshop. That's all I'm saying."

Dad nodded at the compromise: she'd put up with his exuberance; he'd put up with the putting up.

They have been married for thirty-five years, most of them happy. Happy, it seems to me, because they have learned that both faith and love are matters of partial victory. There's a kind of truth in concession; having once hoped to live the perfect lives their vocations required, they have come to know that, even where God is concerned, perfection is a lie.

"Well you'd better shake a leg or we'll be late," Mom said.

"We won't be late, Mary. There's plenty of time."

"Do you remember how to get there?"

"I know how to get there."

"Are you sure?"

The gathering in Framingham was of twenty regulars: eight couples and one widower, led by a former nun turned yoga teacher whose married-priest husband was a good sport, slender and tall, up for anything. He was in quite good shape for a man near seventy, still wearing a crisp little beard like the beatnik priest he once had been, though now it had gone white. Behind the workshop leaders stood a guitar player the yoga teacher knew through a shared acquaintance, their mutual Sufi master.

Following the yoga teacher's instructions, the eager but awkward dance class stood in a circle and joined hands. Today, she told them, they would be singing a new song designed to seem old: the Lord's Prayer translated into Aramaic.

"It's the prayer Jesus taught his disciples in the language he would have spoken," she explained. Never mind that the words had reached this former convent recreation center traveling through the Gospel of Matthew's Greek to St. Jerome's Latin. Never mind that all they knew of the man whose name they invoked they had learned from the tradition they were trying to change. For the moment, they were past worrying about contradiction. The yoga teacher explained that the challenge for her was deciding which parts of their collective past they had been blessed by, and which parts they had merely survived. If it turned out that all of it was both, then maybe they could invent a new past and live it now.

"Who's ready to sing?" she asked.

Earlier in the workshop the group had sat and studied a handout with the words printed in block capital letters. So many years spent memorizing prayers apparently had made them all quick studies, because when the guitar player began to strum a plodding rhythm in a minor key, the circle of married priests and former nuns began to sing, chanting syllables that would have made anyone who happened to see them suppose they were a group of retired suburban witches, a coven circling its cauldron.

"*Ab-woon da-bash maya . . .*" they intoned with careful pronunciation, "*Neth-ka-dash sha-mak . . .*"

From time to time, the yoga teacher added the more familiar words of the prayer, using her lilting soprano to remind the dancers what they were singing. "Our Father, who art in heaven," she sang, "Hallowed be thy name . . ."

As the Sufi guitarist strummed, the group moved together like a halting game of ring-around-the-rosy. Still joined at the hands, they took one clockwise step, bowed to the center, dipped at the knees. They turned to the dancer on the left, turned to the dancer on the right, then looked into his or her eyes.

"See them," the yoga teacher said, "really *see* them."

All the while the circle moved to these strange sounds she insisted were very much like those Jesus Christ would have said the night he taught his followers to pray to God and call him, Abba. Father. "It's a prayer you all know, but now you'll get to know it again," she said, and then continued to sing, responding to each line of Aramaic the group chanted with its English translation.

"*Tetha mal-koo-thak . . .*"

"Thy kingdom come."

"*Ne-we tzev-ya-nak . . .*"

"Thy will be done."

"*Aykan da-bash-maya af-bara . . .*"

"On earth as it is in heaven . . ."

My mother could only take so much of this. She never had much patience for all-day workshops, and, anyway, her knees weren't what they used to be. That was the main thing. In fact, she seemed a little sad she didn't feel up to continuing the dance. Of my parents, she used to be the dancer—before her heart surgery, before that night twenty years before when she blacked out cold and gave us all a fright, she would stay out on the dance floor until the band packed their fiddles. Before then, it was my father who always sat on the sidelines, watching my mother dance with her brothers like she was the Last of Irish Rovers.

With this kind of dance, though, my father was in his element. He closed his eyes as the group circled, bobbed at the knees when the simple choreography required it, chanted the prayer in Aramaic as carefully as he had said his Latin when he was in seminary, as fluidly as he had spoken his first Mass in English after Vatican II, as ecstatically as he had prayed with God's own language when he learned from the Pentecostals about speaking in tongues. The spirit blows where it will, the Gospel says. Dad, as ever, liked to keep a finger in the wind.

After a half hour of dancing and singing and praying, the group took a break in folding chairs and talked about what it was they were trying to do.

"It's not like we don't know this isn't genuine," the yoga teacher said. "We don't have to pretend to be certain that Jesus said these words exactly as we say them today. Quite the opposite: we know this is a translation based on modern scholarship and historical studies. To us, at the start of a new century, that is part of what gives it power, the fact that it is a re-creation, the fact that we create it ourselves from all the material and resources we have been given."

Dad nodded in agreement. "That's when we get past syllogism and into poetry," he said, "and that's where the meaning is. We know that we bring meaning to it with our experiences, with our lives. The Word made flesh goes both ways. The Word is fully incarnate in us, and we need to put our full selves into the words."

The yoga teacher seemed pleased with the notion. "Yes," she said, smiling broadly. "Who's ready to dance some more?"

As the others stood and found their positions on the dance floor, my mother touched my arm and asked if I wanted to see the rest of the convent grounds. Then she whispered to my father, "Bill, we're going to take a walk up the hill. Peter wants to have a look around the old novitiate."

"Have fun!" Dad said, and rushed back to the dancing.

Mom and I slipped out the side door just as the prayer circle started to spin again. Up the hill, through a thick stand of pine, we could barely make out the building I was there to see: the Sisters of St. Joseph novitiate, the place where my mother became a nun. Inside, Mom had suggested we walk up the driveway so I could get a better idea of the size of the campus. Looking at the hill now, though, it seemed it might be difficult for her. A few stairs left her struggling for breath lately; because of her pacemaker, even gentle hills gave her trouble. This one was as steep as a ski slope.

"We can drive if it's too far for you," I said.

"What the heck. If I keel over on the way up there, it'll be a good finish to your book."

The first time my mother climbed Bethany Hill, she had been seventeen years old, staring out the window of her Uncle Pat's car. A postulant's trunk shared the backseat; in the front, her mother kept telling Pat to slow down.

There would be no problem with speed as we climbed up now. Mom took my arm as we trudged along the driveway's steady incline, taking it step by step, pausing often so she could point out the changes the place had been through since she'd lived there.

"There's the new scholasticate," she said, pointing to a long brick block of a building halfway up the hill. "It was new when I was here, anyway. They built it just after my profession. The way they rushed to get that place done! Can you believe they thought they'd need so much space?"

"I guess it seemed they would then," I said.

"It really did. So many new postulants every year." She seemed to add up faces in her mind, all those city girls whose lives were not so different from her own. "Most I knew left years ago, of course. And the ones that stayed in, I wouldn't know them by name—they all stopped using their religious names in the '70s. I guess they got tired of being called Thomas and Richard and John.

"I think the CSJs mainly use the building for meetings now," Mom explained. "Looks like there might be something going on today."

As the hill leveled off, we could see that the area in front of the scholasticate was crowded with cars. When my mother had been known as Sister Thomas Patrick, nuns weren't even allowed to drive. These days they seemed to get around however they pleased: an equal number of hatchbacks, station wagons, and sedans filled the grid of the parking lot. They also seemed free to speak their minds in a way that would have been unimaginable to the girls who became Sisters in 1958. Scattered throughout the collection of nuns' cars were all manner of political and religious bumper stickers: *Pro-Life Means Anti-War, No Blood For Oil, Eve Was Framed.*

Just as we reached the entryway, the doors pushed open and a crowd of women with tidy gray hairdos began streaming out toward the cars. The Sisters of St. Joseph had dropped the habit by then; they dressed like any older businesswoman might for a meeting: colorful blazers; dark skirts hemmed below the knee. Their shoes were unmistakably nunnish, though. In beige or black they were thick-soled and sturdy, and at the moment seemed literally to add a bounce to the Sisters' steps. The women walking toward us were visibly jubilant, talking and laughing in groups of two or three as they came down the stairs.

Mom squinted at one nun in a bright green linen jacket. "Sorry to bother you, Sister," she said. "You look very familiar. Could you tell me what your religious name was?"

When she told us the name she once had used, Mom lit up like a bulb. "Oh! I'm Mary Doherty! I used to be Sister Thomas Patrick."

"Mary Doherty!" the nun called out. "What on earth are you doing here?"

"Oh, I'm just here with my son," Mom beamed. "This is Peter. I'm showing him around my old stomping grounds."

"Your son!" the nun said approvingly. "Well, it's very nice to meet you, Peter. You look just like your mum."

After only a moment of small talk, the nun excused herself. "Wish I could talk more, but we just had a big meeting and there's lots to do. Very exciting," she grinned. "We're ahead of our time!"

A few others approached and it was the same sort of interaction each time. Mom asked each Sister what her religious name had been, and with that bit of information she was able to connect faces and names to a whole universe of shared experiences. One woman had been a year ahead of her in the novitiate; another had served with her friend Judy, who at the time was called Sister Richard Therese.

"Do I remember correctly that you married a priest?" one of them asked, and her voice was only interested, without a note of reproach.

When finally Mom watched them all go their way, her eyes following groups of nuns as they piled into cars and headed off down the hill, it seemed to be with a sense of pride that she still belonged among them. As if the life she might have lived was as much a part of her as the life she'd had.

From the scholasticate we walked across the top of Bethany Hill, soon arriving at the brownish red stone of the main novitiate building.

"This doorway is where we entered the convent our first day here," Mom said, "and then we all trooped up three flights of stairs to get settled. My glory, the way we cried that night! You'd think we'd never see daylight again."

As we circled the building, Mom pointed out the settings for scenes from her first years as a nun: the convent chapel where with eighty other girls she had donned a wedding gown to be married to Christ; the convent kitchen to which they all had dreaded being assigned; the patch of lawn where their luggage had been left like coffins awaiting the grave.

"And back over here," Mom said, turning a corner to the rear of the building. "This is where we had our daily recreation. I remember once when the novice mistress, Sister Elizavetta, was sick with the flu, she stayed up in her room—that window right up there." Mom pointed halfway up the wall to a window with its shade drawn down. "We knew she was up there trying to rest, so all through the recreation hour we kept singing, loud as we could, *Oh jolly playmates, come out and play with me . . ."*

Mom laughed at the thought. "You'd see her peek out sometimes. Oh were we wicked!"

It might have been talk of a sick nun that made her suggest we stop by the infirmary before heading back down the hill; or perhaps she just hoped to run into a few more women whom she used to call Sister. Who knows, maybe even Elizavetta would be there. Whatever her reason, we headed over to the medical facility that was really all that remained of the novitiate as it had been when my mother had arrived. On this hill named for the biblical home of Martha and Mary, the infirmary was the only place where religious women still lived, and they would not be there at all if they intended to live very long.

Inside, we were greeted by a woman of at least eighty-five. She sat behind a reception desk, and was dressed just as all the CSJs we'd met in front of the dormitory had been: bright pastel blazer; tasteful gold cross dangling from her neck; big plastic glasses that covered her cheeks and forehead as well as her eyes. Mom explained that she was a former CSJ, and asked if it would be okay if we had a look around.

"Go right ahead," the receptionist said. "We're always happy to have a Sister come home."

Beyond the lobby, the place had the smell and look of a hospital. Even the pictures of saints that decorated the walls seemed as though they had been sterilized, encased as they were in metal frames that gleamed like surgical tools in the light of the fluorescent tubes overhead.

Everywhere we looked, nuns in a variety of habits—blue, white, gray, black—moved through the halls and the adjoining rooms. Some worked there, it seemed, providing care for their more senior Sisters; others sat slumped over bowls of soup in the dining hall, or upright and eager above Bingo cards in the parlor; one wheeled herself out of the elevator with a potted plant in her lap. Mom moved cheerily from room to room, making conversation, asking questions, bringing a smile to every old nun we met.

"And what was your religious name, Sister?" she would always ask and, before we knew it, we'd had an earful of family secrets and church assignments and the general state of the world. If my father had been in his element down the hill in the experimental worship circle, my mother was certainly in hers here, among her Sisters and their stories.

After almost an hour, we decided we should head back down to the rec center. Dad would start to worry. We said our goodbyes to the Sisters, and made our way to the lobby.

Before leaving, Mom ducked her head into the front office to thank the elderly receptionist. "And by the way, Sister, what was your religious name?"

The woman stared a moment, then said, like she was speaking to a child, which by her lights, she was, "I'm not a Sister, dear. I'm a great-grandmother."

"Oh! Well, good for you!" Mom cheered. "I hope to be!" She put her hand to her mouth in a conspiratorial whisper—"I'm working on it!"—then she hooked her thumb in my direction. "But I need my children to give me some help!"

The great-grandmother smiled, and so did my mother. Pressure from all sides.

"Okay, okay," I laughed. "I'll see what I can do."

With my mother dreaming of grandchildren in the place where she made her vows, with my father down the hill singing a familiar song in a foreign tongue, I wondered if this was the true creed of my family's roundabout religious history: from immigrant ghettos to seminary classrooms, from church basements to street riots, from convent dormitories to wedding beds, that faith is not just loyalty to tradition, but a readiness to become something new.

"Soon," I said. "I promise."

LIST OF ILLUSTRATIONS

ACKNOWLEDGMENTS

This is the kind of book people tend to write after their parents have died. Mine, thank God, are alive and well as of this writing, and so it is especially true that this book would not exist without their faith, courage, and love. Growing up, the story of who and what they were before they were my mother and father served for me as an initiation into a world moved by paradox; that their early promises never to have children led them to each other and ultimately made our family possible caused me endless wonder, the true prime mover of any writer's life. I know now that their decision to marry was not the mystical coming together I once imagined it to be, but it seems to me no less miraculous for that knowledge, and I am all the more grateful. This book is dedicated to them, and to their stubborn hope in a faith that can change not only the world, but itself.

My sister, Kathleen, and my brother, Sean, do not appear in these pages nearly enough to convey their importance in my life. They would have written very different accounts of our shared experiences, and I hope they do.

Many friends and colleagues read rough drafts and false starts and helped me with their comments. Jeff Sharlet, my Buddha-killing collaborator, did me the great service of being my toughest reader. Sean Manseau sat through innumerable editing sessions, making the kinds of suggestions that only another writer could. Betsy Frankenberger, a most considerate spy, never lagged in her enthusiasm. Elana Wertkin read closely and was always honest enough to warn me when I'd gone off course. Other early readers included Paul Morris, Ben Weiner, David Englander, and Catherine Saint Louis; I am grateful to them all for their interest, their effort, and their friendship. Amy Scheibe, whom providence has made my editor, helped me fill in the gaps in the story, much improving the narrative in the process. Maris Kreizman, Carisa Hays, Suzanne Donahue, Dominick Anfuso, Martha Levin, and all at Free Press have been extraordinary in their encouragement. My agent, Kathy Anderson, has been a kind and careful guide through the dark wood of bookmaking; without her I'd be lost.

From a very early age, some of my oldest friends helped me see the humor in my ecclesiastical lineage, especially Jeremy Brothers, Jason Nutile, and Lori Salmeri. It's no surprise to me that, as actors and writers, they all are now funny for a living. In their hands the book would have had a few more laughs. Another old friend, Matthew Ludvino, provided good company and a comfortable couch, making research trips far more bearable.

There is a great deal of secrecy hardwired into Catholic culture, and at times it made research more difficult than it might have been. And so I am particularly indebted to those open-minded souls who went out of their way to assist me. The librarians of the Archdiocese of Boston archives and of Saint John's Seminary were quite helpful in this regard, as was the staff of my mother's childhood church in Dorchester, who shared files of parish history as often as I asked. It's worth noting that my father's childhood church in Lowell declined to do the same, telling me quite honestly they had such files but I couldn't see them; they didn't know what I might find.

Similarly, I am grateful to the many people from my parents' past who shared their time and their memories with me, especially their cronies from the convent, the seminary, and their days in Roxbury: George Spagnolia, Judy Stoddard, Bob McCreary, and others who prefer to go unnamed. My mother's attorneys in the case of *Doe v. Creighton*, Theodore Ornstein, David Dwork, and Adam Berkowitz, were also a great help. If not for their work on my mother's behalf, I might never have known how brave she is.

Finally I want to thank Gwenann Seznec, who has seen me through this project from the start, reading, cheering, and frequently reminding me that even while it is an account of such big subjects as Sex, Love, and the Catholic Church, it is first of all a story of family. She will be my wife by the time these words are published, and with her, God willing, I will keep the promise with which the book ends.

ABOUT THE AUTHOR

Peter Manseau is coauthor of *Killing the Buddha* and a founding editor of the award-winning online magazine of the same name. His essays and commentaries have appeared in the *Washington Post* and on National Public Radio's *All Things Considered*. Raised outside Boston, he currently lives in Charlottesville, Virginia.